The Cultures of Celebrations

The Cultures of Celebrations

edited by

Ray B. Browne
and
Michael T. Marsden

Bowling Green State University Popular Press
Bowling Green, OH 43403

Outdoor Entertainment Series

General editors
Ray B. Browne
Michael T. Marsden

Copyright © 1994 by Bowling Green State University Popular Press

Library of Congress Catalogue Card No: 93-74428

ISBN: 0-87972-651-2 Clothbound
0-87972-652-0 Paperback

Cover art by Gary and Laura Dumm

CONTENTS

INTRODUCTION

Michael T. Marsden
Ray B. Browne

Popular entertainments, like many other aspects of popular culture, can be used as windows into the attitudes and values of the many who participate in them and enjoy them. They function as mirrors or lenses, reflecting/refracting the immediate society and, in some instances, affecting it.

As Foster Rhea Dulles points out in his classic book, *A History of Recreation: America Learns to Play*, it took almost four centuries for Americans to embrace play as a human activity worthy of the spirit as well as of the body. And two hundred years after the founding of the nation, Americans are just beginning to enjoy entertainments without serious moral and political reservations. Inheriting a Calvinist perspective in the structure of our political and social units, we have been uneasy about pursuing entertainment forms which do not also enhance our survival probabilities.

While it would be inaccurate to suggest that our Puritan forebearers were devoid of a spirit of fun, it would be correct to suggest they were convinced of the fact that their earthly success or lack thereof constituted evidence of their eventual fate in the hereafter. In strict Calvinist terms you could not earn salvation; you were simply either among the chosen or you were not. But how you lived your life did matter, not in terms of the ultimate outcome in the hereafter, but in terms of symbolic salvation or damnation. Coupled with the basic tenets of capitalism, Calvinism was a powerful motivator, for you worked hard not only to succeed in this life, but in the next as well. To be a failure in this life was a clear indication of your immortal bankruptcy.

While our Puritan forebearers frowned on entertainments which distracted the faithful from the ultimate goal of salvation, they also faced a hostile environment which required hard work and careful planning. Such strenuous demands left little room for frivolities which did not sharpen survival skills. The only types of entertainment which were encouraged were those which developed skills, such as target shooting or moral dramas. While the grimness of the Puritan existence

1

has certainly been overstated by historians, the "blue laws" which have survived into the 20th century give testimony to the effectiveness of their moral strictness about certain entertainment forms.

Attitudes towards leisure certainly influenced many early American laws, and may well have been a contributing factor to the Civil War as Northerners and Southerners fought about styles and forms of play as well as about the compelling reasons of preserving the Union and ending slavery. Given the failure of the Southern mode of leisure to prevail and the underdeveloped Northern consciousness about the importance and value of play, a truly mature sense of play in America occurred only along the line of the moving frontier as people sought sanity through play in an otherwise hostile environment. Mountain men, for example, arranged for their annual two to three weeks of play (the rendezvous) where they would match survival skills and cavort in relative drunkenness. But their play, like that of children, was all seriousness, for they were re-establishing their ties to the human condition from which they had been isolated for most of the year.

The spirit of play has to be rekindled in most Americans who love their leisure time and their leisure pursuits but who are fearful they will have to account for their leisure time in some constructive manner. Vacant time is frightening to Americans, and retirement, while a desirable goal, is troublesome to many who are unused to dealing with large amounts of unstructured time. As a people Americans seem unprepared to deal creatively with their leisure time.

Entertainment forms which satisfy do so by engaging us in a process of "flow" whereby we become one with the activity. Some people experience "deep flow" where a merger occurs between the individual and the event to such an extent that all reality except the event itself fades. This union allows the spirit of play, a common experience for the child, to surface and take control of our adult moment.

According to Frank Manning in the introduction to his *The Celebration of Society*, celebration has four major components: 1) it is performance, 2) it is entertainment, 3) it is public and 4) it is participatory (4). Manning sees celebration as a text to be interpreted (6). He reminds us of the anthropological concept of being "thrice born"—first into our own culture, then into another culture we study, and finally back into our own culture with new insights about both cultures. This is the perspective the true student of popular entertainments must develop in order to read the entertainment texts which surround us and which can reveal more about ourselves and our neighbors than we ever imagined. For Manning and other cultural analysts, such as Victor Turner, entertainment forms reverse the normal state of things and convert the mundane into a symbolic playing field where we act out our innermost attitudes, beliefs and values.

In his book, *Celebration*, Victor Turner reminds us that "objects speak" (15) and that rituals which employ special symbolic objects provide an organized way of "binding for the moment the opposing forces within the community and tying together the past with the present" (27). According to Turner, celebrations are always framed, either within literal or figurative boundaries, so that our expectations as players or spectators can be met (28).

"Homo ludens" is indeed an appropriate topic for study and analysis because people at play reveal a great deal about themselves. Of the six classic theories of play Thomas Kando recounts in his book, *Leisure and Popular Culture in Transition*, the recapitulation theory is the most intriguing for it suggests that through play we relive the history of the human race (29). While the surplus-energy, instinct-practice, recreation, catharsis, and relaxation theories all have their significant appeals, the recapitulation theory alone provides play with the role of high theater. In learning to read the language of play, we are learning to read the texture of culture in all its complexities and subtleties.

The particular case studies which follow provide ample exemplification of the rich sociocultural information close examinations of popular entertainment forms can provide. These studies also provide details of how societies, both consciously and unconsciously, give shape and form to peoples' deepest desires in entertainment form after entertainment form. It is through our entertainment forms that we reveal most about ourselves. Although anchored in analyses of American entertainment forms, this volume provides insightful studies of non-American entertainment forms as well.

In the first essay, "Light and Dark of the Sunroad: Feminine Processions and Masculine Parades," Anne Kaler points out how since the beginning of human consciousness, symbolizing and activating the two gender halves—female and male—in outdoor activities have been necessarily united to create the needed whole in human imagination and symbolic/ritualistic action. "The configuration of the union of opposites occurs in the parade and the process," she says, "when seen as the process of conception." The egg and the sperm of potential human imagination and action are needed to be united to create the full "healday" necessary for humankind's continuance and growth.

4 The Cultures of Celebrations

In the second essay, "Political Activism and Quietism in Shi'a Rituals: Versatility in Paradox," Mehran Tamadonfar demonstrates how rituals may be used to cloak attitudes or to spark and energize them. Often when outward manifestations of deeply felt attitudes would be dangerous, rituals provide a treasure chest in which they are stored, to be polished and burnished against the time they can safely be brought out. These rituals are especially important when used by a cultural and political minority.

Rituals become inanimate develop into icons. Stonehenge in England, as we all know, has for millennia been the site of some kinds of strange beliefs and activities, exactly what is perhaps even now not fully understood. Partially because of our lack of full comprehension, Stonehenge has become an icon of England's past and a symbol of our, sometimes desperate, drive to understand our history through these symbolic roots. David Crouch and Adam Colin in "Re-presenting an Old Outdoor Entertainment: Stonehenge" trace the development of an old field of activity to its latest uses.

From the very ancient to the nearly new cultures is not a long step in the seven-league boots of rituals, as Judith Kapferer points out in "The Dream of Community: Folk Festivals and Ideology in Australia." Her argument, clearly and powerfully made, is that there is an eternal conflict between the State and everyday people. But in order to survive, societies need to minimize conflicts. One way to do that is to reach back through the differences in modern cultures to the sameness which apparently existed at least to a greater degree than now in folk cultures. To be sure, differences existing today are real. And it is imperative for the people in order to protect society from the abuses of the State to understand these differences. Otherwise the State will continue to manipulate these events for its own purposes: "Despite widespread historical, political, economic and social divergencies, the People, wherever they may be, are still forced from time to time, and sometimes incessantly, to engage in struggles of autonomy, and equality in social formations which, however subtly, would deny them those freedoms." But "The establishment and maintenance of society-wide harmony and consensus, of *an identity of interest* among groups whose interests are often in fact deeply opposed, is vital to the survival of the democratic State, and to its legitimation."

In what might be thought an example of Kopferer's thesis, Terry Smith, in "Popular Culture and the Visual Messages of the Lord Mayor's Procession," examines a yearly ritual of 16th- and 17th-century London to determine its audience, symbols and meanings and results. He ably demonstrates that, as Kopferer points out in her article, sometimes the most physical rituals and entertainments can be used for broad political and social ends.

Rituals and entertainments among the Puritans in America could contribute to the ligatures which held together and articulated community life. Exactly the nature of these entertainments has not always been known or acknowledged. The Puritans, presumably a straight-laced and pragmatic people who did not want to waste time, have not always received high marks on the ritualgram and laughmeter. But it is time that all of us understand the part that outdoor entertainment played in forwarding the purposes of their lives. Bruce Daniels, in his essay "Parties for the Common Good: Civic Socializing in Puritan New England" provides good coverage and details in forwarding that needed understanding.

Entertainments that occur only every 100 years are especially informative because they reveal what a society at a particular time holds important and how those beliefs differ from the beliefs of a former century. The celebrations of Columbus' first trip to the New World in the form of the Columbian celebrations is especially useful in this regard. "How an event is commemorated matters," says George Weddell in his essay "National Portraits: The Columbian Celebrations of 1792, 1892-93, and 1992 as Cultural Moments." "It matters," he continues, "who controls the definition of an event, what symbols they choose to emphasize, and it matters who has a voice in deciding the terms upon which participation in the event is allowed." With Columbus these criteria are especially important because ethnicity, nationalism and politics are creating a new dynamic which may recreate all observations of Columbus' event. It will behoove us to understand.

In addition to some people, some events seem to embody a whole people—their dreams, hopes and dynamic spiritual and physical energies. Such was the American circus. "The circus was more than a mere outdoor amusement," says Doug Mishler in his article "'It Was Everything Else We Knew Wasn't: The Circus and American Culture,'" "It's enduring allure was linked to the turbulent and energizing forces which affected United States Society." Someone has said that in order to understand America today one must understand baseball. True or not, it is almost certainly proper to say that in order to understand this country for the five decades before and after the turn of the 20th century one must understand its circus. Mishler brings to the fore much understanding of the phenomenon.

Often the myths and legends that are reenacted in various forms of rituals and entertainments are personified in one person who understood them in bone and blood. P.T. Barnum was such a person.

Another, perhaps even truer exemplar, was Buffalo Bill Cody. He fed on living myths and legends, gave them greater significance and projected them into the future. "The fact that these myths and legends continue to survive and influence our lives," says Susan Clark in "The Menace of the Wild West Shows," speaks eloquently of their magnetic and pervasive qualities." If America has always been larger than reality, at least a part of that accomplishment must be attributed to Buffalo Bill Cody. America without him, at least the myths and legends of the American West, would be a far different place. As Tennyson's Ulysses says that he was a part of all that he had met, so it can be said that America is a part of all its mythic characters that it has experienced.

Sometimes rituals seem to run so close to the surface that many wilful non-participants tend to scoff and bad-mouth them as being without significance. Beauty pageants have generally been held to be only skin deep and unimportant. Michael T. Marsden, in his essay "Two Northwestern Ohio Beauty Pageants: A Study in Middle America's Cultural Rituals," demonstrates that all events have significance if people will only learn to read them. "Community-based beauty pageants are dramatic events," Marsden says, and are rituals "of cultural attitudes and values which contestants have learned to dramatize most effectively..."

The community festival is one of the least understood areas of celebration, as Marsden says, and needs to be studied: "The Community festival," Marsden says in "Summer and Winter Festivals in Thompson, Manitoba," "might provide a significant window into the culture of a community. It may well provide us with a narrative about the community's cultural essence."

One community festival that has created a magic and ambience all its own, New Orleans' Bourbon Street, and its extension the French Quarter, has an antic quality that ties it into reaches of the extreme and near-pornographic. Bourbon Street is a permanent festival in a city known for its bacchanalian Mardi Gras and its generally laid-back approach to life. Bourbon Street is the permanent land of flesh and music, of shake-rattle-and roll, in a near approach to rawness and risqueness that to many persons symbolizes the extremes of the genre. As Les Wade says in his essay "New Orleans' Bourbon Street: The Evolution of an Entertainment District," Bourbon St. is the theater of the performing body. Having survived many changing attitudes about it by the outside world, the Street has survived and, as Wade says, "No longer so beleaguered by charges of immorality of indecency, the street has shed its image as a public menace and now stands as a New Orleans signature, a civic asset, as indispensible to the city's vaunted cultural uniqueness as Mardi Gras, shrimp Creole, mausoleums, and streetcars." The change says more about the visitors than about the Street.

If Bourbon Street is an outdoor theater of sounds and moving bodies, other kinds of outdoor theater have long-since contributed mightily to American entertainment as alternative theater. They are far off Broadway, generally not within sight of New York City and often not within sight of any skyline. But they have been important in the development and continued life of America. It is time they were fully known. In "Alternative Theatres in Kentucky" Marilyn Casto provides much needed information on such places of entertainment both in Kentucky and elsewhere.

All forms of outdoor entertainment have had as their purpose to delight and instruct. Perhaps nobody has taken more seriously the possibilities of delighting and instructing than Walt Disney, called by Max Rafferty, Superintendent of Education of the State of California, "the greatest educator of the twentieth century." No American—and almost nobody anywhere—of the last half of the 20th century has failed to attend the Disney school and to learn there. Disney's concept of the theme park is probably the most effective, directed-learning school of all times. Disney hovers over the world of entertainment and education like a giant eagle, ready to teach us all to fly higher. He is an icon, a ritual, almost a religion and a whole way of schooling. "Properly plumbed and connected," Margaret King says at the end of her essay, "Instruction and Delight: Theme Parks and Education," "the resources of the theme park offer exciting channels for the transformation of education into the well-rounded, interactive, and integrated adventure it must become in modern life."

There are many forms of outdoor entertainment discussed in this collection of essays—and much more. The 15 articles, written by some of the leading authorities in the fields, contribute to our much-needed but elusive understanding of the nature and use of non-work time in modern life.

The need for understanding the nature of non-work time becomes more and more urgent every day as people insist on extended time away from work, more time away from home and more facilities for using that recreation time which we look upon as a Constitutional and God-given right. But we do not want to "waste" our time. People like to plan, see and do. We see a lot and do a lot, and sometimes we plan. Ours is a world filled with foreground and background noise and sight. The electronic media—especially television—have inured us to what we hear and see and changed the nature of reality. As Mark Twain once remarked, it is amazing what we can look at and still not see. We do not "read" all we look upon. Consequently we understand or misread much that goes on around us. But the way people desperately dig after ethnic roots and national heritages demonstrates that we think we need to cling to concepts that we believe helpful in our lives. People may be racked with cynicism, but they are strongly influenced by the electronic media around them because of its omnipresence. Comedian Will Rogers made a career out of voicing the American belief that reading filled our needs: all he knew, he said, was what he read in the newspapers. Now we are more likely to believe what we see on television: seeing is believing. We all know anecdotes about unsophisticated people thinking that what they see on television and movie screens is the actual world, and we know how the "virtual reality" on television and movie screens today fools us all.

So it is convincingly apparent that we need to get away from the enclosed "reality" of the screens and get back into the society of human beings as participants. We have neglected the reality of the outside world. That world speaks in thousands of voices and languages, with the many tongues of all creatures and phenomena. To understand them we must first experience them. Outdoor entertainments lure us out again into the society and nature that constitute the real world.

Society is driving rapidly toward more leisure time and more non-work activities. A growing number of these activities develop around icons and rituals in which we anchor our faith and purpose in life. All work and no play may make people dull and insensitive, as the old adage teaches. But all play and no work, especially non-directed play, unless those activities are fully understood, may create chaos and destroy an environment, a nation and a world.

Homo ludens needs to be understood. These essays help in that understanding.

Works Cited

Dulles, Foster Rhea. *A History of Recreation: America Learns to Play.* Chicago: U of Chicago P, 1965.

Kando, Thomas M. *Leisure and Popular Culture in Transition.* Saint Louis: The C.V. Mosby Company, 1975.

Manning, Frank E. *The Celebration of Society.* Bowling Green, OH: Bowling Green State University Popular Press, 1982.

Turner, Victor, Ed. *Celebration: Studies in Festivity and Ritual.* Washington, D.C.: Smithsonian Institution P, 1982.

LIGHT AND DARK OF THE SUNROAD: FEMININE PROCESSIONS AND MASCULINE PARADES

Anne K. Kaler

Men parade in groups: a solitary woman is a procession.

The masculine parade and the feminine procession alternate as dominant symbols of the seasonal changing of light. The symbolic and symbiotic balance between light and dark—male and female, Mother Earth and Trickster Son, life and death—is mirrored in the feminine procession and the masculine parade.

In seasonal celebrations of light and dark, the basic configuration lies in the symbiotic relationship between the larger feminine figure of the Mother Earth and her physically smaller Trickster Son. Religious iconography stresses the Madonna as the woman holding the smaller male; the fairy tale of Sleeping Beauty shows the princess isolated by a thorny hedge until the one unremarkable prince besieges her fortress. The human mind can be said to possess the larger feminine "egg" of creativity in the right brain and the smaller and more numerous "sperm" of the left-brained masculine reason in the many guises of the Trickster Son. Both are needed to energize the mind into creativity: both are figures of the human personality—the contemplative creative side of solitary intuition and the active ordered side of reason; both are needed to bring the world of idea to birth. The pendulum of the seasons sways between the Trickster Son and the Fruitful Mother to achieve the harmonic balance of creation.

Popular culture and literature solidify this balancing act by portraying parades and processions as predominantly masculine or feminine. Just as the earth needs the sun and the rain to fertilize her, during conception the tiny sperm and the large egg mutually dissolve the walls of their being to become one new being. The uniting of the Trickster Son with Mother Earth recreates and restores the health of the community and the individual. This union takes place at the seasonal shifts when changes in the solar and lunar calendar are noticeable and are celebrated by feminine processions and masculine parades.

Calendars are artificial devices. Scratch a "holyday" and uncover a "holiday" perched on top of an agricultural "healday" phenomenon. A "healday" stems from the hearth goddess Helle whose name indicates both the "wholeness" and "holiness" of a day of recreation and celebration, a day which restores holistic health to both the individual and to the community.

Humans seem to work on a natural cycle of seven—seven days of creation, the division of the lunar month of 28 days into four weeks of seven days, the menstrual cycle. The same concept can be applied to a diet calendar—six weeks of fasting relieved by one week of feasting—or an academic calendar of six-week semesters broken by mid-semester breaks. Holidays, Holydays, and Healdays occur at the natural breaking points within the 13 weeks between solstices and equinoxes, appearing at the midpoints between the masculine or solar celebrations when a change in light is perceivable. These weaker or lesser feasts have traditionally been celebrated as major feasts by those believing in feminine elements of the universe such as Wicca. Even within Christianity, though, this seven-week phenomenon is noticeable. For example, Ember days and rogation days, three days of fasting for the success of the harvests, announced the change of seasons in pre-Vatican Catholic practices. Their dates were embodied in the rhymed ditty: "Post-Lentem, Post-Pentem, Post-Crucem and Post-Lucem." "Post-Lentem" indicated the Wednesday, Friday, and Saturday fast and abstinence days after the beginning of Lent (February); "Post-Pentem" was after Pentecost (May-June); "Post-Crucem" was after the Feast of the Holy Cross (September); and "Post-Lucem" celebrated the feast of St. Lucy (December). Yet, rather than allowing the four feminine feasts of light to complement the solar calendar's solstices and equinoxes, the liturgical calendar often overrides the feminine feasts of the waxing and waning of light by renaming or rededicating them with parades rather than processions.

The calendar shows two periods of the sun's waning—August and October—and two of the sun's waxing or strengthening—February and May. The first two—August and October—have suffered a transformation or rechristening into orthodox masculine feasts of patriarchal religion. A calendar of such feasts looks like the chart on the top of the next page.

The first two feasts of the waning celebrate the dying sun and the darkness of winter by ritualistic processions. Heralding the feast of the dead, the Halloween days imitate their feminine origin from the dark side of the Terrible Mother. The eve of All Hallows or All Saints when the dead are reverently remembered was first intended to assuage grief

Winter Solstice, December 21

February
Bride, St. Brigid
Groundhog Day,
Return of Light

November
Samhaim, All Souls,
All Saints, Halloween,
Dying of Light

Spring Equinox
March 21

Autumnal Equinox
September 21

May
Mayday, Law Day (US),
Workers Day (USSR),
St. Joseph The Worker

August 15
Assumption of Mary,
August 13, Diana,
Shooting Stars

Summer Solstice, June 21

MASCULINE ——   FEMININE ——

and to insure the continuity of the life/death cycle. However, the natural death process of the autumnal moon and the sun's decline has been weakened by the positioning of the feasts in the Christian church. By insisting on All Saints' Day as November 1, the Church anticipates the Resurrection motif of the spring without fully acknowledging the natural waning process of death as a cessation or slowing of the life force. This denial of death is "postponed" until the last day of the *triduum*, the Feast of All Souls on November 2, when the possibility of souls in transition from one state to another is finally given recognition. But, by reducing the angel of death to a minor devil, the effect of the cycle of nature is upset. All living things need a rest period, a cessation, a journey underground, a death; absence of such a period results in an unhappy emphasis on the baneful aspects of skeletons, witches, black cats, and demon-faced pumpkins. Rather than the orderly formation of a parade, the straggling trick-and-treaters is a sporadic procession of individual attendants, celebrating the grotesque face of the Terrible Mother by their burlesqued masks, distorted costumes, and antic dances of her stripped-to-the-bone Trickster Son's skeleton.

In contrast, the masculine version of the winter celebration rejects the feminine death motif for that of the noisy parade: Thanksgiving day parades, football homecomings, fall marching band festivals, early Christmas shopping parades, bonfires, and hayrides. While such parades are usually a blend of male and female participants, there is little sense of a feminine religious procession in such celebrations because the Trickster Son temporarily triumphs over his Mother. Pre-Christmas parades introduce another archetype of the Dionysian reveler in the image of the overweight Lord of Misrule who dominates the season—Santa Claus atop his sleigh of material goods. While old St. Nick does not directly represent the drunken excess of Dionysian revelry, his body image in America suggests excess—doesn't everyone leave cookies for him—yet the European original of St. Nicholas pictures a lean and ascetic Bishop of Myra who distributes money to the poor.

At this beginning of the winter solstice season, certain festivities are totally feminine. In the textile industry in Europe, women paid homage to St. Catherine of Alexandria by taking her November 25 feast day as a holiday. In groups and carrying distaffs, they would prowl the streets in the short winter sunlight looking for hapless young men whom they would hold captive. For women trapped indoors, sewing or lace-making for most of their lives, the brightness of the winter day threatened by the dark months ahead must have been a necessary outlet for their bodies and minds. In England, circular cakes or cookies called Cattern cakes were baked and decorated to honor the sun-goddess aspect of the fiery wheel with which St. Catherine was threatened.

In the August festivities, however, the procession takes precedence over the parade and the feminine is relatively unthreatened by a patriarchal take-over. Originally, on August 13 the natural phenomenon of the Aurora Borealis, the showers of dying stars in the last two weeks of August in the Northern Hemisphere, was attributed to the sky goddess whom the Romans celebrated as the virgin huntress Diana. A cluster of female saints connected with light surround these August days. For example, the mid-August feast of St. Clare of Assisi celebrates the first woman received by St Francis. Her name in Italian means "light" or, more correctly, "radiance" and she is often pictured holding a round sun-like monstrance containing the Holy Eucharist with which she halted a barbarian invasion. So also, when the Christian church selected August 15 as the Feast of the Assumption of the body of Jesus' mother Mary into heaven, artists pictured her in the act of being "assumed" into heaven surrounded by stars, clouds, and angels. (Notice the distinction made between the "Ascension" of Christ, body and soul, 40 days after His death and the "Assumption" of Mary's body to preserve it from incorruptibility. Christ "rose" from the dead; Mary was "raised" into the heavens. Earlier matriarchal religions see the opposite as happening—that the Mother "raises" the Son to her after rescuing him from the under-world.)

Even modern songwriters refer to such heavenly happenings as mystical experiences, the result of hallucinogenic drugs, in "Lucy in the Sky with Diamonds." The symbiotic relationship persists in Mary Poppins who descends from the sky by means of a theatrical *machina* of her practical umbrella; her son/lover is the English folklore character of Jack-in-the-Green, whose dance with his chimney-sweeps clears the London sky of soot and clouds. Traditional female heroines "drop" from the sky: Dorothy in *Wizard of Oz* lands on the wicked witch while the good witch glides in on a pink bubble; Alice "drops" into Wonderland through her rabbit hole; Dolly "descends" the staircase; Mame rides her "crescent moon" in her stage play. In literature, the procession occurs in the production or dance numbers that the heroine undertakes: Dorothy is surrounded by the Munchkins. Many times these sun-goddesses of literature are accompanied by small token males: Dorothy has Toto, Mame has her nephew, Dolly has her attendant waiters; Mother Rose in *Gypsy* has her bevy of boy dancers, St. Margaret has her dragon on a chain.

Long hours of waning August sunlight encourage outside activities like church festivals, revival meetings, and family reunions. Within some ethnic communities like the Italian-American, the feast of the Assumption features major three-night festivals and parades, culminating in fireworks imitative of the shooting stars. A particularly feminine procession occurs along the Atlantic shores where the sea is "married" to the land by throwing wreaths of flowers on it. Processions, usually of old women, make their way to the Atlantic beaches, parading a lengthy rosary of beach balls and rope, reciting Marian hymns, to dip ailing bodies in the surf and to fill jars with holy water for the coming year. Perhaps this event derives from the sacredness of the month of August to the European vacationer, as Labor Day marks the end of summer festivities for Americans.

The strongest points of light are in the waxing or growing periods of the light—February and May. During the first few days of February, the midpoint at which the hours of sunlight become noticeably longer, the return of the sun appears as the revival of Mother Earth. The Druidic celebration of the Irish goddess Bride by the igniting of bonfires across the hills of Ireland was Christianized into the feast of St. Bridget, whose flaming cross was woven of reeds. Notice how fire saints cluster around this date—St. Agnes on January 21; St. Blase on February 3; St. Agatha, who was rolled on hot coals, on February 5; St. Bridget on February 1; St. Dorothy, whose eyes were torn out, on February 6. (Recent changes in the calendar of the saints have caused some dates to shift slightly.)

Yet, men have claimed this February feast of light. For example, in Punxatawney, Pennsylvania, the groundhog "predicts" six more weeks of winter weather if he sees his shadow on the second of February. The custom of annoying a sleeping groundhog came about because of the natural process of groundhog courtship. The male groundhog wakes up about a month before the female groundhog and goes in search of a mate. Handled by men in top hats and tails, the groundhog is a male symbol although women's liberation has secured the existence of a Punxatawney Philomena to match Punxatawney Phil. Her name ironically is one drummed off the rolls of the saints by the Bollandists who claimed she was a vestigial cult of a local sun goddess. The recent movie *Groundhog Day* has a cynical weatherman repeat the day until he catches on to compassion, catches his mate, and decides to settle down in the small town of Punxatawney. Only when he "relaxes" enough into the slower pace of the procession by sleeping with his mate does his fortune change.

Four times a year the light is celebrated in its death or waning or in its waxing or strengthening. The Jewish feast of Purim, the defeat of Esther over Hammon, is celebrated by the tricorned filled Hammontasch cookies. Until recent years the February feast was mostly feminine in character while retaining its light imagery as Candlemas because candles used throughout the year are blessed on this day. Whereas the feast of the Purification of Mary arose from the Jewish necessity for ritual cleansing a mother of the "stain" of childbirth, the Church now stresses the second feast—Christ's Presentation—as a symbiotic balance of the mother presenting her child to the community of believers. In Catholic churches until quite recently, a woman was "churched" several weeks after giving birth. This ceremony involved a priest's meeting the woman at the church door with prayers and a candle which she carried to the altar to light in gratitude for the successful birth.

It took creative engineering to impose Christianity onto the calendar. Having placed the celebration of Christ's birth smack in the middle of the unruly December Saturnalia, the Church counted backwards nine months to use the vernal equinox or March 25 as the moment of His conception when the Incarnation (the taking on of flesh by the Godhead in Christ's body in Mary's womb) took place. The feast has always been called the "Annunciation" because of the angel's message to Mary of Nazareth. If Christ was born in December, then eight days later his circumcision must occur on January first, since Jewish males are usually circumcised on the eighth day. (Interestingly, medical science has recently proven that this is the time period it takes for the baby's blood to develop a sufficient clotting factor.) Thus, to offset the final days of the Saturnalian feasting, the first of January became a Holyday of Obligation, the Circumcision or Naming of Christ, sometimes referred to as the Presentation of Christ to the Temple. In Eastern Christianity, the January 6 Feast of the Epiphany delayed Christ's Circumcision until February 14, the date when the birds start to notice the change of light.

To realign the symbiotic balance of masculine and feminine, the Church recently rededicated January first as the Solemnity of Mary as the Mother of God and moved the Feast of the Circumcision to February second. By linking the Presentation of the Child Jesus in the Temple with the Purification of Mary, the church removed the distasteful concept of a woman needing to be cleansed of childbirth and instead celebrated the offering of the firstborn son to God and the ritual of readmittance of the woman to religious community. Look at the phrasing of the feasts. The "Presentation of Christ to the Temple" takes place at the same time as Mary's "Purification" from the "stain" of childbirth. But the term "Presentation" has an older feminine history which predates the modern "Presentation of Christ." Originally, the Presentation referred to the legend that Mary was presented to the temple in Jerusalem to be trained as a temple virgin, skilled in weaving and sewing the sacred cloths. The legends come from apocryphal stories of Sts. Joachim and Anne, Mary's parents, who promised her to God because they had been barren for so long; notice the similarity to the story of Elizabeth and Zachary, Sarah and Abraham, Hannah and Samuel. It even appears to be a vestige of the Roman Vestal Virgins who preserved the sacred precincts and flame. Paintings of Mary's presentation show the three-year-old child ascending the steps of the temple into the arms of an old priest, often her uncle. Mary is seldom shown as an infant, except in the rare paintings of her birth. The more familiar configuration is of St. Anne as the older woman, Mary as the Virgin-Mother, and the Christ Child in her arms. Even in the gospel of the "Presentation of Christ," the characters of the old blind Simeon and the ancient prophetess Anna, appear to complete the symbiotic balance. Simeon becomes the moribund Old Year holding a New Year's infant Christ while old Anna consoles the young virgin-mother Mary.

Good configurations never die. In the Irish mumming plays and the English St. George plays, the return of the sun is reenacted by having St. George split open the casque of the dark knight to release the young blond youth of the new year. In Pynchon's *Gravity's Rainbow*, the blond youth is entombed by the old German scientist in a V2 rocket aimed at a theater of English children. Old Father

Time ushers in the babe of the New Year. Such symbolic welcoming back of the sun by parades is typified in the splendor of the Philadelphia Mummers' Day parade with its sparkling sequined marching brigades. But the origin of the Mummers' Day parade was a noisy informal procession of black-faced and costumed revelers touring from house to house, begging food and drink. Although the Mummers' Day Parade has turned into a televised formal march up Broad Street, the Mummers always stop at the hospitals, like St. Agnes' and the Mercy Hospitals, to perform their special patterned dances for the patients and nuns. Thus the male parade returns to its feminine roots.

During the Middle Ages, the midwinter festivities of young boys replaced the older feminine celebration of the return of the light to the land. The feast of the Holy Innocents on December 28 engendered the students' feast of the Boy Bishop during which authority was overturned while the young men mocked their teachers and clergy. Rather like the current student government day, the boys ruled for a day or so by relaxing rules. Consider that the trickster-son always needs an audience or community before which to perform his tricks. Six weeks later another break from routine is needed when the first change in the sun's rays becomes evident.

Shakespeare's *Twelfth Night* and the feast of the Boy Bishop broke the monotony of the house-bound people by suggesting physical movement from place to place. Liturgically the first weeks in February which introduce the black fast of the Lenten season begin with a celebration or carnival similar to the Feast of Fools or of the Boy Bishop in the Christmas season. Since "carnevale" means abstaining from meat and dairy products (a neat way to lower blood cholesterol and triglycerides prior to spring planting), different societies ease into abstinence with festivities of varying length: Venice, for example, has a ten-day festival; Rio de Janiero has three days. Notice how these festivities such as Mardi Gras, Fat Tuesday, and *Fastnacht* encourage the eating of fatty foods, like round donuts and hot cross buns. (Again, all these are primarily male endeavors. The only activity women get to do is to flip pancakes in an English Shrove Tuesday race.) Where the feminine feasts celebrate Mother Earth and her ever-changing relationship with the Sun, the male feasts center in celebration within a community. For example, young scholars—teenagers and tricksters alike—in the university cathedral schools needed to break their concentration every six or seven weeks. When the middle of February rolled around, pre-Lenten festivities of Mardi Gras provided an outlet for boyish tricks, masquerades, and frolic.

Literature reiterates this male prerogative to frolic in groups while the woman stays solitary. The Viennese operetta of *The Student Prince* has the hero woo and nearly win Kathy, the barmaid of Heidelberg. He leads his drinking buddies in *carmen burana* while she lugs beer steins; he parades with his "fraternity" brothers while she waits tables; he fights a duel over her while she patches up his wounds. Sentiment wins out as he sacrifices her to marry for duty, a kingdom, and a princess rather than for love. Kathy is always seen alone, never with a woman companion; at the end of the story, she is alone, the Mother Earth figure surrounded by the horde of students. She is named for St. Catherine of Alexandria in whose honor Cattern cakes, round cookies representing the fiery wheel of the sun, are baked. At the end of *West Side Story* Maria is alone on the stage, walking off into the temple halls of the city streets. Mame Dennis is off to India with her small grandson, Rose in *Gypsy* leaves her successful daughter, Alice tumbles out of her rabbit hole and back through her mirror, and Dorothy goes back to the farm in Kansas.

Or take Franco Zeffirelli's *Taming of the Shrew*. The opening shots include the young scholar Lucentio entering Padua to attend the opening ceremony of his university term when the piazza erupts with the carnival spirit. Notice how the three vices ascribed to young men—wine, women, and song—attempt to banish winter. Wine flows freely; bottles are passed from hand to hand. Even death must wait for frolic: the skeletally lean man in his nightshirt dragged from his death bed on a stretcher is paraded as the *danse macabre* figure of dying winter. If someone is dying, a jolt of life from the students will surely revive him. The pigs' masks of the churchmen, the enlarged puppet heads of the paraders, and the oversized costumes increase the carnival atmosphere. Finally, the blond and buxom Venetian courtesan, complete with bawd and maidservant, is both a dramatic stock character representing sexual excess and a Renaissance ideal of earthly beauty and early death. In direct but complementary contrast is the figure of the beautiful Bianca whose unmaidenly recognition of the goliardic song sung to her forecasts her deceitful character; she is the Renaissance concept of heavenly beauty and earthly desire.

The schoolboys' festival spills over from the street into the garden where the light-hearted student Lucentio (his name means light) woos Bianca (whose name means white). On the other hand, Petruchio's serious wooing of Kate for his fortune guides the viewer on a tour of Puritan standards of wealth and status—the broken lyre, the thrown dishes, the stained glass, the bulging storeroom, wool bins and poultry scattered, ending finally on the tile roof and the plunge into the woolen fluff of their "marriage bed." Shakespeare uses Kate's journey to and from Petruchio's country house as a solitary procession, horses following horses in a line, the bedraggled Kate on a mule. Her isolation is a necessary device to bring her into alignment with her society. On the other hand, the carnival "parade" of Bianca's wedding feast turns into the arena for the masculine ritualistic battle as to who has the most obedient wife. Notice the wedding guests milling around, the crowded streets, the lushness of the costumes and the food—all set the stage for the dethroning of the "love goddess" Bianca for the Puritan Kate.

European street parades often seem to contradict the religious impetus of procession. The statue or relics of a local saint might be borne on the shoulders of young men; if that saint were female, she became the courtly love idol but often the local women were not allowed to participate. Running the bulls at Pamplona is an exercise of machismo. So strong is this masculine tradition that not until 1993 were minorities or women allowed on the krewes of the New Orleans' Mardi Gras parade; the same restrictions plagued the centuries-old Philadelphia Mummers' parade until recent years. The men parade and the women sew and cook.

In *Animal House* or *Police Academy*, in boot camp or prep school, the trickster is alive and well and living in the frat house where the tradition of mocking administrators or faculty resurges during that section of mid-winter called the Spring Break. Occasioned by the seven-week semester, the college boys' trooping to the sunny beaches has the reputation of wild drinking, wild parties, and wild, wild women. Where the panty raids of the fifties and sixties replaced the fraternity hazings, the Boy Bishop and the Fool's Feast melded into New Year's Eve costume balls. *Ferris Bueller's Day Off* offers some insight into the Boy Bishop feast. Outwitting authority, Ferris maneuvers his friends into a glorious day of youthful freedom from high school. The poor principal who wants to capture this trickster becomes the predictable butt of the physical jokes; his secretary is equally befuddled; the entire school system is disrupted by the trickster. Yet Ferris' parents, oblivious to his misdeeds, respect his privacy so much that he escapes all punishment and the audience, knowing his good heart, admires and envies his clever manipulation of the system. The final proof of Ferris's Lord of Misrule guise occurs in his frenzied dance with the "maiden" on the parade float. With all its frivolity, the story transmits a lesson—a time for celebration refreshes and renews the individual. The real hero, Cameron, summons up strength to confront his father after demolishing his prized car. Telemachus has to confront Odysseus and

Stephen Dedalus has to meet Bloom. While none of these heroes openly confronts the Mother—Motherland, Mother Church or mother-wife in Penelope/Molly—the feminine procession of reconciliation hovers in the background.

Notice that all the examples have been male. Do women need the same festivities as men? Is their role different—separate but equal or of different emphasis? Or are they just excluded like the mummers' wives who got to make the costumes in the earlier days. Do women ever assume the role of the Lord of Misrule or the Boy Bishop? Women can't be bishops, can they?

Often the feminine version of the parade appears in the religious procession; the only way a woman can to lead a parade or a procession is because she is a) beautiful or b) the tallest or shortest in her class. For example, European customs stress a girl's First Communion day when she is outfitted as a miniature bride. In some countries any woman who dies unmarried is dressed in bridal white for her funeral as if the concept of the *sole femme* is unnatural or, perhaps, as if ultimately everyone is a "virgin bride" to the experience of death. Even an apparent "parade" is often a procession in disguise because the woman is solitary: the prima ballerina in a dance recital, the strutting of the bathing beauty contest, the riding around the stadium of the homecoming football queen.

Women don't belong in parades, custom seems to say. Take the filmed musical version of *Hello Dolly* where Dolly is shown as an interloper in Horace Vandergelder's annual Fourteenth Street Day Parade. She cannot march in step, she tries to adjust her pace to that of the men but fails, she makes him misstep. The pulling back by the camera pits the lone woman against the background of uniformed marching men. Like Venus rising from the foam of the ocean, Dolly's dress is mauve overlaced with a fishnet pattern which replicates Venus' seductive fish imagery. Her song "Before the Parade Passes By" brings to a climax her decision to re-enter the stream of life not as just a participant but rather as the sun goddess returning to a winter earth. Isn't she the matchmaker, *par excellence*? Doesn't she, like manure, encourage "young things to grow?" Doesn't she appear in splendorous sequins, fishtail train, and feathered headdress like the rays of the sun? Doesn't she pause at the top of the steps to receive the adulation of her attendant waiters to the cries that it is "so nice to see you back where you belong?" Dolly is an example of the symbiotic mother and her many sons/and lovers—Cornelius and Barnaby and Ambrose—all of whom she marries off to her worthy "daughters." And who is a more fitting consort for her Trickster Lover than the wily Yonkers Yankee peddler merchant, small in his mind and cheap with his money, that money which will permit her to be fruitful in spreading fertility.

When a woman leads parades, parades ultimately lead back to her. Women's festivities may center around about light but they suggest that the important activity takes place in the dark, namely the regeneration of the community. And it is to enhance a new generation by widening the gene pool by indiscriminate sexual encounters that leads to the final celebration of symbiosis—the first of May.

Mayday is one of these feasts. Halfway between the vernal equinox in late March and the summer solstice of late June, the first of May is a feast of light and growth of light. In literature, Mayday has symbolic and verbal significances. The Earth Mother's ultimate title of May Queen is that of a minority—a woman among women—a goddess or a god-bearer. The Church dogma of the Immaculate Conception set Mary of Nazareth aside as one kept sinless and spotless from her mother's womb. Elizabeth's cry to Mary of Nazareth that she is "blessed among women" reinforces the special quality of her maternity: "blessed is the fruit of your womb." In literature, when fantasy writers create a solitary female character, such a woman is "misbegotten" or marked in some way by her conception: Joan D. Vinge's summer queen is marked by her psychic powers; Jo Clayton's Serroi is born in the wrong season and her Alytys is a half-breed on a planet which does not want her. Hardy's Tess is first seen on a Maywalk with other women yet she is singled out by the red ornament on her dress and is the one not chosen to dance with Angel Clare. (Notice how the man is the light image here). Tess, Anna Karenina, Hester Prynne are reduced to Earth Mothers and forced to walk the solitary path of the outcast woman.

Within the last 30 years, a national card manufacturer tried to revive Mayday festivities by promoting the giving of May baskets of candies or flowers to a loved one. Americans resisted the commercialization of a feast about which they had deep-seated suspicions. Hawthorne's tale of the Puritan Maypole apparently had a lasting effect because nothing is heard of May baskets today. Many older towns and villages however sport the vestige of a phallic Maypole in the granite war monument or statue and Memorial Day serves as the final tribute to the dead soldiers of the Motherland. Some places have demoted Mayday from a day of maternal fertility to a prosaic one still suggestive of its symbiotic duality. In Russia, the day is known as the day of the worker, much like the American Labor Day. In America, May first is Law Day; within Catholicism, the first of May is dedicated to St. Joseph the Worker, the foster father of Jesus, whose March 19 feast falls during Lent. Like Friar Tuck and the other attendant protectors, St. Joseph is the patron of virgins.

Often around Mayday, the Trickster splits himself into two archetypes, physically and emotionally distinct. The small lean figure is reduced to the son/lover like Eros is to his mother Aphrodite. He may, for a while, become the full-sized lover bound by heroic duty like Robin Hood. He most often becomes the celibate protector, obese because he is the Lord of Misrule, drunk because be is a Dionysian offshoot, celibate because of his vows as an attendant priest to the Mother Earth figure.

Such pairings of opposites occurs frequently. Maid Marion and Friar Tuck came into English literature in fourteenth-century ballads along the song road of the troubadours by way of the dances held on Mayday. The names of these dances changed as the characters grew or lessened in importance; they are referred to as the Maid Marion dances, Mayday dances, and Robin Hood Day dances. All the ceremonies involve weaving an intricate pattern of ribbons around a Maypole or forming a dance pattern led by the Hobby Horse or Lady Betty figure, both androgynous figures. Because any ring or carol dance accompanied by a song or chant is a form of procession or parade, the symbiosis is continued.

In the dances, Maid Marion is a euphemism for Christ's mother, a woman honored as an eternal virgin despite her motherhood. The similarity between the month named after the Roman goddess Maia, the word "maid" and the name "Mary" whose German form is often "May" makes it is easy to see the devotion to the Marian figure. "Mother, mother, mother, pin a rose on me/For I am to be Queen of the May" is an old folk song which captures the essence of May Day. Traditionally the month opened with the young women scouring the countryside for the first flowers of the spring season to "bring in the May." Even an innocent child like Heidi searches for them and the modern musical "Camelot" features a lavish production number on the lusty month of May sung by young Guinivere.

The maid of May is never threatened sexually by her Trickster Son or her stalwart Trickster protector, such as Friar Tuck. Stained glass pictures in Salisbury cathedral show the Mayday dancers with a full-sized Marion and a smaller leaner figure of a boy archer, who may be a vestigial Robin Hood. Friar Tuck is resplendent in his role as Fraser's king of the wood, the attendant priest at the goddess' shrine. He may have grown old in her service, inclined toward a midriff paunchiness, lax toward his religious duties and too fond of wine, but he is Maid Marion's protector still. Like his fellow Lord of

Misrule, Friar Tuck becomes rotund, rosy and roisterous, a caricature of Dionysus and Bacchus, complete with vine leaves, tonsure, and wine jar.

Kevin Costner's Robin Hood movie sees Tuck as driving a wagon of wine or beer, entering the city draped in ivy wreaths of Bacchus, wielding the quarterstaff with the outlaws. In most stories he is a sorry representative of organized religion but a fine messenger of God. With the trick of mythic remembrance, folklore rewrote the Robin Hood legends to include Friar Tuck although he did not appear until the 14th-century ballads. Most Robin Hood stories center around the rescue of Richard the Lionhearted who died in 1199. The Franciscans did not come into England until 1224 yet most assume that Friar Tuck is a Franciscan when, in fact, he is a renegade monk; i.e. one who has broken his vow of stability by leaving his monastery without permission. No wonder he is hiding in the forest. Even so, he wears a brown habit, a cord with three knots and sandals. Because Franciscans were known for their joyful dancing and singing, Friar Tuck first enters England as a "dancing friar" in his encounter with Robin Hood where they confront each other over a stream and "dance" around each other physically and verbally. Whatever his entrance, Friar Tuck is connected with the spirit of frolic.

Edith Wharton's *The Age of Innocence* uses Mayday terms for her characters' names. The hero is Newland Archer, a modern Robin Hood in the "newland" of America who marries May (Maid Marion) Welland. He lacks the outlaw's spunk because he is unable to leave his wife to follow his love to Europe. Rather like Robin Hood who bled to death at the hands of a faithless prioress, Newland Archer bleeds slowly to emotional death until he is too weak to climb to his love's apartment. Robin Hood shot an arrow out of the window to mark his grave as Archer marks time. In *The Handmaid's Tale*, Margaret Atwood also uses Mayday as a password for the underground resistance to her handmaid's totalitarian regime, carefully explaining that Mayday comes not from the month but from the French cry for help, "M'aidez moi." In one sense Atwood's Mayday is a procession because her narrator is so solitary. Although it has fallen into disuse, the May procession used to be a ritual for students in Catholic schools. Someone was selected as the May Queen, often accompanied by a male escort grudgingly called the "King" because a "Queen" needed an escort to crown the statue of Mary, the high point of the ritual. Any memory of the pagan "King's" unfortunate fate was expunged by the Christian ritual.

Although it is easy to take a jaundiced perspective that religion usurps feminine holidays as masculine holydays, the continued presence of the symbiotic and complementary natures of most change-of-season feasts tends to soften any criticism. The union of opposites is desirable and, if one holiday should reflect the masculine more than the feminine or if a holyday should seem more feminine than masculine, the end and intent of both is achieved if a "healday" soothes an individual or a community to a better peace.

The configuration of the union of opposites occurs in the parade and the procession when seen as the process of conception. When the lone egg leaves the ovary for its winding journey down the Fallopian tubes to the uterus, "she" is the creative intuitive aspect needing the male element to fertilize her into full being. The crowd of energetic sperm stroking their way toward the egg is mirrored in the image of men marching around a central or larger female. When the procession meets the parade, when the egg and the sperm dissolve their mutual walls, when conception and regeneration take place, the world celebrates a "healday." And a new individual and a new community are brought into being; in literature, the romantic comedy ends with dancing and feasting and the hope of a renewed world.

POLITICAL ACTIVISM AND QUIETISM IN SHI'A RITUALS: VERSATILITY IN PARADOX

Mehran Tamadonfar

Introduction

From the outset, the Shi'is, as the minority in the Islamic community, developed political styles and attitudes that were manifested in their rituals with deep cultural roots. These rituals demonstrate two paradoxical orientations: one activism and rebellion, and the other quietism and submission to authority. This paradox provides the Shi'is with an exceptional versatility in adopting any, even contradictory, political attitudes. Historically, the Shi'a self-perception of an oppressed minority has resulted either in subjugation to or revolt against authority. They have even developed a doctrinal justification for this paradoxical attitude.

Currently, activism marks the Shi'a political orientation; thus, identification of the Shi'is as the militant Muslims. The quietist doctrine of *Taqiyyah* (religious dissimulation) is attacked by the forces of activism for being reactionary and counterproductive. According to the activists, Islam has always been a revolutionary movement committed to changing the existing non-Islamic orders. This revolutionary attitude is vividly manifested in the Shi'a rituals.

Rituals and Political Quietism and Activism

All organized religions contain certain exoteric elements that might not be intrinsic to the central message of the religion, but might play a crucial role in the internalization of the message by the followers. Shi'a rituals play such a critical role, since they are the cultural link between Islam and specific Muslim communities. On the one hand, these rituals facilitate the expression of Islamic values in terms that are understandable to the community and, on the other hand, they incorporate certain communal traits into the body of Islamic beliefs and practices. The Shi'a rituals in Iran, for instance, illustrate how Islam has influenced the development and direction of Iranian culture since the beginning of the 16th century,

25

and how this cultural tradition has shaped the exoteric dimensions of Shi'ism.

Most Shi'a rituals, especially the 'Ashura rituals, add greater political and emotional content to the Shi'a practices (Zonis and Brumberg 55). These rituals are criticized for their un-Islamic or even anti-Islamic connotations that not only endanger Islam, but also leave the Shi'a community open to manipulation by its leaders for political purposes (Kasravi 44). However, such rituals as Rawda-Khani (Narrative Recitation), street processions, and Ta'aziyeh are dynamic and powerful components of Shi'i cultures that, on the one hand, keep the community focused on its minority (oppressed) status, and on the other hand facilitate their mobilization in resistance to such an oppression.

While these rituals are practiced primarily by the I thna 'Ashari (Twelver) Shi'is, other extremist and moderate Shi'is also exercise these rituals. They are common among such extremist groups as Bektashis, Kizilbash, and Shabak who commemorate the events of Karbala by fasting, weeping, and beating their breasts. Chants of praise for Ali and cursing of Yazid are integral parts of these rituals. The Nusayri sect, extremists who worship Ali as God (Ali Allahis), have transformed the observation of Hussein's martyrdom from a day of sorrow and lamentation into a day of festivity and joy because, being divine, Hussein has triumphed over death (Moosa 125, 390).

The Twelver rituals may be classified according to the time or frequency of their occurrence. Namaz (prayer) occurs on a daily basis; Friday prayers are performed weekly; fasting is observed during the month of Ramadan annually; Aza-dari (mourning for Imam), joyous celebrations such as Ba'athat (anniversary of Muhammad's appointment to prophecy), and Imams' birthdays are performed annually; and Ziyarat (pilgrimage to Mecca and other holy shrines) is sought irregularly.

Rawda Khani (Narrative Recitation): This ritual that is practiced throughout the year, but with most intensity and emotion during the month of Muharram, is simply a dramatic narration of the life, deeds, suffering, and death of Shi'i martyrs. Historically speaking, these rituals that began early after the events of Karbala flourished and developed under the Safavid rule in Iran (Chelkowski 3). Almost always linked, though sometimes slightly, with the Karbala events, these stories were initially taken from the book of Rawzatu'l Shuhada (The Garden of Martyrs), which was written in Farsi. Gradually, professional narrators creatively added to their sermons and largely underscored the suffering and heroism of the Imams.

Rawda-Khani is a stationary performance by a narrator who is usually seated on a raised pulpit and his audience is gathered in a semicircle beneath his feet. These sermons are held in private homes, mosques, or Husseiniyyahs (normally an educational institution for the study of religion). The *Rawda-Khan* (narrator) is expected to excite and manipulate the emotions of his audience through the choice of episodes and modulation of his voice. The audience's emotions are raised to the point of weeping, lamentation, self-flagellation, and calling for Hussein and salvation.

Street Processions: Mainly a Muharram event, street processions entail narrative recitation, but they mostly involve public self-flagellations including *Sine Zani* (breast-beating), *Zanjir Zani* (beating with chain), and *Qameh Zani* (beating one's forehead with a sword). These processions carry a simulated body or a replica sarcophagus (*Tabut*) and are, in effect, ritualized funeral processions for Hussein and his companions. These processions go through streets and the bazaar jammed with spectators chanting eulogies and threnodies to the martyrs while groups (*dastas*) of men (women do not participate in these processions) beat themselves rhythmically with sticks, chains, and swords until the blood flows from their backs and foreheads.

The procession music and poetry exemplify the sufferings and deeds of the Imams. In reference to the fate of the youth in Karbala, this poetry says:

> My Akbar returns from the Euphrates with parched lips;
> > My young Akbar!
> Flow forth, O fountain of my moist eyes;
> > My young Akbar!
> While the turquois vat [of heaven] has dyed
> > the robe of thy life with red blood;
> The world has dyed my veil black with the indigo of mourning;
> > My young Akbar! (qtd. in Eqbal 201)

Ta'ziyeh: As the only indigenous drama engendered by the Islamic world, *Ta'ziyeh* is a "ritual play" that has its form and content deeply rooted in the religious and secular traditions of Muslim societies, especially those of Iran. Although these plays cover the whole array of Islamic history and traditions, as understood by the Shi'is, the nucleus of the plays are the events of Karbala and martyrdom of Hussein.

After Hassan, Ali's older son and his rightful successor, his brother Hussein set out to expose the illegitimacy of the Umayyad dynasty and to restore the legitimate right of the Family of the Prophet to authority. As the *Ta'ziyeh* projects, then Hussein refused homage to Yazid, the Umayyad leader, and along with his family and 70 of his companions left Mecca for the City of Kufa, a city near today's Baghdad, to organize his opposition. The Caliph's forces ambushed them at the plain of Karbala and denied them water for ten days in the burning desert. Unsuccessful to get oath of allegiance (*Bay'ah*) from Hussein for Yazid, the Umayyad forces cut Hussein and his male companions to bits with arrows and swords, and took the females and remaining children to Damascus as captives. The culmination of this event is on the tenth day of Muharram (*Ashura*) in 680 A.D. Ever since this event, Hussein's and his companions' martyrdom symbolize the injustice of the Sunni majority against the Shi'is and the Shi'i obligation to resist this injustice.

Ta'ziyeh is neither performed in all Shi'i communities, nor does it involve the same rituals. To the Shi'is in India, *Ta'ziyeh* is not a dramatic theatre, rather it is an actual object, a reproduction of the tomb of Hussein (Jaffi 222). In Iran, however, *Ta'ziyeh* has evolved into a highly stylized theatre with extensive poetry, music, and production.

There is no consensus about the historical origins of these plays. Some date them back to 963 A.D. and the opposition to the oppression committed by the Umayyads against the Family of the Prophet by Ahmad-ibn Booyeh, the ruler of Baghdad (Browne 30-31). Much of this emotion was initially expressed through narrative recitation and street processions. At the popular level, inherent in these ceremonies was a community of shared feeling and participation in the tragedy and fate of Hussein. For some time, the objective was opposition to the power and establishment of the Sunnis. But, with the passage of time and changing conditions, theatrical enactments of the struggle replaced real fighting (Baktash 97). By the 18th century, street processions and narrative recitations were fused into a new dramatic form.

In Iran, these plays had their roots in funeral songs and commemoration of deceased heroes. However, with the official support of the late Safavid leaders (1501-1722 A.D.) and the Qajar dynasty (1779-1920 A.D.), these plays gained an Iranian character, and were later spread to Iraq and southern Lebanon. During the

Nasseruddin Shah's rule (1848-96 A.D.), *Ta'ziyeh* gained great significance in Iran largely due to the official sanction and growing professionalization of the performances. Hundreds of places such as *Takkiyyehs, Husseiniyyehs,* and *Maydans* were established to perform the Ta'ziyeh. The Qajars prided themselves in building an elaborate *Takkiyyeh* called *Dawlat* and sponsoring major productions there (Humayuni, *Ta'ziyeh* 20). With the growth of Ta'ziyeh, the greater dramatization of religious performances was gradually accepted, and individual creativity found its way into the content and styles of performances (Baktash and Ghaffari 7-8). This growth also led to the emergence of humorous *Ta'ziyehs,*[1] collection and completion of *Ta'ziyeh* poetry, and reconcilliation of this poetry with the classical Persian music and songs (Mashhun 39). These developments gave primacy to the theatrical dimension of *Ta'ziyeh* over its religious one, and enhanced the non-Islamic influences on the future development of these plays.

The origins and early developments of the *Ta'ziyeh* can be attributed to the Persian, Mesopotamian, Anatolian, and Egyptian myths (Yarshater 93). However, it was the pre-Islamic Iranian—predominantly Eastern Iran—traditions that provided a solid and ready-made framework for the future development of these plays. The Zoastrian workship of Mitra that, like *Ta'ziyeh,* was performed on a raised platform clearly gave roots to these passion plays (Rezvani 23-24). The pre-Islamic epic stories were also most likely instrumental in the popularization of the Ta'ziyeh. At least the two dramas of Yadegar-e Zareran (The Memorial of Zareran), a Middle Persian epic that was of a Parthian origin, and the *Blood of Siyavush* (Khoon-e Siyavush) contributed to religious ceremonies.[2] The symbolisms found in Ta'ziyeh are also seen in similar fashion in the epic stories of Bijan and Rooin (Ferdowsi 1238-39). The use of the title of *Shah* (King) and *Shahzadeh* (prince) for Hussein and Hassan and their sons respectively also indicates the Iranian cultural influences.

Non-Middle Eastern religious and secular practices also influenced the content and styles of *Ta'ziyeh*. The presence of lions and dragons might conceivably be the result of the influence of the Chinese theatre (Janatti Ata'i 3-4). Puppetry in Ta'ziyeh also reminds one of similar theatrical practices in Japan and other parts of Asia. European theatre seems influencial in the later development of *Ta'ziyeh* in Iran (Mahjub, "Effect" 148).

Ta'ziyeh Production. Ta'ziyeh is often a broad and comprehensive spectacle that embraces the entire community. As such, the popular beliefs determine the parameters of the content and styles of these productions. In the beginning, these plays consisted of a few loosely connected episodes with long elegiac monologues followed by some dialogues. There was little action other than recitation and singing. The actors read their lines from prepared scripts. This practice that continues even today largely reflects the Muslims' proscription against representation of living things, especially the Prophet and Imams. With the passage of time, especially under the Qajar support, the production became professionalized with the establishment of *Takkiyyehs*. With the decline of the royal patronage, two types of *Ta'ziyyeh* productions are found: One by the professional groups and the other by the non-professionals. Today, professional productions are played throughout the year in both urban and rural areas. These troupes are usually a family business with actors trained from their childhood. The non-professional productions are usually organized on or around the day of 'Ashura by an ex-professional or semi-professional Ta'ziyeh actor who brings the villagers together to perform, most commonly, the martyrdom of Hussein. To the actors and spectators, this is an act of communal piety and has very little artistic value.

From the outset, the interplay between the actors and spectators was the central attraction of the popular Ta'ziyeh. The *Takkiyehs* preserved and enhanced this feature. The main action takes place on a curtainless and raised platform. Surrounding this platform are narrow secondary platforms used for sub-plots and for indication of journeys, passage of time, change of focus, and special events. The spectators surround these platforms and passageways, which itself symbolizes the ambush of Hussein by the Umayyad forces. The audience, thus, plays the dual roles of a symbolic villain and, at the same time, the mourners of the martyrs. In the *Ta'aziyeh* of *The Marriage of Qassem*—Hassan's son who was to marry Hussein's daughter Fatemeh at his father's will—there is extensive audience participation and interaction with actors. As the fighting goes on, both actors and spectators make preparation for the wedding on the central stage and in the area surrounding it. They participate in this joyous event collectively until the horse that Ali Akbar, Hussein's son, was riding in the battlefield appears without his rider. At the sign of death, the spectators freeze into position. With the return of Ali Akbar's body, the audience weeps as it participates in the last rites of the dead. In line with rituals in the Shi'a funeral processions, the audience assists with the carrying of the coffin and performing funeral rites and, at the same time, continuing with their participation in the wedding festivities by turning from side to side and changing from weeping to laughter.

The audience normally knows the story and adds to the emotional component of the drama by its explicit, forceful, and sometimes violent expression of grief and mourning that is lacking in the actual production. Communal participation—whether in the form of financial backing for the event, playing in the drama, or being an active spectator—is viewed as an instrument of salvation and redemption. Thus, there is no scarcity of participation. In fact, the productions at the *Dawlat Takkiyyeh* during the Qajar period were extravagant events (Chelkowski 7-8).

Acting in the *Ta'ziyeh* has rarely been realistic, since the events were so extraordinary that the plays could never achieve realism regardless of the quality of acting. Actors are usually men and children, not women. Given the nature of characters they play, including the holy leaders and villains, these actors never seek to nor could they realistically portray them. An actor who is a devout Shi'i, can never conceivably become one with the Imam. This is normally viewed as blasphemy (Mamnoun 157-58). Also, the actor who plays the villain—Yazid, Shemr, etc.—has very little artistic desire to identify with the role, because he not only rejects the villians' acts and deeds but also wants to avoid violent reaction from the spectators. To the latter end, it is not uncommon for the actor playing Shemr to announce at the beginning: "I am not Shemr, nor is this the land of Karbala; I am just playing the role." This formula is partly used to fend off the danger that the spectators would become so enraged at his killing of their beloved Imam that they would kill him, and partly as a preparation for the role (Fischer and Abedi 15).

Although there are examples of women's acting in the *Ta'ziyeh* in southern Iran (Baktash and Ghaffari 4), women have generally not acted in these plays since W.W. II. Before, women did partake in the Ta'ziyeh, especially in the south. Evidently, during the reign of Fathali Qajar (1797-1834 A.D.), the Shah's daughter sponsored *Ta'ziyehs* for women in which women were the main players and portrayed the central female personalities in the Islamic/Shi'a traditions like Fatemeh and Shahrbanu (Massoudiyyeh 19). Female personalities are portrayed as heroic and self-sacrificing individuals who set aside their own needs and natural inclinations as mothers, sisters, wives, and relatives in order to carry out the will of God, to promote Islam, and to support the righteousness of Hussein's actions. In the afore-mentioned play of *The Marriage of Qasem*, his mother begs Hussein to allow her son who is getting married to participate in the *Jihad*.

When Qasem leaves for the battlefield, his mother says: "O brave lion cub so worthy of my milk. I am one thousand times fortunate to have a son of such ilk" (Humayuni 20).

The Language of Ta'ziyeh. While the specific Ta'ziyeh stories are set and well known, the language may vary sharply from one story to another and from one production to another. The language covers a fairly broad spectrum of ideas and feelings from expressions of sorrow for the sufferings of the Family of the Prophet, to appeals to the villains for ceasing the injustice, to calls for revolt against tyranny and oppression. Initially, the *Ta'ziyeh* language was simple and concentrated on universal truth. Gradually, however, during the 19th century, they became more developed and refined as literature. This developed form of language became increasingly secular in content, and reflective of the Iranian folk traditions (Chelkowski 8).

This literary language and its link with the Persian literary traditions has not been adequately studied. There is no doubt that this language was derived from religious rituals of processions as well as literary sources dealing with martyrdom of Hussein and related events. The books of the *Rawzatu'l Shuhada* (15th century), the *Haft Band* (16th century), and such poetry works of Qa'ani and others are among the major literary sources of these plays (Hanaway 182-83). However, there is no comprehensive published source containing these stories available. Even for what is available, no direct link can be established with the Persian literary traditions. However, even those who suggest that the *Ta'ziyeh* language is—in contrast to Persian poetry—general, direct, and simple, do admit to the influence of that poetry upon the Ta'ziyeh language (Forough 80-81).

Like the earlier Ta'ziyeh writers, modern writers incorporate activism and quietism, love of the Family of the Prophet and hatred for the oppressive tyrants, the redemptive nature of martyrdom for Islam and mourning for its martyrs, fatalism, and free will into their plays. In one version of the Ta'ziyeh of the *Martyrdom of Hussein*, when asked for the reasons for his revolt against the oppression of the Umayyads, Hussein answers: "...because of the sins of the Nation of believers." In another version, he states: "Fate and the will of God dictated thus" (Shahidi 59). A much more enlightened response is furnished by another writer in the *Martyrdom of Ali Akbar*, when, in response to his sister Zainab, Hussein stated:

> ...to revolt is better than to endure,
> Hatred of this infidel must not destroy our faith.
> Even Solomon's kingdom was transitory.
> Although the fiend works hand in hand with the Devil,

if Allah had not wanted Islam to spread
You and I would have no life.
Those who have not been struck by the Devil
Never ascend to Solomon's throne,
Summon young Ali Akbar, without him I have no life. (Shahidi 59)

There is undoubtedly a qualitative difference in the philosophical components and styles of the *Ta'ziyeh* literature. Some use questionable language in an attempt to downgrade the villians and the community and to elevate the Family of the Prophet and establish their right to authority. In the *Martyrdom of Ali*, the author quotes Ali as having said to Muhammad in his dreams:

O Cousin, the people, after thou wert gone, had no regard for thee. A certain dog [referring to Abu Bakr, the first Caliph] stretched forth the hand of cruelty and injustice, and made a breach in thy house. He disregarded my nobility and merits, and took the Khalifat from me by force. He aimed at Ali's disgrace, in that he put a rope round my neck. He burned the door of the house with fire, and in so doing grieved thy holy children. (qtd. in Pelly 138)

The most criticized texts of the *Ta'ziyeh* are the ones that demonstrate an unending obsession with the Imams' suffering and their search for pity and reward for such sufferings. Muhammad's response to the above complaint by Ali is:

O Ali! Ali! I am undone! Complain no more, for I cannot bear to hear it. I am consuming away as a burning candle by thy sad condition; I am terribly concerned on thy behalf. O' Ali, I swear by the Lord, the Creator, that mighty God, that I am heartily weary of such people who have not regarded nor honoured thee. By the Lord, I am an enemy of such a nation. Be not sorry; I will advocate thy cause in the Day of Judgement. (qtd. in Pelly 138)

Paradoxically, the same Ali embraces martyrdom when he says:

Come out, O morning, from the bosom of the east, and be not sad owing to Haidar's murder. It is decreed that before dawn my head shall be cloven asunder with the stroke of a scymetar, and my moon-like face be washed with my own blood. But let God's will be done; it is for the Shi'ahs that I suffer all this. (qtd. in Pelly 138)

Similar patterns are found in the *'Ashura Ta'ziyehs*. Hussein complains of injustice, mourns the oppression against his family and followers, and cherishes revolt and martyrdom. In one of the more emotional scenes at the bed of his son, Ali Akbar, he comments:

O' Ali Akbar, thou light of my eyes, thou art in a sound sleep now, disregarding that to-morrow, dear one, thou must become a martyr. O' flower of my garden the palm tree of thy stature shall be struck down from the saddle to the ground with the axe of injustice. (qtd. in Pelly 277)

In rejecting Yazid's request for surrender, however, he bravely calls for resistance and welcomes martyrdom:

Out upon thy tyranny, thou revolutions of time! Fie to thee and thy fidelity, thou faith less spheres! How can I the new rose of the meadows of the illustrious prophet's flower-garden, the esteemed child of Ali the lion of the great Maker of the universe, surrender to Yazid, though my head be severed from the body by the edge of a glittering sword? *I am willing to be killed* for the sake of God's people, that I may intercede for all in the great plain of the last account. It is hard for me that Zainab should be led into captivity; but easier than to surrender to an adulterous generation. (qtd. in Pelly 251)

Self indignation and search for forgiveness and redemption by the villians seem to be integral to most Ta'ziyeh literature, and are largely designed to elevate the status of the Imams and to enhance their legitimacy and justice of their cause. The villain often admits to the greatness of the Imam and his own wrong deeds. In the *Ta'ziyeh of Qasem*, Shemr admits to Hussein's greatness by saying:

Accept my challenge, O gem among men
Accept my challenge, O ruler without a friend
Accept my challenge, ye from whose locks
and face one may learn the Surahs of
lightness and grace. (Humayuni 113)

On the occasion of beheading Hussein, Shemr admits to the Imam:

I am the hard-hearted shameless Shemr,
I have no fear of God;
I have no shame before the prophet;
I have no embarrassment before the cheek of Ali;
I have no fear in my heart of Hassan;
I am not afraid of the lamenting of Fatemeh;
I shall cut off the head of her son;

I shall cause her Zainab to have a scratched
face [from mourning]. (Baktash 110)

This style excites the spectators into a frenzy of opposition to
tyranny. The Imam's merciful response to an indignant enemy
enhances the legitimacy of his claim and the redemptive nature of his
cause. When Hur ibn Yazid, a respected Umayyad commander who
halted Hussein at Karbala, sought Hussein's forgiveness, Hussein
praised him for his noble deeds. In a *Ta'ziyeh*, Hurr is quoted as
having said:

O son of the prophet! Here is the man who did you great injustice in
detaining you at this place and causing you so much trouble. Is it possible
for you to forgive a sinner like me?...when all hopes for peace are gone, I
cannot buy Hell for the worldly gain. Forgive my mistake and allow me to
sacrifice myself for you. Only by doing this can I redeem myself in the eyes
of God for my sin against you.

In response, Hussein embraces Hurr and says: "You are free-
born and noble (*Hurr*) as your mother named you" (qtd. in Jafri 209).
   The poetry of *Ta'ziyeh* combines these ideas into a set of
instructions for communal activism. In the *Martyrdom of Hussein*, the
actors sing:

It is the month of Muharram,
Shi'is revolt! Shi'is weep! Shi'is revolt!
It is the death of Hussein, Hussein the Sun of
the Easterners;
East and West and whatever in between is in mourning.
Without the king of religion, today is my last day on
the earth.
My corps under this ground is without a burial shroud,
Fetch me an old shirt and let me prepare to join
the earth today. (qtd. in Massoudiyyeh 77)

Political Symbolism in the Ta'ziyeh. As in all performance
conventions, the *Ta'ziyeh* consists of certain symbolic elements
designed to convey a sense of time, intensity of evilness and
goodness, and the redemptive value of mourning. The intent is to
transform the audience in some perceived manner: to make them
laugh and/or cry, to create in them a sense of heightened reality, to
elevate their sensibilities, and to generate a powerful sense of
emotion (Beeman 24).

The Ta'ziyeh symbolism in Iran is deeply rooted in the Persian socio-cultural and political traditions. The dualism of good versus evil, symbolized as light versus darkness, prevalent in these plays is undoubtedly rooted in the pre-Islamic Zoroastrian traditions. In these dual images, sacrifice and death are portrayed as darkness, while life is portrayed as light. Hussein's sacrifice of himself (submission to darkness) is to bring salvation or eternal life (light) to the followers at the end of time. This means the final triumph of good over evil (Hanaway 187-88). The use of the titles of *Shah* (king) and *Shahzadeh* (prince) for Ali and members of his family also indicate the influence of the Persian political traditions on these plays. In Iran, these titles were exclusively used for the Persian kings and their sons and not for the Caliphs. The incorporation of these symbols into the *Ta'ziyeh* literature was designed to develop a link (Humayuni 20) between the religious and political establishments and consequently legitimize both in the public eyes.

The performance symbolizes timelessness. In fact, past, present, and future coexist in the *Ta'ziyeh* (Wirth 33). Ali, Alexander, Hussein, and Napoleon appear in the same scene. They could conceivably symbolize the timelessness of good and evil. Colors, clothing and accessories, and physical attributes of the actors are employed to symbolize events and conditions. In the past, strict division into symbolic colors was observed including white and green for protagonists and red for the villains. Red also symbolized blood, sacrifice, and death. Today, black also symbolizes death and mourning. Depending upon the producers' financial resources, costumes' colors and styles are carefully chosen to conform to these symbolic conventions. However, in less elaborate productions, little attention is paid to costly symbolism. When possible, warriors dress in military uniforms, traditionally British officers' jackets. Abbas, the standard-bearer of Hussein's troops, is distinguished by wearing a long white Arabic shirt, embellished by a military jacket, boots, and a helmet. The villains wear red clothes and carry bloodied swords. The martyrs' clothes are stained with blood. Bad characters wear dark sun-glasses, learned people wear reading glasses, and those with eminence walk with a stick. Props often have symbolic meanings as well. A bucket of water usually represents the river, often the Euphrates, Gabriel's umbrella indicates descent from heaven, and an automobile hub-cap is a shield. The choice of the actors is also based on the symbolic meanings of their physical attributes. The actor chosen to play Shemr is usually a tall man with a strong and frightening voice. Preferably, he has blue eyes, most likely symbolizing his infidelity and lack of identity with the community.

Hussein is played by a bearded man in his 40s, and Zain al-Abidin (the fourth Imam) by a sick man, in some villages by a pale opium addict (Fischer and Abedi 13).

Conclusions

The Shi'a rituals have been criticized by not only the secular political establishment but also by the Sunni and Shi'i scholars. Much of the opposition by the clergy is theological and justified on the basis of the principle of prohibition of representing Muhammad and the Imams. While supporting the dynamic and revolutionary dimensions of these rituals, some Shi'i scholars criticize their historical inaccuracies and their quietist components. Regardless of their religious views, these leaders have unceasingly used these rituals in advancing their political and social objectives. This has, of course, made the secular political establishments the most ardent opponents of activism in these rituals, when such activism is perceived irreconcilable with their interests. Dissident political groups have often used these rituals to mobilize support against governments and their policies. In response, governments have sponsored those rituals that reinforce quietism when possible, and have limited such practices when necessary.

The political appeal of these rituals is directly tied to the degree that these rituals are internalized in the Shi'a worldview. In the case of Iran, the expansion of the secular political and nationalistic elements of these rituals, combined with their religious components, have made them integral to the Shi'i-Iranian political orientation. These rituals give the community an opportunity to remind itself of its own shortcomings, and to renew its commitment to its ideal religious and socio-political order. The tragedy of Karbala often reminds the Shi'is of the on-going injustices and prepares them to accept the premise that military victory is temporary, as it was at Karbala, and true and eternal victory is only achieved through suffering and sacrifice that elevate human spirit and consciousness. This premise plays a dual role. On the one hand, it makes the Shi'is cognizant of the imperfections of this life and, at times, quiet in the face of tyranny and oppression. On the other hand, it harvests the seeds of an active community in pursuit of justice by whatever means necessary. Thus, the current Shi'i activism in the forms of revolutions and terrorism is by no means the only or the final form of Shi'i political orientation. In response to changing circumstances, the Shi'is will exercise their impressive political versatility and will adopt quietist and activist orientations in the future, as they have done in their long history.

Notes

[1]Sadeq Humayuni cites 100 Ta'ziyehs in his *Ta'ziyeh and Ta'ziyeh Khani.* 45-63.

[2]For the story of Siyavush refer to: Yahya Gharib. *Khoon-e Siyavush* (Siyavush's Blood). Tehran: Afshar Publications, 1362 A.H.

Works Cited

Baktash, Mayel. "Ta'ziyeh and Its Philosophy." *Ta'ziyeh; Ritual and Drama in Iran.* Ed. Peter J. Chelkowski. New York: New York UP and Soroush P, 1979. 95-120.

Baktash, Mayel, and Farrokh Ghaffari. *Teatr-e Irani, Se Majlis-e Ta'ziyeh* (Iranian Theatre, Three Ta'ziyeh Ceremonies). Shiraz: Entesharat-e Sazeman-e Jashn-e Honar, 1350 A.H.

Beeman, William O. "Cultural Dimensions of Performance Conventions in Iranian Ta'ziyeh." *Ta'ziyeh; Ritual and Drama in Iran.* Ed. Peter J. Chelkowski. New York: New York UP and Soroush P, 1979. 24-31.

Browne, Edward G. *A Literary History of Persia.* Vol. IV. Cambridge: The UP, 1959.

Chelkowski, Peter J. "Ta'ziyeh: Indigenous Avant-Garde Theatre of Iran." *Ta'ziyeh; Ritual and Drama in Iran.* Ed. Peter J. Chelkowski. New York: New York UP and Soroush P, 1979. 1-11.

Dabashi, Hamid. "Ali Shari'ati's Islam: Revolutionary Uses of Faith In a Post-Traditional Society." *The Islamic Quarterly* 4 (1983): 203-22.

Eqbal (Namdar), Zahra. "Elegy in the Qajar Period." *Ta'ziyeh; Ritual and Drama in Iran.* Ed. Peter J. Chelkowski. New York: New York UP and Soroush P, 1979. 193-209.

Ferdowsi, Abulqassem. *Shahnameh.* Vol. V. Tehran: Brookhim, 1314 A.H.

Fischer, Michael M.J., and Mehdi Abedi. *Debating Muslims, Cultural Dialogues in Post-Modernity and Tradition.* Madison: The U of Wisconsin P, 1990.

Forough, Mehdi. *A Comprehensive Study of Abraham's Sacrifice in Persian Passion Plays and Western Mystery Plays.* Tehran: n.p., n.d.

Gharib, Yahya. *Khoon-e Siyavush* (Siyavush's Blood). Tehran: Afshar Publications, 1362 A.H.

Hanaway, William L., Jr. "Stereotyped Imagery in the Ta'ziyeh." *Ta'ziyeh; Ritual and Drama in Iran.* Ed. Peter J. Chelkowski. New York: New York UP and Soroush P, 1979. 182-92.

Humayuni, Sadeq. *Ta'ziyeh and Ta'ziyeh Khani.* Tehran: Sazeman-e Jashn-e Honar, 1350 A.H.

____. "An Analysis of the Ta'ziyeh of Qasem." *Ta'ziyeh; Ritual and Drama in Iran*. Ed. Peter J. Chelkowski. New York: New York UP and Soroush P, 1979. 12-23.

Jaffi, Syed Husain Ali. "Muharram Ceremonies in India." *Ta'ziyeh; Ritual and Drama in Iran*. Ed. Peter J. Chelkowski. New York: New York UP and Soroush P, 1979. 222-37.

Jafri, S. Hussain M. *Origins and Early Development of Shi'a Islam*. London and New York: Longman, 1979.

Janatti Ata'i, Abulqassem. *Bonyad-e Namayesh dar Iran* (The Foundation of Performing Art in Iran). 2nd ed. Tehran: n.p., 1356 A.H.

Kasravi, Ahmad. *Shi'igari* (Shi'ism). n.p.: n.d. [1361 A.H.].

Keddi, Nikki R. *Roots of Revolution: An Interpretative History of Modern Iran*. New Haven: Yale UP, 1981.

Lewis, Bernard. "The Shi'a in Islamic History." *Shi'ism, Resistance, and Revolution*. Ed. Martin Kramer. Boulder: Westview P, 1987. 21-30.

Mahjub, Muhammad Ja'far. "The Effect of European Theatre and the Influence of Its Theatrical Methods Upon Ta'ziyeh." *Ta'ziyeh; Ritual and Drama in Iran*. Ed. Peter J. Chelkowski. New York: New York UP and Soroush P, 1979. 137-53.

____. "The Evolution of Popular Eulogy of the Imams Among the Shi'a." *Authority and Political Culture in Shi'ism*. Ed. Said Amir Arjomand. Trans. John R. Perry. Albany: State U of New York P, 1988. 54-79.

Mamnoun, Parviz. "Ta'ziyeh from the Viewpoint of Western Theatre." *Ta'ziyeh; Ritual and Drama in Iran*. Ed Peter J. Chelkowski. New York: New York UP and Soroush P, 1979. 154-66.

Mashhun, Hassan. *Moosiqi-e Mazhabi-e Iran va Naqsh-e an dar Hefz va Esha'eh-e Moosiqi-e Melli-e Iran* (Iranian Religious Music and Its Role in the Preservation and Expansion of Iranian National Music). Shiraz: Entesharat-e Sazeman-e Jashn-e Honar, 1350 A.H.

Massoudiyyeh, Muhammad Taqi. *Moosiqi-e Mazhabi-e Iran; Moosiqi-e Ta'ziyeh* (Iranian Religious Music; Ta'ziyeh Music). Vol. 1. Tehran: Soroush Publications, 1376 A.H.

Momen, Moojan. *An Introduction to Shi'i Islam, The History and Doctrines of Twelver Shi'ism*. New Haven and London: Yale UP, 1985.

Moosa, Matti. *Extremist Shiites, The Ghulat Sects*. Syracuse: Syracuse UP, 1988.

Pelly, Lewis. *The Miracle Play of Hasan and Hussain*. Vol. I. London: Wm. H. Allen and Co., 1879.

Rezvani, Medjid. *Le Théâtre et la danse en Iran*. Paris: G.-P. Maisonneuve et Larose, 1962.

Shahidi, Anayatullah. "Literary and Musical Developments in the Ta'ziyeh." *Ta'ziyeh; Ritual and Drama in Iran*. Ed. Peter J. Chelkowski. New York: New York UP and Soroush P, 1979. 40-63.

Shari'ati, Ali. *Shahadat* (Martyrdom). Tehran: Husseiniyyeh-e Irshad Publications, 1350 A.H.

Tabataba'i, Allamah Muhammad Husayn. *Shi'ite Islam*. Albany: State U of New York P, 1975.

Wirth, Andrzej. "Semiological Aspects of the Ta'ziyeh." *Ta'ziyeh; Ritual and Drama in Iran*. Ed. Peter J. Chelkowski. New York: U of New York P and Soroush P, 1979. 32-39.

Yarshater, Ehsan. "Ta'ziyeh and Pre-Islamic Mourning Rites in Iran." *Ta'ziyeh; Ritual and Drama in Iran*. Ed. Peter J. Chelkowski. New York: New York UP and Soroush P, 1979. 88-94.

Zonis, Marvin and Daniel Brumberg. "Shi'ism as Interpreted by Khomeini: An Ideology of Revolutionary Violence." *Shi'ism, Resistance, and Revolution*. Ed. Martin Kramer. Boulder: Westview P, 1987. 47-66.

RE-PRESENTING AN OLD OUTDOOR ENTERTAINMENT: STONEHENGE

David Crouch
with
Adam Colin

Introduction

Stonehenge in the UK has been the site of an outdoor festival for at least three and a half thousand years. Originally erected for spiritual celebration, perhaps also for time-keeping, this structure has survived to become a World Heritage Site that is visited by a thousand people an hour during the summer months. Over one and a half million people visit the site each year. It is the site of the annual Summer Solstice celebration, where, for decades, thousands of people from hundreds of miles around have gathered to experience the moment of Midsummer as the sun rises through the far Stones at Dawn on June 21. This is accompanied by the movement of the Druids, a people who claim an ancient tradition and worship. Their tradition of worship has become linked with Stonehenge now synonymous with the tradition of the Druids, pagan worshippers who have enjoyed periodic revivals since the 17th century rediscovery of the mythical quality of Stonehenge (Mitchells 10 et seq.).

The way the monument will be presented for our gaze during the next phase of its history is the subject of continuous debate in Britain, because its great attraction make it a vulnerable site. It has come to be an icon of contemporary Britain's fascination with its past. In this process, Stonehenge ("The Stones") becomes of major interest in the way our contemporary culture places its heritage; how it seeks to enjoy outdoor entertainments and what its festivals actually mean.

Southern Britain, in the corner around Wiltshire and Dorset especially, has numerous burial mounds, henges and other ancient and mystic sites. Of course, there are sites of central historic importance all over Britain, but the huge scale of the site, and the massive blocks of stone at Stonehenge has captured the imagination more than most. It is considered the richest prehistoric site of Europe and is designated a World Heritage Site. It rises from the surrounding vast plain of Wiltshire, not far from the cathedral city of Salisbury. It is mainly a collection of huge stones, positioned in a circle. Originally, the circle of vertical stones was topped by horizontal stones of similar thickness. The view is impressive and, not surprisingly, has inspired many artists as well as travelers and tourists.

Stonehenge 1930. Postcard. British Railways.

The site is adjacent to the main road from London to the West country countries of Somerset, Devon and Cornwall and so is very accessible to large numbers of people in a holiday mood. It provides a convenient stopover for people traveling and many of these spend a few hours around the site. Central to the way we use Stonehenge today is the question of who owns the past; how the past may be drawn into the experience we have of it today, as an outdoor experience.

Long ignored as old stones in open pasture, the site attracted the interest of inquiries during the 17th century. John Aubrey was first to realize that the henge was built by the Britons and interpreted it to be a temple associated with the Druids (Mitchells 30). A century and a half later, William Stukeley mixed together the growing interest in ancient monuments, the stories of the Druids collected since classical time, ancient mythology and the patriarchal religion of the Old Testament. In a way generally favored by antiquaries, artists and poets in the 18th century, he leaned towards an idealized vision of nature or "natural religion." Thus it became opened as an outdoor entertainment, visited at that time by antiquaries, collectors (parts of the monument were taken by wealthy amateurs), and increasingly by middle-class tourists during the 19th century.

From Outdoor Entertainment Back to Spiritual Site

In the 1920s this interest was built further with a book by Watkins that directed astronomical interpretations of the importance of the Stones towards Earth Mysteries (Chippindale 35 et seq.). This argues that the legends and local customs of the countryside and the dates and places of festivals, fairs and seasonal gatherings and other traditional components in pre-industrial society are part of an enduring inheritance that is manifested in the sites and landmarks of the landscape. It is felt that these landmarks retain a spiritual, sacred significance. These arguments are shared most significantly by people who have adopted the label "New Age." For these people, Stonehenge has become an icon not only of ancient British Heritage and Culture, or even of English Landscape, but of the nature of civilization—with the idea that these megalithic sites are somehow to do with observatories, even computers, in a previous scientific culture (Mitchell 29).

Amongst a wider population, the iconic significance of Stonehenge is formed by paintings. Turner and Constable both painted dramatic and atmospheric images of Stonehenge. Both capture a mystical, spiritual quality typical of their Romantic period, but in both cases revolutionary in their depiction of landscape. This was not a distant drama of an Italian "Other," visited by wealthy heirs on their Mediterranean Tour, but at home amongst a farming landscape that was very British. It is not surprising that these images contributed to the power of Stonehenge for new generations. No longer were these being seen as isolated from the contemporary world. They had been reintroduced into popular culture.

These have been informing threads in that they have structured the special place that Stonehenge has in popular imagination and explain why it has become a feature of culture so widely enjoyed by a wide population in Britain and amongst visitors from overseas. The way in which it has become an important contemporary outdoor entertainment is the result of several influences coming together over more recent years.

The gathering of Druid members revived and increased during the twentieth century, drawing increasing numbers interested in early faiths of this kind. By the 1960s, this had become a spectacle where thousands of people each Summer Solstice journeyed, usually by car, to the site, mainly to watch the Druids celebrate, something that has become a unique outdoor entertainment. At this time the phenomenon changed from being a site of outdoor religious festival and sometime visited curiosity to being also a major outdoor entertainment. Large numbers could gather without disturbance and participate in the drama of the event. This combined with the growing popular interest in more diverse meanings and by the late 1960s many of these "onlookers" were sharing the spiritual significance of this event.

Whereas the Druids celebrate a religious event in a sacred and very organized way, there is a new community of people with a deeper interest in the Stones involved in a very extensive Outdoor Festival. People who associated themselves with New Age ideas and who were influenced by the growing phenomenon of outdoor festivals, especially rock concerts and alternative values, began a Free Festival, coinciding with the Summer Solstice, at Stonehenge in 1974. This became an annual event that attracted thousands of people to celebrate the deeper significance of the place. The event grew in size and by the 1980s had become more structured. However, in 1985 the festival was banned.

This legal action was in response to expressed concern about the behavior of some of the participants, for whom the derogatory term of "hippies" was used. Some of them were associated in the popular tabloid press with the occult, others simply with seeking an alternative

Icon of Stonehenge; by Turner.

Druid Ceremony.

lifestyle. Many of them came from ordinary suburban homes for the weekend, to which they would return on Sunday night. There was alongside this a concern for the safety of the Stones themselves and the surrounding landscape. The very idea of a Free Festival—implicitly free in order as well as in price—was anarchic for many observers. As people tried to reach the site for the festival in Summer 1985, a thousand people were arrested, 200 vehicles impounded and a police cost of over a million pounds. The legal ban on the event has continued for the last decade, and the struggle has been repeated, but with less fervor, as members have moved to other outdoor sites with similar mythical/spiritual association. Still, in the 1990s, the paths of these travelers are followed by police to where they seek to "organize" "alternative" outdoor festivals.

Re-establishing a Site for Mass Entertainment

Since the 1980s the site at Stonehenge has been fenced off from the general public. No longer is it possible to walk within the circle. Access to the surrounding field is by way of car park, tunnel and turnstile. On the way to the tunnel, the visitor is positioned in history by a series of large hoardings that depict man in space, Henry VIII, and a man dressed in Norman clothing. This is now a managed site, where the entertainment is closely interpreted by the owner/guardian, English Heritage

The site on which the Stones themselves sit is owned by English Heritage, a Government body, with the responsibility of protecting what its name implies. Adjacent land considered important in the wider outdoor experience of the henge is owned by the charity, the National Trust, who lease out the land to farmers for pasture. The Trust is equally concerned to maintain the environs of the Stones to preserve its unique quality. English Heritage has the uneasy role at Stonehenge of securing the public access to the site, while protecting the site from damage. With the powerful combination of spiritual, mythical and iconic significance and wide popularity this task is not easy. The Stones are one of the most visited outdoor locations in Britain.

This complexity provides English Heritage with a dilemma that is exemplary for the future of Heritage enjoyed as entertainment anywhere, and which poses interesting questions concerning the position of outdoor entertainments and festivals in contemporary popular culture. That popular culture is re-shaping the significance of special locations, and what people want to do when they visit them. Thus each age has had a different Stonehenge, with different measures of festival and of entertainment.

Books and articles, as well as television programs and school projects on Stonehenge abound. Stonehenge is continually prominent on the tourist route, for the home and overseas visitors alike. It is a valued symbol of the strength and continuity of British Culture. These promotions shape and re-shape the position of Stonehenge in popular culture in Britain. The power of the art icon is being joined by other forms of cultural representation, notably in advertising.

One major biscuit manufacturer has depicted Stonehenge in its promotion of its thick sandwich biscuit called Bourbon. Titled "Biscuithenge (Bourbon on the Rocks)," the advertisement strips the Stones of all their mysticism. They become something with which we are all familiar, a household biscuit. The biscuit is positioned as the horizontal stone along the top of two vertical stones. The significance of this is not lost on the reader, as several of the Stones are well-known to have fallen, or been moved during the last few centuries. But the use of the Stonehenge image in this advertisement is clever. It represents solidity, reliability and a thickness that people associate with and enjoy in the biscuit advertised (rather than a quality that breaks teeth!). Moreover, there is a strong sense of Englishness, tea and biscuits, too.

Another feature of these stones is captured in another ironic way, in their use to advertise windows used to promote double glazing. The Stones are used in this advertisement because they impress the image of a "permanent feature." The windows have a long life, and Stonehenge places this message breathtakingly. Symbolic of a different lifestyle, these windows are presented as up-market; they offer much cultural capital in terms of neighborly impression.

The solidity, reliability and power of these Stones is matched by the timeless competence of human beings to measure perfectly; to construct sound principles for permanence; indicative of the secrecy and hidden powers that surround the image of the Druids. This is the way that the Royal Institute of Chartered Surveyors uses Stonehenge as its badge of professional competence in their present promotional materials.

The twin qualities of competence and being well informed are at the center of the computer company IBM's advertisement "There's no mystery when you know how." In a drawn image it features the Stones surrounded by sketches of their imagined construction notes. The high-class lens manufacturer Zeiss has similarly used the image of Stonehenge in its advertising. It asserts the perfect accuracy and, again, durability of their product.

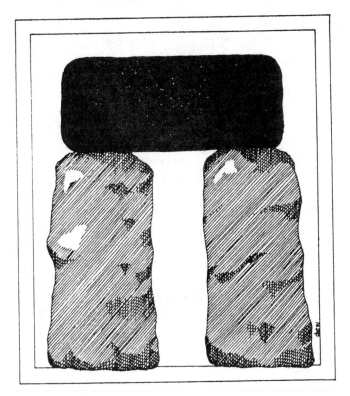

BISCUITHENGE

(bourbon on the rocks)

Symbol of Stonehenge 1990 Biscuithenge.

The messages in these advertisements influence our general perception as much as draw on our awareness of the Stones. The postcards that people buy at the gift shop by the Stonehenge car park include the Romantic paintings of Constable and Turner and drawn images of Summer Solstice, complete with Druids at worship. There are also Rock cakes on sale and postcards that depict the more humorous imaginative stories of dinosaurs being used to move the huge Stones, otherwise thought impossibly moved from their origins hundreds of miles away.

The deeper spiritual significance of the place continues to be a deep influence upon artists like John Eaves. His Stonehenge Watercolour Drawings and Collages were exhibited at Bath Gallery, UK, in 1991. English Heritage allowed him to draw within the stone circle provided he finished by 9 am. The early morning light gave long shadows or dark, rain filled skies which he recorded in a series of powerful drawings which convey the brooding atmosphere and sense of awe invoked by the monument.

These Stones, and their surrounding landscape, have become an icon of the English landscape. They are also a repository of all sorts of cultural values. This is contained in the way people are attracted to the Stonehenge site and how they want to use it. There has been increasing dissatisfaction with the way Stonehenge is presented for popular enjoyment. In this case, "entertainment" is a circumscribed notion, as the site is of Heritage value that extends beyond ephemeral fun, but that does not diminish its value as entertainment in the widest sense of the term.

The current introduction that the visitor gets to Stonehenge— turnstile, ramps, unimaginative office and barbed wire—represents a short term response to the huge numbers visiting and the Free Festival, rather than any considered program of presentation and protection. The then Chair of English Heritage said in 1985 that the site needed a permanent solution that will "protect Stonehenge for all time, as well as allowing visitors to enjoy the full and unique fascination of the site whilst not placing its preservation in jeopardy" (English Heritage 2).

Theme parks have come to be a popular means of exhibiting and interpreting Heritage in Britain (Urry 104 et seq.). Mainly modeled on the Disney formula, theme parks have become a widespread version of outdoor entertainment. However, this has not been without criticism. Concern over theme parks applies particularly to their use in Heritage and concerns the integrity of the way that the parks may selectively interpret and present heritage, and dilute or even frustrate its meaning.[1]

A theme park has been suggested for Stonehenge itself. The idea is that the structure itself could be left open or covered, and the whole site "represented" in the form of the Early Briton, or Druidic, period. It has been argued that such a treatment would close off the wider meaning that people hold of the site, and change the ways in which people can experience this monument that has spiritual and mystical quality; that the wider positioning of the site in its landscape would be lost if it were "built-in" and too much activity close to the

Gateway to Stonehenge, Photograph by Andy Kirman, 1991 (kind permission of photographer).

site is considered to diminish its quality. The commitment of English Heritage to the wider and non-commercial meaning of the site means that this form is unlikely.

The British archaeologist Glynn Daniels has suggested an alternative solution that would be a theme park, but in a very different sense. This suggests an outdoor entertainment to be called Foamhenge. This would consist of a fun structure that replicates the Stones in foam, built two miles from the site itself, for visitors and mass participants in the Solstice Festival. Although mentioned ironically, this may offer an alternative to increasing the number of people concentrating close to the site itself, while at the same time enabling mass outdoor entertainment linked with the iconic significance of the site. People who find the spiritual significance of the greatest importance may, however, not find this helpful.

Although English Heritage is mindful of costs and is not adverse to commercialising its sites, it is careful to note the distinctive character of an outdoor site like Stonehenge. "Our main aim is to conserve and display to the public, and there is no reason why these two objectives should clash unless we were crude enough to let them. As it is, we do not go in for th Disneyland approach" (Adam Colin interview with English Heritage 1990). However, the commercial issue may influence the way that outdoor entertainment is presented at this site. Stonehenge is being reinterpreted as a site of outdoor entertainment in new ways, and may no longer be available as a site of Festival.

A former President of the Royal Institute of British Architects expresses the concern of placing together an outdoor entertainment site with a site of significant Heritage value and spiritual significance. He likens possible re-presentation of the Stones to the recent history of some of Britain's great railway stations, which have strong historical associations for many people, sustained by their physical form. Many have been converted to absorb large shopping malls. "What you see is a shopping centre which just happens to have trains running through. We need to know how many franchises there will be in any scheme (for Stonehenge) and only then judge whether the site will end up as a major tourist facility which just happens to have Britain's most important monument on the outskirts" (Adam Colin interview with Max Hutchinson 1990).

This raises important questions about how different sections of popular culture can be related in the experience of outdoor leisure and indeed whether they can be on such a scale. These sections include a preference for religious celebration; free festivals, organized viewing and commercial entertainment.

These concerns are placed in sharp focus by the British Government's insistence that English Heritage seek up to 50 percent commercial funding for the project. Recognizing that the present turnstile and subway design needs to be replaced by something more "appropriate" and the limits on the number of people the site can accommodate, English Heritage proposes a visitor Interpretation Centre that will accommodate the 4-5000 visitors that currently visit the site at National Holidays, and a projected doubling of the annual visitor number. The Centre would be located up to a mile from the Stones themselves. Visitors would not need to go to the stones, as the Centre would provide the background explanation, viewing-points and shops.

In taking this approach, the strains are evident between achieving what English Heritage calls a "heritage management project," the popular interest in the site as an outdoor entertainment and the special interest groups for whom it remains a significant calendar festival. A survey of visitors conducted by English Heritage in 1991 showed support for replacing the present facilities and for the proposed Centre (Colin). It is, however, difficult in a survey like that to engage the deeper kinds of significance associated in the imagination of popular culture. Jeffrey Jellicoe, a prominent English

Six designs for Stonehenge visitors' centre

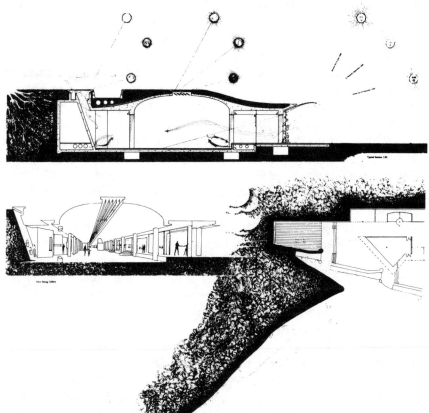

Edward Cullinan Architects

An exhibition of the six shortlisted entries for the design of a new visitors' centre at Stonehenge opens at the RIBA today. On display are six very different approaches which nevertheless share an appreciation of landscape and history, combined with a disarming sense of discretion

EDWARD CULLINAN ARCHITECTS
The winning architects regard the scheme as 'less a building and more a gateway or portal'. Set south-facing and turf-roofed into the chalk hillside, it is made from heavy materials with substantial insulation on the outside, while overhangs on the south side give protection from the sun. Rising exhibition terraces lead to a large, round, grass viewing platform

FUTURE SYSTEMS
The design's goal is to 'restore dignity to Stonehenge and its setting, and to heal the landscape through design'. The 'no-building building' involves a gently curved steel and grid shell structure clad in glass. The degree of heat and natural light that enters is controlled through a system of fish-like scales, suspended over 75 per cent of the roof area

New Designs for Outdoor Entertainment? *Journal of Royal Institute of British Architects.* 6 January 1993. Reprinted with permission.

Landscape Designer, argues that money is irrelevant to the future of a site of such acknowledged importance. "You must decide what you really want from Stonehenge." For him, that depends on who owns it; "That is absolutely clear—the nation, everybody" (Colin). However, the site as an outdoor Festival has limits. These result from its vulnerability as Heritage if huge numbers regularly walk around it. Moreover, there is a contradiction between its mystical appearance on the Plain, and its focus of thousands of people. For many, Stonehenge is a heavily peopled place.

The postcards and contemporary paintings press interest in the future of the site and in the conflicts during the time when the Free Festival was banned, and advertisements are themselves all mythic representations of the landscape and countryside. They provide the fragments of the backcloth of what makes the site so important as outdoor festival and as outdoor entertainment. The ritual use of landscape extends to many other sites that host religious and festival activities, and include Glastonbury and Lindisfarne off the Northumberland coast in the UK; Little Bighorn, Niagara Falls and Mount Rushmore in the USA.

Stonehenge itself now inspires very directly at least five places of outdoor entertainment in the USA. Two Stonehenge replicas have been built in Missouri and Texas, and very recently there are two Stonehenge constructions built of cars. One carhenge in Nebraska was built by an engineer in 1987. An Autohenge was built in Ontario in 1986. The locations of these motor henges are important and both are in flat open landscape like Stonehenge (the original), and have processional avenues as their approaches, to preserve their sense of the sacred. In 1987, mystic people from around the world visited Autohenge. Another in Washington State is a gathering place for Motorway gangs, another kind of outdoor entertainment (Chippindale 60-61).

Conclusions

As outdoor sites become attractive to commercial entertainment, the form that they take may be changed or focused in new ways. Their role in our popular culture may change too. For those sites that have wide popular significance that celebrate the secular and the spiritual; that extend beyond the commercial world to religion and myth, there is a diversity of the culture values such as an outdoor festival may serve. Moreover, there is growing concern about the way that history, common heritage, is interpreted, reinterpreted and re-presented. Ironically, as the renowned English landscape photographer Fay Godwin has remarked, there is potentially more damage to the Stones from the defenses constructed around them to protect them from visitors than the more ephemeral litter that is associated with the large festival (Godwin 52). That festival could well be better organized, and perhaps placed at some distance from the Stones themselves without needing to be banned.

The increasingly widespread popular interest in places like these demonstrates how people continue to find new ways and means of entertainment out-of-doors. This happens in ways that are as diverse as the popular culture in which people participate. It draws upon a varied supply of icons, in this case produced over thousands of years. In addition, outdoor sites are being reinterpreted; through advertising, organizing, theming and through the available presentation of the icon as postcard, pop videos using dry ice and Stone forms. People make different popular cultures with the help of these Stones.

In modern times, Stonehenge has slipped from casual outdoor entertainment to serious religious festival; a religious festival reinterpreted in contemporary thinking and more spontaneous event, to a mass outdoor entertainment with a multiplicity of purpose, and becoming increasingly organized. The present debate about its future collides these different popular cultures. Part of this process is the reshaping of outdoor entertainment, where the issues are concerned with organization and commercialization; access and presentation and values. Stonehenge typifies the present preferences for offering places as spectacle, where people come to gaze and enjoy at a distance. The kind of experience that people obtain thereby may be very different from the informal, sometimes impromptu event, as a special kind of modern day Pilgrimage. For Stonehenge, huge, unique and the focus of so many icons itself, this alternative may no longer be realistic. The continued value of Stonehenge as a site of major outdoor entertainment and continuing festival is not in doubt.

Note

[1]Sharon Zukin. *Landscapes of Power*. University of California UP, 1991. This text includes fascinating accounts of the landscapes created by Disney and by Miami Vice, both physically and symbolically. Patrick Wright. *On Living in an Old Country*. Pluto, 1985, Robert Hewison. *The Heritage Industry; Britain in a Climate of Decline*. Methuen 1987.

Works Cited

Chippindale, C. *Who Owns Stonehenge?* London: Batsford Books, 1982 and 1990.

Colin, Adam. These interviews are quoted from "The Stonehenge Experience." Unpublished dissertation, Anglia University, 1991.

Crouch, David. "Culture in the Experience of Landscape." *Landscape Research* Spring 1990.

Crouch, David and Adam Colin. "Rocks, Rights and Rituals." *Geographical Magazine.* June 1992.

English Heritage. Stonehenge Study Group Report, 1985.

Godwin, Fay. *Our Forbidden Land.* London: Jonathan Cape, 1990.

Mitchell, J. *Megalithomania.* London: Thames and Hudson, 1982.

Urry, John. *The Tourist Gaze.* London, New York: Sage, 1990.

THE DREAM OF COMMUNITY: FOLK FESTIVALS AND IDEOLOGY IN AUSTRALIA

Judith L. Kapferer

I begin this discussion of national identity with two views of the Antipodes, propounded by the 17th-century Utopian anarchist Gabriel de Foigny and the 20th century liberal phenomenologist Richard Rorty.

First, the description provided by de Foigny in his *A New Discovery of Terra Incognita Australis*, published in English in 1693, and in French in 1676, almost 100 years before James Cook's landing at Botany Bay on the east coast of Australia in 1770:[1]

What is more surprising in the Australian Dominions, is, that there is not one mountain to be seen; the natives having levelled them all...[At thirty five years of age] they are perfect in all sorts of sciences, without observing any difference amongst them, either for capacity, genius or learning...[The Australians] make a profession of being all equal, [their] glory consists in being all alike, and to be dignified with the same care, and in the same manner; all the difference that there is, is only in divers exercises to which [they] apply [themselves] so as to find out new inventions, that the discoverers may contribute them to the public good. (Berneri 191-95)

For a contemporary view, published in 1979 by the American philosopher Richard Rorty, I offer the following:

In the middle of the twenty-first century, an expedition from Earth landed on this planet. The expedition included philosophers...[who] thought that the most interesting thing about the natives was their lack of the concept of mind. They joked among themselves that they had landed among a bunch of materialists, and suggested the name Antipodea for the planet, in reference to an almost forgotten school of philosophers, centring in Australia and New Zealand, who in the previous century had attempted one of the many futile revolts against Cartesian dualism in the history of Terran philosophy. (Rorty 70-72)

I address in this paper the question of national identity. I argue that such an identity is *created*, in and through the discursive practices of both people and state, and in laying out this argument I want to take the characterizations advanced by de Foigny and Rorty seriously. Both the Enlightenment anarchist de Foigny (who refers to the Australians as hermaphrodites, denying all difference) and the contemporary American philosopher Rorty (who calls the Antipodeans "a bunch of materialists" and "Persons without minds") depict a people who elevate the Natural above the cultural or the artificial, merging the physical and the mental, and finding identity and equality—even glory—in being *all alike*. Phrased in these terms, this is a portrait in which most Australians would discern at least a grain of authenticity.

Both de Foigny and Rorty, in their very different ways, take the problem of community, the agreement about how things seem to be, as central. The quest for a sense of fellow-feeling, the dream of community, of shared sentiments and mutual understandings, and the comfortable familiarity of face-to-face relations is an age-old human concern. Whether taken for granted, or denied by loss or exile, the warmth, solidarity and fellowship of family, kin and neighborhood, the sense of belonging and identification, have long provided a bulwark against the terrors of loneliness, alienation and despair, and fueled the human imagination of both community and society.

And this is so, not only for individual beings and primary groups, but also for those larger and unseen groups—religious, ethnic, occupational, regional or national—in which they live and which daily affect their well-being and their social relations. It is the task of the State to evoke in its citizens the same sentiments of attachment, loyalty, even devotion, as those which are routinely applied to families or local communities. The establishment and maintenance of society-wide harmony and consensus, of *an identity of interest* among groups whose interests are often in fact deeply opposed, is vital to the survival of the democratic state, and to its legitimation.[2]

So I focus here upon some of the ways in which national identity, and a nationalist ideology, are constructed by both People and State. A national identity is not something static and fixed. It requires continual negotiation and adjustment among competing groups with varying and shifting degrees of power and influence in any social formation. But at the same time, in order to be effective, it must speak to the most basic understandings of human nature held by the members of these groups.

My use of the term "construction" must not be taken to imply pretense, or unreality, or false consciousness or fiction.[3] The folk festivals I examine here are not representations or symbols of some deeper underlying truths of social "realities." Nor are these practices to be taken as mere superstructural phenomena in the vulgar Marxist sense. They *are*, in and of themselves, social realities; they are the very base of social relations. Embedding taken-for-granted, unquestioning definitions of democracy, egalitarianism, individualism, autonomy, community and society, they nevertheless gather up and focus particular ideological understandings of being in the world.

Raymond Williams makes the point that

[W]e have to recognize the alternative meanings and values, the alternative opinions and attitudes, even some alternative senses of the world, which can be accommodated and tolerated within a particular effective and dominant culture. (10)

The more alternative meanings and values can be incorporated into the public culture, the more powerful the ideological hegemony exercised by the ruling group through the State. In juxtaposing People and State, I am propounding the idea that, in Australia, as in some other egalitarian societies, the Australian people and the Australian state are not to be thought of as the same, with identical interests and aims. On the contrary, the relation between People and State in Australia can be characterized as one of conflict, of mutual suspicion and deeply divided loyalties. It is a relation in which Nature (the human individual) is pitted against Culture (the artificially imposed social order).

I define the State as both an object and an idea, as the sum of all those structures, processes and agencies, both political and administrative, which maintain and underpin the social order and social relations of, in this case, capitalist production. As well, I consider the State to be *the* agent, almost the embodiment, of a modern ruling class. Such a ruling class, fractionalised and divided within itself, with shifting alliances and hostilities between dominant and subordinate fractions, may only rarely, at times of danger to its continued hegemony, be brought to act in concert. (See Althusser, Poulantzas.) Following Althusser, I take the apparatuses of the State to consist in repressive apparatuses (which act by violence or the threat of violence: police, armed services, etc.) and ideological apparatuses (which act through the construction and reconstruction of ideas about the world and its so-called realities, for example, education, the Church, the mass media, the family and so on.) It is the role of the Ideological State Apparatuses, particularly the entertainment and sporting industries, upon which I focus in the analysis which follows.

The idea of People in conflict with the State raises questions of community and society, of elite culture and mass culture, and their inter-relations. As I have already suggested, these concepts are themselves culturally and socially constructed. For my purposes in this essay it is sufficient to note the ancient distinctions utilized by Toennies in his *Community and Association*, of *Gemeinschaft* and "natural will" on the one hand, and *Gesellschaft* and "rational will" on the other, and the ways in which the means and ends of human association are differently perceived and evaluated in the two ideal types of society based on these distinctions. The mapping of rational, business-like, contractual, means-end relations on to urban, metropolitan or cosmopolitan cultures, and of affective, customary, ends-in-themselves relations on to rural, peasant and proletarian cultures, has been paralleled by assumptions of a radical distinction to be made between elite culture and mass culture respectively. What must be stressed here is that these concepts are all ideal types, in the Weberian sense, to be utilized and manipulated by both dominant and subordinate social groups in the furthering of their own projects. It is the project of the State, through the operations of its ideological apparatuses, to establish and maintain an idea of the Nation which melds both Gemeinschaft and Gesellschaft, elite and mass into one harmonious whole wherein community, civil society and the State are conceived of as synonymous and indivisible.

History, Heritage and Hegemony: Celebrating the People

The construction of a national identity utilizes a few fundamental broad understandings of as many citizens as possible. These understandings, or definitions, or meanings center upon the place of the individual in society. Thus individuals, as themselves or as representatives of particular sub-groups and communities, are conceived of as having rights and duties which "need" (for social harmony in societies which profess egalitarianism) to be balanced with the rights and duties of others to whom they might otherwise be opposed. (In Australia, such sub-groups have included Catholic and Protestant, English-speaking and non-English speaking, black and white, bosses and workers, rural and urban dwellers, men and women.) While much such balancing may be done by force or repression, giving greater advantage to one or the other group, the social order is the more stable the more competing parties *believe in* the rightness and legitimacy of the dominance of one over the others.[4]

The fundamental, constantly challenged and constantly reiterated source of national identity is that of history. The location of power blocs in historical time is central to the understanding of the rightness and appropriateness of claims to territorial ownership, political and economic dominance and social control. Australia's recorded history as a nation state is short—less than 100 years; as a geopolitical entity, as a colony of Great Britain, it is slightly longer: 200 years. The indigenous inhabitants refer to more than 40 thousand years of settlement, while the later immigrant groups have their own cultural heritage—British, Italian, Irish, Chinese, Serbian, Croatian, Greek, Turkish, Polish, Cambodian—from which to draw and with which to identify. They have each, in Bourdieu's word, their own habitus, which is always, to a greater or lesser extent, being challenged, protected or modified in relation to the habitus of others, particularly in an immigrant society like Australia.

The ability to define and to celebrate the salient conjunctural moments in the making of the Australian nation, and thus of an Australian identity, lies with those who wield the greatest political and economic power. Since 1788 and the founding of the first British penal colony in New South Wales, that power has rested with the owners and controllers of the means of material and ideological production: white, English speaking, Christian (Protestant, for most of the period) and male. Until very recently, school history texts, always a useful source of information concerning the ruling ideas of the ruling group, privileged the conquest of nature in a hostile environment as the master narrative of Australian history. Tales of intrepid explorers and resourceful pioneers abound, drawing upon gold rushes and land booms, ceaselessly utilizing the metaphor of taming both the land and its Aborigines, and the metaphor of continuing progress, both of which themes are hymned in the national anthem, "Advance, Australia Fair." The story culminates in the great epic of ANZAC (a tale of heroic military defeat at the hands of the Turks in the Dardanelles in 1915) when, it is said, the Australian nation—an independent state since 1901—"came of age." Australian literature and Australian painting, I note in passing, pursue a similar course, celebrating the natural and the land itself; debates about Australian architecture, town planning, landscaping and industrial design also center on these questions of naturalness and authenticity.

At the same time, however, streams of alternative cultural senses and meanings were and continue to be, in Williams' word, accommodated. Children are now permitted, even encouraged, as they were not 40 years ago to study seriously events such as the uprising of gold diggers at the Eureka Stockade in Victoria in 1854; the bitter shearers' strike at Barcaldine in Queensland in 1891 and the subsequent formation of the Australian Workers' Union in 1894; or the sporadic massacres of Aborigines and Chinese laborers which occurred well into the 20th century. The once strongly condemned opposition of convicts, bushrangers (outlaws), squatters (illicit land-holders) and strikers, to the colonial authorities and capitalist bosses, and their eventual acceptance as ideal types of autonomous egalitarian "freedom fighters"—social bandits, in Hobsbawm's admiring phrase—all such opposition has been ideologized as indicative of a basic democratic temper common to all Australians. Thus an outlaw like Ned Kelly, hanged at Melbourne Gaol in 1880 for a series of daring bank robberies, becomes the subject of songs and ballads and even films, and is constituted as a symbolic type of the autonomous and egalitarian individual. The incorporation of oppositional elements, and the appropriation of their political and social programs by the ruling class is crucial to the continued hegemony of that class.

Identity is now a global issue. For millions of people around the world, identity, whether personal or national or both, has become the dominant force in the formulation of individual and social goals. In what President Bush of the United States of America called "the new world order" of democracy, free enterprise and global capitalism, the circumstances and conditions of ideological incorporation have changed radically. A profusion of new nationalisms and unstable economic relations, has produced the disinterment and refurbishing of a number of folk traditions in the attempt to re-attach ordinary people to the political and economic process of multinational business relations.

John Bevan, a senior executive at Sony's Bridgend plant in Wales illustrates the problem of ideological incorporation in the following terms:

> We decided at the beginning that we weren't going to be British, Japanese or Welsh...We were going to be something new called Sony Bridgend. (Wheatley 31)

The history of the multinational corporation and its cultural heritage is not yet deeply ingrained in the popular imagination, despite the fantasies of business management and international finance. So-called "corporate culture" has yet to replace the dream of community at the center of human yearning and endeavor, or as the peg upon which to hang the incorporation of resistant or oppositional streams of thought. For the time being, the State remains largely dependent upon more traditional methods, such as the religious ceremony, the sporting contest, or the eating-drinking-singing-dancing ethnic fiesta, of maintaining hegemonic understandings of national identity as signifying *and creating* multicultural and communitarian harmony.

Three Folk Festivals: Myth and Ideology in a Changing World

I turn now to an examination of three events which I have categorized, very broadly, as folk festivals. They are the annual Australian Folk Festival, which I take as a traditional people's celebration of Australian identity; the Melbourne Cup, a horse race in the capital of Victoria for which the entire country comes to an annual three-minute standstill; and the Australian Formula One Grand Prix, staged in Adelaide, South Australia since 1985. My aim here is to elucidate the ways in which specific understandings of "Australian-ness" are incorporated to a greater or lesser extent by the dominant ideology. The extent of incorporation is dependent, I submit, upon the extent to which the State is able to dominate not only the organization, but also the mythical content of the event in question, and thus to turn its enactment into a popularly supported statement of national identity and nationalist value.

The Australian Folk Festival

The Australian State prides itself on its policies of multiculturalism, developed over long years of struggle with immigrant ("non-Anglo") communities and the indigenous Aboriginal community. These minority groups have steadily resisted attempts to incorporate their ethnic identities and their cultural heritage into a so-called cultural "mainstream"—strictly, a monolithic and monocultural dominance. Policies which have articulated such attempts, variously labeled "assimilation" and "integration" have given way to programs which claim to celebrate difference and diversity, though still within an overarching unity. Over 100 "community languages" are taught in the schools; hard-won "ethnic" broadcasting is fiercely protected; the big cities support various "ethnic" newspapers, soccer teams and cultural centers like the Dante Society, the Celtic Club or the Dom Polski Centre.

These centers underwrite a number of "ethnic"[5] events in which the members of other communities are invited to share—displays of traditional dance forms, performances of folk musical repertoires, and, most popularly, the consumption of "ethnic" cuisines. To all of this, members of the dominant cultural group, usually called "Anglo-Celtic," readily respond. The racism which lurks in the abhorrence of difference can be tempered by the recognition of such differences as being no more than a variation upon a common natural theme: a triumph of multicultural tolerance and egalitarianism.

In its numerical and cultural dominance, the Anglo-Celtic descended population has little need of a specific "ethnic" festival of its own. But in class society those who lack political and economic power seek to establish and uphold community traditions of their own, to formulate a sense of solidarity and identity among those of like situation.[6] The working-class tradition of struggle against oppression cuts across lines of gender and of ethnicity, and in Australia has been mythologised and enshrined (in some ways even incorporated) as a national tradition. It is this working-class tradition, more than any other, which is celebrated at the annual Australian Folk Festival.

This festival, as befits its egalitarian themes, takes place at a different venue every Easter, most often in small country towns, many of which stage their own local productions throughout the year. The site may be the local showground or football field; at Kuranda, in Far North Queensland in 1990, it was the state primary school and its sports field. Venues like these, combining nostalgia and informality, imbue the occasion with an atmosphere of cheerful improvisation and co-operation, an atmosphere heightened by the mythologies of the folk festival itself.

The Folk Festival celebrates, through music, dance and story-telling, the lives of "the battlers"—ordinary working men (and sometimes women) struggling against the vagaries of Nature and the arrogance of power. Its recurrent themes are those of the land and its people, the mythologies of the Bush and its toilers. The old songs are about convicts, bushrangers, (sheep) shearers and (cattle) drovers and stockmen, drought and flood and industrial strife. The new songs cast their net wider, but their themes remain the same. They are about oppression in other lands (students in Tienanmen Square, freedom fighters in Indonesia) and global problems of pollution and land degradation and conservation. Always they are about the efforts of ordinary people, "the folk," to wrest some control over their lives and livelihoods from the tyrannies of banks and markets, laws and regulations and policies designed for the benefit of local, national or global ruling groups.

Participation in the Folk Festival is widespread. Audience and performers intermingle, and much informal teaching and exchange of material and technique takes place; the separation of performers and spectators is much played down, though there are, as always, popular stars who draw the largest crowds. Organization is in the hands of the local folk society members, with support (including some financial support) from the national society. Sponsorship is limited to local businesses and industries. Small children and the elderly, black and white, physically disabled people and raucous teenagers and alternative lifestylers, establishment "folkies" and passing tourists, all mix in an atmosphere of open friendliness and goodwill which is produced by the ethos of the folk festival itself.

The national folk festival may be conceived of as a ritual of resistance (cf. Hall and Jefferson). But it can also be understood as a ritual of incorporation of the People by the State. The characteristics of "real Australians," of the ordinary folk—mythologised as mateship (comradeship) and identity with friends and neighbors (cf. de Foigny's hermaphrodites), physicality (cf. Rorty's people without minds), egalitarianism, self-sufficiency, individualism, natural autonomy—all these can be, and are, transposed as "National" characteristics, evoking sentiments of loyalty to the State, and the values of social democracy, free-market competition, liberal choice, tolerance and diversity.

The Melbourne Cup

The so-called sport of kings—horse-racing—provides a quite different, but nonetheless complementary, perspective on rituals of incorporation and resistance. In Australia everyone may be a king, ideologically speaking, and festivals which may be thought of in other societies (I am thinking of France and Britain, particularly) as the domain of the nobility, are in Australia conceived of as belonging to all. The Melbourne Cup, run every year since 1861 (and significantly, since 1985, sponsored by Carlton United Breweries, manufacturers of Fosters beers) has been lauded as "Australia's premier sporting event." This, in a nation which prides itself on its athletic prowess in fields ranging from football and hockey to swimming and cycling and tennis. The jockey, or the horse, is not the first image of athleticism that springs to mind in the depiction of sporting champions. Yet the combination of the two, of horse-and-rider as one unit, has particular force in a society which sanctifies The Natural and endows those animals thought of as "noble"—like the horse—with human traits, and accords them an honoured place in history. *The Sydney*

Morning Herald characterizes the winner of the 1991 Melbourne Cup, Let's Elope, in the following terms.

> She is somehow both flashy and demure, a filly of hot ice and cold iron...She has the head of a duchess, the bum of a ballet dancer, and walks like a woman with business on her mind...In their own way, all great females are mysterious. (11 June 1991: 58)

The Melbourne Cup is big business and high society; it is also for the small (once-a-year, in many cases) punter and for ordinary people across the country. In this way, participation may be thought of as democratically widespread, in that young and old, rich and poor alike have a sporting interest and a monetary investment in the final outcome of the race. Those who cannot be physically present at the racecourse watch the event on television in bars and betting shops, schools and factories; others—in hospitals, cars, or offices—listen to the radio broadcast.

But in a more usual sense, of course, participation is strictly limited. Trainers, jockeys and horses are the only real participants in the sense of competing in a sporting event. For the owners, for the bookmakers and for the course officials, The Cup, as it is always called, is part of their daily business round, albeit the highlight, for many of their business year. It is also the highlight of the social calendar, with international guest lists, luncheons, balls and champagne breakfasts.

The Melbourne Cup provides a grand spectacle, in which spectatorship is the dominant activity. Spectatorship, not only of a horse race, but of naturally occurring skills and talents, polished to a high gloss by dedication and training. A major element of the spectacle is provided by the parade of opulence and high fashion, the conspicuous consumption and the conspicuous leisure activities of the ruling class, lavishly recorded on television and in the press. (One recalls Veblen's caustic commentary on the quite similar activities of the turn of the 19th-century "leisure class" in the United States.) Millions of dollars are won and lost, emphasizing the centrality of chance and fortune in a culture which routinely—and in a predictably egalitarian and individualist way—employs the concept of Luck to explain both success and failure (cf., in a quite different context, Connell, Davies). It is Luck, for example, which can explain and even, to some extent, legitimate the persistence of social classes in an avowedly egalitarian society. And the Melbourne Cup is a folk festival which makes sense of just such contradictions, justifying the existence of winners and losers by reference to a basic underlying, and natural, equality (cf. Kapferer).

So the Melbourne Cup is a festival of the Australian ruling class, a festival into which the subordinate classes are drawn. In this process, a kind of two-way incorporation may be seen to be in operation with the working class racegoers (and young people in general), subverting the more obvious pretensions of the establishment with displays of "outrageous" or merely "inappropriate" outfits and conspicuous drunken revelry. While the aristocratic pretensions of the Melbourne Cup may be, indeed are, threatened by the participation of the proletariat, the dominant ideology of egalitarian individualism actually achieves renewed force and vigor in its enactment and through that very participation.

The Australian Grand Prix

Since 1985 the Australian Grand Prix has been staged in Adelaide, the capital of the state of South Australia. It is the final event of the international Formula One motor racing championship year, and as such attracts motor racing fans from *all over the world*, especially when the outcome of the championship remains in doubt. Adelaide's—and therefore Australia's—participation in what the press is fond of referring to as a "world class" event expresses an important preoccupation of the Australian State. This is that Australia be counted as an important member of a global community, particularly in political and economic terms.

The Grand Prix is a celebration of a dominant global culture of high technology and high speed, and it would appear to have little relevance for the construction of a specifically national identity. And indeed it has not, except in the limited sense of "putting Australia on the map" in terms of blanket television coverage, as one in a series of sites selected for a festival which could as well take place in hundreds of other towns around the globe. The teams of drivers and crews represent automobile manufacturers multinational corporations none of which has anything to do with Australian tradition or sports or even Australian industry. A totally new (id)entity is being constructed, in the same manner as the "something new" of Sony Bridgend. While folk festivals and horse-races are an essentially modern phenomenon, the Formula One motor-racing championships are post-modern and post-nationalist. Vociferous promotion of the event as a period of incessant partying in which "Adelaide comes Alive" (as the city's advertising slogan has it) cannot disguise the fact that the Grand Prix forms one link in an international chain for the marketing of technological development as both an economic panacea and a moral duty, to the capitalist State.

The Grand Prix, which is not at all the creation of the ordinary people, can also be seen as a mechanism for their control. As Paul Virilio notes, citing Goebbels in 1931: "Whoever can conquer the streets also conquers the State!" (4). The movement and circulation of the mass of city dwellers is generally controlled by traffic laws and regulations, signs and signals, traffic police and parking police. The changed regulations of the Grand Prix period include, on the one hand, a relaxation of liquor licensing laws and on the other hand, a restriction on the movement of local traffic. The latter is the price the People pay for the former; and in most cases we willingly do so, taking on the worship of speed and motion which gives us a brief illusion of autonomy and freedom of movement while being, in fact, severely confined.

Australia's role in the advancement of global economic processes is limited to the support of the international giants and their sponsors. The government of South Australia and the local organizers of the event both stress the critical importance of the Grand Prix in attracting high-spending tourists to the region—a project in which the local casino operators, hoteliers and restaurateurs concur. Concern is continually expressed at the possibility that the international controlling body of Formula One racing (F.I.F.A.) might at any moment rescind the honor granted to Adelaide in 1985, and relocate the Australian Grand Prix, if the race does not meet their expectations.

The event can be seen most clearly as a festival of international capital and Australia's place as a client state (see Crough and Wheelwright) within it. It is a glorification of a style of life which fetishizes speed, movement, luxury and fame and has little relevance to either the traditions of local ruling groups—as in the atavistic celebration of Nature and the rural life in the Melbourne Cup—or the traditions and potentialities of the Australian "folk"—as in the working-class mythologies of the folk festival. The attempt (by the Australian State and its own economic and cultural colonizers) to utilize The Grand Prix, a postmodern phenomenon detached from any historical or mythological narrative, in the creation of a national identity is doomed to failure. In a context of ideological confusion— national culture? global culture? corporate culture? technical culture? (cf. Bell, Abercrombie et al.)—the project of nationalism cannot be separated—if it ever could—from the political and economic interests and aspirations of the (increasingly technocratic) ruling class.

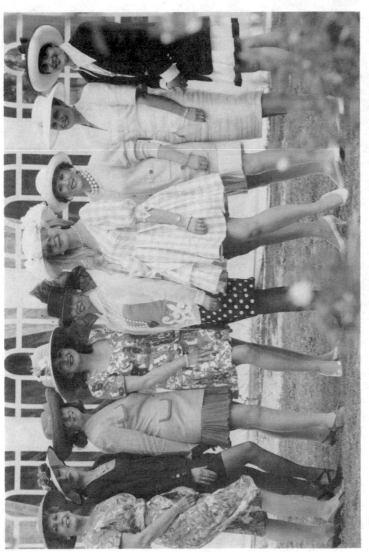

Ladies Day at the Adelaide Grand Prix. In striking counterpoint to the unrelieved machismo of the races, socialites provide a clear demonstration of the relation between conspicuous consumption and conspicuous leisure, as they do at the Melbourne Cup. Photo credit *The Adelaide Advertiser.*

The Young Gentlemen at Play. The relaxation of the rules of speed on the racetrack and of sobriety on the streets achieves a carnival atmosphere in 'the city of churches.' Preferred dress styles for male Formula 1 afficionados (and for national folk festival fans too) are notably more down-to-earth and utilitarian than those of the Melbourne Cup racegoers, numbers of whom still affect the formality of morning suits, in keeping with the studied outrageousness of their female partners' attire. Photo credit *The Adelaide Advertiser.*

Conclusion: People and State, Community and Society

What I have presented here has been a brief analysis of the place of folk festivals—very broadly defined folk festivals—in the construction of national identity and nationalist ideology. In doing so, I have suggested that the celebration of The People, particularly those which suppress class and ethnic divisions, speak to what I have called a dream of community in a way that State-imposed or State-sponsored festivals cannot do.

Yet it is just this dream of community that the ideological state apparatuses work ceaselessly to invoke on behalf of the State. For it is essential for the long-term viability of the capitalist State and its economic project that people and State, community and Society be understood as synonymous, each operating on behalf of the other for the benefit of all, for the common weal.

The joyously inarticulate (according to Jackie Stewart, former World Champion on Channel 9 television, 7/11/93) heroes of the raceway celebrate victory with a traditional champagne shower—but Foster's beer remains dominant. Photo credit *The Adelaide Advertiser*.

I have explored here some of the ways in which the conflict between People and State—a conflict manifested in a way which I take to be characteristically Australian in its affirmation of natural equality and its denial of socially imposed differentiation—can be at least partially and temporarily overcome. I have also examined some of the ways in which alternative or resistant meanings and values can be accommodated and even incorporated by a dominant culture. The three festivals I have described here—the National Folk Festival, the Melbourne Cup and the Adelaide Grand Prix—vary in their effectiveness as tools for the creation of national identity; but I would suggest that it is the Melbourne Cup, in the universality (and the doxicality, to borrow from Bourdieu's usage) of its impact, which is THE national festival. It embodies and resonates with the meanings and values—with the culture—of a nation of hermaphrodite materialists who worship the natural and the physical and deprecate the mental and the spiritual.

However, I should not like to conclude this essay with an impression of Australian culture, and Australian ideologies, as vastly different from the cultures of other western nations in the late twentieth century. Australia is only one moment in the formation of egalitarian societies which place a high, even a supreme, value on the individual. The idea of the Australian Antipodes, as a distinctive social and cultural reality, let alone one of global consequence, may not be widely familiar to those who live beyond its shores (except, perhaps, as an imagined mythological territory, as for de Foigny and Rorty). Yet the analysis of rituals of incorporation and resistance, of ideological hegemony and the legitimation of the capitalist democratic State which I have presented here, has import beyond the cultural experience of a single nation state. Despite widespread historical, political, economic and social divergencies, the People, wherever they may be, are still forced from time to time, and sometimes incessantly, to engage in struggles for autonomy and equality in social formations which, however subtly, would deny them those freedoms.

Notes

This paper is a revised version of a lecture delivered at the Netherlands Institute for Advanced Studies in the Humanities and Social Sciences in February 1992. I acknowledge with gratitude the support of NIAS, and the interest of other Fellows. I am also particularly grateful for the advice and encouragement of Professor Bruce Kapferer, of University College, London, whose 1988 work, *Legends of People, Myths of State* continues to inspire me and many others working in the field of contemporary nationalism.

[1]Although there is evidence of Portuguese and Dutch contact with the unknown southern continent in the 15th and 16th centuries, this was fleeting and unproductive; there is no reason to suggest that de Foigny had any knowledge of these contacts, or of the English ex-buccaneer Dampier's journal of 1688 which recorded the west coast natives as being "the miserablest people in the world" (cited in Hughes 48).

[2]For a stimulating discussion of crises of legitimation in the modern State, see the work of Claus Offe.

[3]My understanding of construction has affinities with Benedict Anderson's use of the word imagination, in his now classic work on nationalism, *Imagined Communities*, and also with Castoriadis' term, coined in 1964, "the social imaginary." Of this phrase Castoriadis says,

> The imaginary does not come from the image in the mirror or from the gaze of the other. Instead, the "mirror" itself and its possibility, and the other as mirror, are the works of the imaginary which is creation *ex nihilo*...The imaginary of which I am speaking is not an image *of*. It is the unceasing and essentially *undetermined* (social-historical and psychical) creation of figures/forms/images on the basis of which alone there can ever be a question of "something." What we call "reality" and "rationality" are its works. (3)

[4]This is a consummation devoutly to be wished on the part of the current ruling group, and is a phenomenon which has been much documented, especially in studies of the "embourgeoisement" of the English working class since the 1950s, and the practice of working class Toryism. See, for example, Goldthorpe and Lockwood's classic work *The Affluent Worker in the Class Structure*.

[5]The term "ethnic" is utilized as both noun and adjective in common parlance to designate the members of minority ethnic groups once referred to by a variety of terms ranging from "migrant" through pejorative appellations like "DP," "Reffo" and specific national terms like "Balts."

[6]See, for example, the work of Hoggart, or Clarke et al., and in Australia the work of Connell et al., on the widely debated concept of working class culture. One might also note in passing the attempts by women in patriarchal society to establish a bond of "sisterhood" which cuts across class, or ethnic, or religious boundaries.

Works Cited

Abercrombie, N.; S. Hill; and B. Turner. *The Dominant Ideology Thesis*. London: Allen and Unwin, 1980.

Althusser, L. *Lenin and Philosophy and Other Essays*. London: New Left Books, 1971.

Anderson, B. *Imagined Communities*. London: Verso, 1983.

Bell, D. *The End of Ideology*. Glencoe: Free, 1960.

Berneri, M.L. *Journey Through Utopia*. London: Freedom, 1950.

Bourdieu, P. *Outline of Theory of Practice*. Cambridge: Cambridge UP, 1977.

Castoriadis, C. *The Imaginary Institution of Society*. Cambridge: Basil Blackwell and Polity P, 1987.

Clarke, J.; C. Critcher; and R. Johnson, eds. *Working Class Culture*. London: Hutchinson, 1979.

Connell, R.W. *Ruling Class, Ruling Culture*. Cambridge: Cambridge UP, 1977.

Crough, G. and T. Wheelwright. *Australia: A Client State*. Harmondsworth: Penguin, 1982.

Davies, A.F. "The Child's Discovery of Social Class." *ANZ Journal of Sociology* 1 (1965): 21-37.

Goldthorpe, J. and D. Lockwood. *The Affluent Worker in the Class Structure*. Vols. 1-3. Cambridge: Cambridge UP, 1968-69.

Hall, S. and T. Jefferson, eds. *Resistance Through Rituals*. London: Hutchinson, 1976.

Hobsbawm, E. *Bandits*. London: Weidenfeld and Nicholson, 1969.

Hoggart, R. *The Uses of Literacy*. Harmondsworth: Penguin, 1958.

Hughes, R. *The Fatal Shore*. London: Collins Harvill, 1987.

Kapferer, B. *Legends of People, Myths of State*. Washington: Smithsonian, 1988.

Offe, C. *Contradictions of the Welfare State*. London: Hutchinson, 1984.

Poulantzas, N. *State Power Socialism*. London: Verso, 1980.

Rorty, R. *Philosophy and the Mirror of Nature*. Princeton: Princeton UP, 1979.

Toennies, F. *Community and Association*. London: Routledge, 1955.

Veblen, T. *The Theory of the Leisure Class*. London: Unwin, 1970.

Virilio, P. *Speed and Politics*. New York: Semiotext(e), 1986.

Wheatley, K. "Back from the Pits." *Sunday Times Business Magazine* n.d. (1991).

Williams, R. "Base and Superstructure in Marxist Cultural Theory." *New Left Review* 32 (1965): 3-16.

POPULAR CULTURE
AND THE VISUAL MESSAGES
OF THE LORD MAYOR'S PROCESSION

Terry Donovan Smith

During the 16th and early 17th centuries the Lord Mayor's Show of London celebrated the new mayor's installation each 29 October.[1] Contemporaneous accounts are from the vantage point of the elite and most analysis tends to rely on these as well as the extant scripts. However, the popular reception might not have been determined by the texts. If the words did not determine the "street level" interpretation, then perhaps an analysis of the visual elements will aid our understanding.[2] From year to year, the shows of the late 16th and early 17th centuries were very similar. Besides the obvious and necessary similarities between each year's procession (i.e. the same companies using the same barges employing the same musicians playing the same instruments wearing the same costumes, etc.), the writers would borrow characters, story-lines, and concepts, not only from their own previous work, but from other pageant poets, as well.[3] Arthur Clark points out: "Originality in Lord Mayors' pageants would have been misunderstood in Heywood's day, and he did not try the experiment" (117).

William Smythe, a participant in the festivities of 1575 and alderman of the Mayor's company, recorded a detailed account of the procession that year. There were 16 barges on the Thames, seven musical groups, eight groups of men of up to 100 (each group wearing matching gowns), parade marshals, at least three carriages, several large banners, and a pageant wagon reminiscent of medieval processional stagings. According to Smythe: "In this order they pass along through the city to the Guildhall, where they dine that day, to the number of 1000 persons" (qtd. in Hone, 248). Several of the entries indicate that the men were "two by two" which gives the impression that it was a tight squeeze down the narrow lanes. One of the bands was, however, "eight and eight" and "whifflers," or parade marshals were employed to clear the route. The whifflers employed in 1617 were "men masked as wild giants who by means of fireballs and wheels hurled sparks in the faces of the mob" (Bergeron, *Venetian* 45). Obviously, crowd control was necessary.

By 1600, the use of rolling shows had been amended with the addition of three to five temporary (but substantial) stages on land and one on the Thames. Since the procession began with the river journey, this show was first. The characters of the water show would occasionally reappear at the end of the day to bring an element of closure to the festivities.

Thomas Heywood's 1631 show, *Londons Jus Honorarium,* is a representative example of a contemporaneous Lord Mayor's Show. It began on the water where the barges of the mayor approached "two craggy Rockes, plac'd directly opposit, of that distance that the Barges may passe betwixt them" (lines 87-88). On these rocks were serpents and other monsters "spitting Fier" and "vomiting water" (89-90). There were "Syrens" playing instruments and singing and "Ulisses [who] personate[d] a wise and discreete Magistrate" (107). (Although occasionally, especially after the Restoration, adults performed, the actors were primarily children.) Ulisses gave a speech that described the scene and supplied a moral: "evade malicious envie" (126-27) and "shunne th' extreames" (148).

"The first show by Land [was]...a greene and pleasant Hill" (153-54) where the characters of Summer, Faith, Hope, Charity, Time and Truth lounged. Under Truth was "this inscription; *Veritas est Temporis Filia, i.* Truth is the Daughter of Time" (167-68).

> Time speaketh
> Fruitfull trees, greene plants, flowers of choise smell
> All Emblems of a City Governd well;
> Which must be now your charge. The Labels here
> Mixt with the leaves will shew what fruit they beare:
> The *fear of God*, a *Magisgtrate discreete*,
> *Justice*, and *Equity*: when with these meet,
> *Obedience unto Rulers*, *Unity*,
> *Plaine* and *just dealing*, *Zeale* and *Industry*: (184-91)

In opposition to these positive concepts were representations of such negative concepts as pride, malice, and envy.

"The Labels" alludes to the fact that the underlined words and phrases were printed on signs that hung beneath or near the character to which it applied. This emblematic format was extremely important to the reception of the message.

In any abbreviated performance medium, ideas must be

Virtue and Fame. From Henry Peacham, *Minerva Brittana* (London, 1612).

Ulysses. From Geoffrey Whitney, *A Choice of Emblemes* (Leyden, 1586).

projected quickly and succinctly (e.g. a political "sound bite"). The poets and designers of the Lord Mayors' Shows achieved this by using emblematic representations. David Bergeron reports that "Englishmen of the late sixteenth and early seventeenth centuries... took great delight in emblem books" (*Emblematic* 167). An emblem book is a collection of iconographical pictures usually with moral or religious overtones. Bergeron explains:

The typical emblem is essentially tripartite in arrangement. It must have a picture—usually allegorical, symbolic, or mythological in content. Frequently there is an accompanying "word" or "motto," a brief epigraphic summary of the meaning of the illustration...[and] verses which attempt to bring the picture and the motto together. (168)

Most of the texts of Lord Mayors' pageants call for mottos nearby.

> *London*, the speaker
> Will you know whence proceeds this faire increase,
> This joy? the fruits of a continued peace,
> The way to thrive; to prosper in each calling,
> The weake, and shrinking states, to keepe from falling,
> Behold my motto shall all this display,
> Reade and observe it well: *Serve and obay.*
>> (Heywood, *Honararium* lines 250-55)

In a study of 17th-century "Allegories of Truth," Sheila Williams says:

Certain tableaux devised by several other pageant-poets had all three elements—picture, motto, and verses—and usually the motto was placed above or before the tableau in emblem-book fashion. If we allow that the essence of the emblem was a picture plus a verbal explanation, and accept either the motto or the verses as fulfilling the second function, then the normal method of the pageant-poets was the same as that of the emblem writer. (qtd. in Bergeron, *Emblematic* 169)

The Lord Mayor's Show, then, could be seen as a living emblem book.

Most of the Pageant Poets, in some way, took the presence of the common person into account when planning the shows, even if it was in a condescending manner. For his 1637 Pageant, Heywood wrote that "the third pageant or Show meerly consisteth of Anticke gesticulations, dances, and other Mimicke postures, devised only for

Truth. From Henry Peacham, *Minerva Brittana* (London, 1612).

Envy. From Geoffrey Whitney. *A Choice of Emblemes* (Leyden, 1586).

the vulgar, who are better delighted with that which pleaseth the eye, than contenteth the eare" (*Londini Speculum* lines 256-59). Thomas Dekker was even less complimentary: "The multitude is now to be our audience, whose heads would miserably run a wool-gathering if we do but offer to break them with hard words" (qtd. in Burke, *London* 44). But, if some aspects of the show were designed to pander to common tastes, most were not. The ultimate arrogance was displayed by Ben Jonson who presented shows which "might, without cloud or obscurity, declare themselves to the sharp and learned; and for the multitude, no doubt but their grounded judgments did gaze, said it was fine, and were satisfied" (qtd. in Burke, *London* 44-45). (It is interesting to note that Ben Jonson was retained to write only one pageant.)

But who were "the multitude?" A generic member of the popular culture was an unemployed (or under-employed) "blue collar" worker. Due to immigration from rural areas, they lived in increasingly crowded conditions. Most had little education, but surprisingly the majority could read.[4]

In a contemporaneous account, the Venetian Ambassador, Horatio Busino, saw the crowd as "a fine medley: There were old men in their dotage; insolent youths and boys...; painted wenches and women of the lower classes carrying their children, all anxious to see the show." The ambassador is disturbed by "two ugly Spanish women...ill dressed, lean and livid and with deep set eye balls, perfect hobgoblins." In an entry that sheds light on the deportment of the crowd, he notes that a "wicked woman in a rage" attacked someone from the Spanish embassy "with a cabbage stalk" (qtd. in Bergeron, *Venetian* 45).

Anthony Munday recognized that crowd noise was excessive. For the 1611 show, he introduced interpreters in the forms of St. George and St. Andrew. However, these interpreters rode with the Lord Mayor for his pleasure: to explain and restate what he may not have understood or heard. Munday says that "the weake voyces of so many Children...in a crowde of such noyse and uncivill turmoyle, are not any way able to be understood" (qtd. in Bergeron, *Anthony Munday* 354). It is clear that the crowd heard few, if any, of the shows' words.

If the words were lost, then the visuals must have determined popular reception. The most popular type of character portrayed during this period was allegorical anthropomorphic representations of positive concepts or character traits (Table 1). Roughly 60 different characters were represented over 140 times. The second largest

Table 1
Allegorical Character Sets
("( )" indicates number of shows which character was used.)

<u>Positive</u>
<u>Concepts</u>
Ambition
Candor
Charity (4)
Commiseration
Conscience
Constancy
Councell (2)
Courage
Custome
Discipline
  eight
  Beatitudes
Equity
Expectation
Faith (5)
Fame (6)
Fortitude (3)
Fortune
God's Truth
Graces (3)
Harmony
Health
Honor (5)
Hope (5)
Hope (4)
Humility (2)
Humor
Industry (3)
Justice (6)
Knowledge (2)
Learned Religion
Learning
Liberalitie (2)
Love (2)
Loyalty
Magnanimity (2)
Majesty

Meekness
Mercy
Modesty (2)
Nobility
Patientia
Philosophica
Peace (4)
Piety (2)
Placabilitie
Plentie (3)
Providence (2)
Prudence
Religion (4)
Reward
Science (4)
Simplicity
Temperance (2)
Tranquility
Truth (5)
Vertue (3)
Vigilance (2)
Wealth
Wisdom
Zeal (5)

<u>Negative</u>
<u>Concepts</u>
Barbarism
Calumny
Death
Desire
Disdain
Envy
Error
Excess
Falsehood
Fear
Folly
Hostility

Ignorance (3)
Impudence
Malcontent
Mutinie
Oppression
Riot
Sicknesse
Sloth
Superstition
Treason (2)

<u>Government</u>
<u>and Power</u>
Authority
Civil
  Government
Commonwealth
Genius of City (2)
Homebred
Husbandry
Lawe
Military
  Discipline
Navigation
Policy (2)
State
Victory

<u>Time</u>
Antiquity
Season (7)
Time (5)

<u>Human</u>
Auditus
Five Senses
Humanitie
Olfactus
Tactus

Visus
Visus [sight]

<u>Non-living</u>
<u>Physical</u>
Ayre
Clothing
Fire
Nature
Properity
Water
  Famine
  Mansuetudo

<u>Spatial</u>
Aglaia
Albania
Bellona
Bristoll
Britannia
Cambria
Country
Earth
Exeter
Humber
Lincolne
London (7)
Oceanus
Oxford
several Citties
Severn
Thames (2)
Trent
Troya Nova
Westminster
Yourke

category was spatial representations with 20 places (mostly towns and rivers) filling 30 character slots. "London" was the most represented appearing in seven shows. Similarly, negative concepts and traits came in third. These were represented 25 times with little duplication. What was surprising was the relative scarcity of characters representing power and government. A most telling set included characters that were based on temporal concepts and physical human traits: seasons were represented only a half-dozen times and "Humanitie" and the "Senses" were used in only two shows.

The list of historical characters (Table 2) shows that almost every one is a former mayor, royalty, or a saint (with one writer thrown into the mix). And the characters representing living types were generally uncommon: eunuchs, Indians, Russians, soldiers, doctors, moors, et al.

The parade consisted of three basic visual sets: men, objects, and clothing (Table 4). The men are all aldermen, craftsmen, musicians, or officers. The clothing is either bright and colorful or dark and somber. The objects were either military oriented musical instruments, political banners, or weaponry.

The procession and its shows were, of course, not the only things to see: the crowd itself must have been a strong visual stimulus. Lining the streets were people of every description. They were, for the most part, of the lower classes. A little imagination will conjure up a crowd, pushing and shoving, jockeying for position. Street entertainers would probably have taken up positions to make some money. The elite spectators would have been a completely different visual element. They were generally separated from the street level, but some accounts show that this separation was by no means complete.

The spatial elements of a Lord Mayor's Procession can be seen as consisting of four distinct areas: two for the participants and two for the spectators. The participants were confined to the middle of the street and elevated stages. The spectators were either lining the sides of the street or watched from balconies and windows above street level. Divisions of these areas were generally distinct: men were employed to keep a the spectators back from the stages and the participants. Reports indicate that the stages were sturdy, quite impressive structures. (They even seemed to have gotten in the way of normal commerce and part of the fees paid to the organizers was for post-parade demolition.) For ease of viewing, the stages were usually high above the crowd.

Table 2
Historical, Mythological, and Living Character Sets

Historical			
Ancient Brittish	Gunner	four nymphs (2)	Severne
Barde Edward	Indians (7)	Gogmagog	Sideros
Confessor	judge	Golden Fleece	Sol
Eliza	master of shippe	Griffons	Syrens: Telsipio
Farrington	men & officers	Hercules (2)	Telamon
former mayors	Moors (4)	Humber	Telamon
Henry III	old lord	Iligi	Thamesis (2)
his queen	pastoral couple	Janus	Golden Fleece
Jack Straw	[red feathers	Jason (3)	The Nimph
John Lepston	and tiger]	Jove	Euphemes
Pythagoras	Russian prince	Juno	Titan
Queene Irene	Russian princess	Jupiter (3)	Tritons
Richard II	sailor (2)	Lemnos	two mer-maids
Richard I (2)	Shepheard (2)	Locrine	two angels
Robin Hood	Shipwright	Luna	Ulisses
[Robin's] men	soldier	Mare-mayds	Unicorne (2)
in green	Spaniard	Marine nymphs	Venus
Sir John	University doctor	Mars	Virgo
Norman		Medea (2)	Vulcan
Sir William	**Mythology**	Mercury (3)	water
Walworth (2)	Aglaosi	mermaids	nymphes
Sir Henry Fitz	Albanact	Mulciber [god	wild giants
Alwin (3)	Amphion	of mines]	Zethes
St. Andrew	Amphitrite (3)	Neptune (3)	
St. Katherine (3)	Andromeda (2)	Nilus	**Animal**
St. Dunstan	Apollo (2)	Oceanus	beasts
St. Andrew	Argurion	Orpheus (3)	birds
St. George	Ariadne	Pallas	camel
various famous	Arion (2)	Pandora	dolphins
mayors of	Bellona	Perseus	estridges
London	Brutus	Pollux	[ostriches]
	Calais	Pollux	Leopard
	Calcos	Proteus	leopards
Living Types	Camber	Royall Eagle	lion
Astrologian	Cassiopeia	Sagitarius	lizards
Philosopher	Castor (2)	sea-symphs	luzern [lynx] (2)
attendants	Corinaeus	sea horses	Lyon (2)
Champion	Cupid (2)	Sea-nymph	Snakes
children of pageant	Cyclops (2)	Sea-goddesses	Woolves
comely eunuches	Dragons	Serpents	

Table 3
Object Sets

Animal/Nature		Musical	
arbor (2)	Rinoceros	three-forked	golden Purse
Beasts	rock (3)	Thunderbolt	golden Scepter
Birds	Scallop	**Musical**	horse-shoe
Cammells	Sea-Monster	bugles	Lemnions Forge
claud	Sea Lyon	drum and flute (2)	Masts
Cocke	Sea Horses (3)	fifes	mirrors
confections	sheep	Harp (2)	rich Booke
craggy Rockes	shel-fishes	oboes	rod with two snake
Crocadile	shell of a	pipers	twined sceptres
dates	siluer Scollup (2)	trumpeters (3)	Sheep-hook
Dog (2)	snakes	**Clothing &**	silver rod
dolphin (3)	sugar	**Jewelry**	sparks
dove	sunbeams	blew coats (3)	Staffe
dragon	Swans	colored gowns (11)	Tacklings
elephant	tortois	gold/silver chains	Tobacco pipe
estridge	tree (6)	(3)	torches
Flocke	Turtles	Coronet/Crowns (5)	wheels
flowers (3)	unicorn	model of a fair	**Set Pieces**
forest	whale	temple	Apollo Palace
fruit (3)	wings (2)	pendants (2)	Britannia's
furs	Wolfe (2)	phantasticke	Watch-Tower
ginger	**Weapons**	dressing made	Castle of Fame
Goddesses	Armour (2)	out of fishes red	or Honour
golde Tinsell	arrows (2)	sleeves & caps (3)	Envy's Castle
golden leopard	bows (2)	ribbon	fountaine of Vertue
human heart	shield (5)	rich attire	golden Cave
Lambe	Crooked Sword	silver collar	green hill
lemon tree	dart	**Tools**	Hill
Lyon	emblematic	Anchors	Imperiall Fort
Marine Nimphs	fireballs	Booke	Isle
new slaine deere	Lances (2)	bottle	Mine
nutmegs	Mace of Triple	burning lamp	mount of Fame
Owles	fire [Jove]	Cables	mount of Gold
palm brand	Ordnance (2)	Cordage	Mownd
Palme Tree	pike	distaff	pillars
Peacocks	siluer Trident	forge	proud swelling
Pegasus	spear	glass	Sea
pelican	staves (3)	globe	The Bower of Bliss
Plants	sword	golden ladder	Throne of Virtue
	target	golden hammer (2)	tomb (2)

Table 4
The Procession Sets

People
poore men (70-80)
livery in their long gowns
aldermen scarlet gowns
Bachelors (60 -100)
Whifflers ensign of the city
mayor
sheriffs (2)
officers mayor's
officers sheriff's
officers other
sword-bearer [of the city]
waits [musicians] of the city
drum and flute of the city (2)
trumpeters 12 & 16
Hautboys [oboes]
Wyfflers [pipers]

Objects
pike
great standards
white staves
target
banners

Clothing
scarlet gowns (4)
blue gowns (2)
red sleeves (2)
caps (2)
velvet coats
chains of gold
gowns with crimson hoods of satin
silver collar
black gowns

There are two messages to understand: one transmitted and one received. Also, there are certainly different levels of awareness of the different messages. The visual evidence shows that the messages conveyed were adherence to positivism, the relative unimportance of the common experience, and the glorification of service. While the crowd was distracted and distracting, each of the emblematic morality tales could be seen and understood at a glance. Similar to the way a modern viewer understands the messages of a television commercial, the person in the streets was capable of grasping the implications quickly. It is acknowledged that the common spectator probably looked at the emblems, responded, and went on to the next picture. Indeed, that is what would be expected. Effective propaganda requires obfuscation: the message is best hidden behind the veil of entertainment.

The largest group of characters represented positive character concepts: the common man was certainly being sent a lesson in the importance of these to a healthy psyche. Since many of the images were almost duplications from emblem books, the visual "bites" would have been immediately identifiable. It seems probable, then, that the message conveyed would be the one received. (The *results* of this reception, however, may have left something to be desired.) The second and third largest sets of characters were anthropomorphized geographic locations and negative character attributes. These, too, would have fit into the emblem book structure and would have gone toward building up the conveyed meanings.

Hard work was something to be endured. "Time" and "humanity" counted less than the "city" and the "company." "Nature," was either represented by fantastic, other worldly ostriches, elephants, and "marine nimph[s]," or elements from the now distant country-side in flowers, trees, and sunbeams. (The average daily encounter with nature was more likely to be cats, rats, and fog.) The encoded messages all seem to add up to telling the common person to look beyond the everyday experience. What was important was a positive attitude and dutiful obedience.

With the exception of "ordnance," the items of war bore no relationship to contemporaneous modern warfare, harkening the spectator's thoughts to days of by-gone glory. There was music, but it was martial in nature and probably engendered impressions of the importance of those in the procession (and, by deduction, the lack of importance of the spectator). All of these lists seem to reinforce the worthlessness of the human element: spirit and sacrifice take precedence over the pleasures or pains of the body. The people in

South-east prospect of Westminster Bridge, Lord Mayor's Show Day, 1747: The Water Pageant.

A view of Cheapside as it appeared on Lord Mayor's Show Day, 1761.

power had a solemn duty and were sacrificing for those not in power. The common person, then, should be happy to sacrifice for the realm. Even the clothing in the procession gave the impression of colorful, medieval monks, further deepening the respect for the position that the performers had attained. From "golden hammers" to "imperial forts" to "Sea-Chariots," the common people saw wonderful tools they could not use, far-off places they had not seen, and marvelous vehicles in which they could not ride.

The mythological characters probably served a dual purpose. As expressed by Ben Jonson, the learned would have been able to understand the references to commerce, history, and government. The person in the street may not have understood this, but the characters would have been interesting to see. The condescending attitude that precipitates exclusion of the common person from a large element of representation may have reinforced the more deprecating message; but even if it did not, the average Londoner was certainly not receiving any positive message about his or her condition. Indeed, not once was there a character in any of the *tableaux* that bore any resemblance to a common person. Even adding in the roughly 1000 men marching in the parade, if one was not a member of one of the guilds, these would appear to be just another form of royalty to an unemployed, hungry Londoner.

Reinforcing the basic visual message were the spatial elements. The crowd was, for the most part, segregated from the participants. Unlike medieval festivals where the demarcation between players and audience was sometimes almost undefinable, the difference at a Lord Mayor's Procession was clear and unmistakable. The elite were above; the performers protected. The crowd was kept away— sometimes, by force.

There are, of course, many possible interpretations. Some aspects of these messages are admittedly more subtle than others and would have only been received at a subliminal level. Many spectators may not have understood anything, others may have been inspired by the messages to work hard to become one of the elite. It is clear that the overall message being sent was one of obedience and hard work. The overall message received probably broke down into two basic models. After being presented with a picture of power and obedience, the common Londoner may have returned to the daily grind with an odd sense of defeat. The world may have at once seemed larger, yet less available. Conversely, a forward thinking young Londoner might have been inspired to work hard to get ahead: to be one of the elite in the "scarlet gowns."

"The Chariot of Justice," in the Lord Mayor's Pageant of the Goldsmiths' Company, 1690.

The Lord Mayor's Show, 1747: Hogarth's version.

Heywood's 1639 presentation was the last before The Interregnum. The unrest that preceded and surrounded the Civil Wars preempted these spectacles. But even though hostilities had ended by 1647, it was not until 1655 that another Lord Mayor's show was staged. It was a rather weak demonstration, presenting only one pageant (Withington, *Pageantry* 44). The processions continued to gain their lost splendor and, by the Restoration in 1660, had once again achieved the glory of the pre-Commonwealth years. But the fact that they were done away with for so long could be telling.

Before the Civil Wars, London had been a Puritan stronghold. According to Harrison:

The growth of radicalism, political and religious, advanced fastest in London.... The intervention of the people in politics was decisive in December 1641. Crowds of Londoners, mainly the lower sort of citizens and apprentices, demonstrated against the king in support of the commons... [and] formed rank and file of the parliamentary army. (193-94)

If the popular reception had been one of defeat and demoralization, then it seems logical that, while they were in power, the commoners would eschew so offensive a display as the Lord Mayor's spectacle. But, why did it return (even in an abbreviated form) while the Puritans were still in power? One can speculate that the realities of a self-governing Commonwealth had finally hit home: the English were beginning to lament the loss of spectacle and ritual. In a contemporary parallel, only months after the fall of the Soviet Union, conservative Stalinists demonstrated in favor of a return to communism (ironically, employing a forum unheard of under Stalin). Similarly, in 1655, the same year as the return of the Show (however anemic), there was a failed royalist insurrection. Perhaps the people of London, were harkening back to "better" times: when order ruled and one knew where one stood. Indeed, the apocryphal "stiff upper lip" may have been in its germinal stage: the crown was repressive, but the trappings helped define society.

Notes

[1]The analytical tools of this study were taken from Helbo. See especially chapter IV: "Pedagogics of Theatre."

[2]The mayor was selected from among the leading aldermen of one of the 12 merchant companies that controlled manufacturing and trading in England. For a thorough history of the Lord Mayors' Shows, see Withington, *English Pageantry.*

[3]For one very specific treatment of this see David M. Bergeron, "Thomas Dekker's Lord Mayor's Shows." *English Studies* III (1970): 2-15. He compares Dekker's shows to those of Thomas Middleton, John Webster, Anthony Munday, and John Squire.

[4]Harrison points out that, based on the ability to sign one's name (and the fact that reading is taught before writing), "overall literacy figures for London [in 1642] were 78 per cent" (164). Though they could read, they certainly did not read much. Quaker library records indicate that "avid readers borrowed eight books in ten years" (Reay 7). It is reasonable to suppose that the common person was not an avid reader. However, it did not take much time, nor a great deal of reading ability, to read an emblem book. Therefore, if it is reasonable to assume that they would not fathom much of the more esoteric content of the show, it is also reasonable to assume that they would recognize a good portion of the characters from emblem books and understand their symbolic references.

Works Cited

Bergeron, David M. "Anthony Munday: Pageant Poet to the City of London." *Huntington Library Quarterly* XXX (1967): 345-68.

____ "The Christmas Family: Artificers in English Civic Pageantry." *ELH* XXXV (1968): 354-64.

____. "The Elizabethan Lord Mayor's Show." *Studies in English Literature* X (1970): 269-85.

____. "The Emblematic Nature of English Civic Pageantry." *Renaissance Drama I.* Ed. S. Schoenbaum. Evanston: Northwestern UP, 1968. 167-98.

____. *English Civic Pageantry: 1558-1642.* Columbia: U of South Carolina P, 1971.

____. "Symbolic Landscape in English Civic Pageantry." *Renaissance Quarterly* XXII (1969): 32-37.

____. "Thomas Dekker's Lord Mayor's Shows." *English Studies* III (1970): 2-15.

_____. "Venetian State Papers and English Civic Pageantry 1558-1642." *Renaissance Quarterly* XXIII (1970): 37-47.

Burke, Peter. *Popular Culture in Early Modern Europe*. New York: Harper, 1978.

_____. "Popular Culture in Seventeenth-Century London." *Popular Culture in Seventeenth-Century England*. Ed. Barry Reay. London: Croom Helm, 1985. 31-58.

Clark, Arthur M. *Thomas Heywood: Playwright and Miscellanist*. New York: Russell & Russell, 1967.

Drake, Dr. Nathan. *Shakespeare and His Times*. Ms. Vol 2. 164. Qtd. in William Hone. *Ancient Mysteries Described, Especially the English Miracle Plays* 1834. Detroit: Singing Tree, 1969. 246-48.

Harrison, J.F.C. *The English Common People: A Social History from the Norman Conquest to the Present*. London: Croom Helm, 1984.

Helbo, Andre, J. Dines Johansen, Patrice Pavis, and Anne Ubersfeld. *Approaching Theatre*. Rev. Trans. Bloomington: Indiana UP, 1991.

Heywood, Thomas. *The Dramatic Works of Thomas Heywood Now First Collected with Illustrative Notes and a Memoir of the Author in Six Volumes*. New York: Russell & Russell, 1964.

_____. *Thomas Heywood's Pageants*. Ed. David Bergeron. New York: Garland, 1986.

Reay, Barry, ed. *Popular Culture in Seventeenth-Century England*. London: Croom Helm, 1985.

Williams, Sheila. "Two Seventeenth Century Semi-Dramatic Allegories of Truth the Daughter of Time." *The Guildhall Miscellany*. Qtd. in Bergeron *Emblematic* 169 (Oct. 1963): 220.

Withington, Robert. *English Pageantry: An Historical Outline*. 2 vols. New York: Benjamin Blom, 1926.

_____. "The Lord Mayor's Show for 1623." *PMLA* XXX (1915): 110-15.

PARTIES FOR THE COMMON GOOD: CIVIC SOCIALIZING IN PURITAN NEW ENGLAND

Bruce C. Daniels

New Englanders gathered together inside the meetinghouse to worship and offer public testimony to their faith. Beyond all other occasions, these congregational meetings symbolized the Puritan way of life both to themselves and to posterity. New Englanders, however, also met outside the meetinghouse. They gathered together for non-religious purposes: to work collectively, to perform civic duties, to affirm community values, and to celebrate patriotic events. These secular gatherings outside the meetinghouse had more in common with religious ones inside than might at first be apparent. They both expressed the communal spirit of a covenanted people; they both reflected the essence of the Puritan belief that the best recreation combined duty and enjoyment; and they both had a serious purpose as well as a social function. These meetings constituted a type of gathering particularly congenial to colonial New England society—parties for the common good. In theory, duty ranked first at these gatherings, fun second. In reality, as the colonial period progressed, New Englanders shifted the relative weighting of the two components. Rather than gathering together to do their duty and have a little fun at the same time, they used duty as an opportunity—sometimes as a pretext—to justify having a good time on the town. This change bespoke neither hypocrisy nor hedonism. Instead, it represented the emergence of more worldly, secular views of recreation. These views, however, remained embodied in forms based on Puritan ideals.

The Productive Party

In a hazy way, almost all Americans have some notions of house- and barn-raisings. Particularly associated with life on the 19th-century prairies, raising parties still go on today and have been much publicized in the 1980s through Project Habitat which puts up low-cost housing with voluntary labor. Although not prominent in the folkculture about Puritanism, raisings were ubiquitous throughout colonial New England's history. In the 17th century, the frames for most buildings—personal homes, barns, shops, meetinghouses, mills and so forth—were constructed and hoisted into place at these communal parties. In the 18th century the custom became less prevalent in large towns as professional housewrights took over design and construction of ambitious buildings. Still, the practice continued to some extent in all communities including Boston and Newport and it remained commonplace in small towns and rural areas.[1]

Despite the hard work that had to be done, raisings were parties replete with food, drink, frivolity and some lighthearted ceremony. Houseraisings customarily began with a woman—often a bride—driving in the first pin of the frame. The work part of the party ended when a selected local hero shinnied out the ridgepole to hammer home the final beam. Spring months constituted the raising season, after the melting of snow in March but before planting time in late June. Raisings commonly took place in two stages, one of preparation, one of construction. John Ballantine, the Westfield, Massachusetts minister wrote in his diary that in February of 1761, 25 men came to hew and stockpile the timbers for his barn. In April, they returned with wives and families to build and raise the frame. The primary gathering was short and all work; Ballantine served no refreshments. For the second meeting, people brought a "plentiful supper...more provisions than was needed" and turned the construction into a real party. At this as at most raisings, the host supplied rum and other alcohol although virtually never did any problems of drunkenness or misconduct arise.[2] These were family parties with serious purposes.

Raisings were the most pure and poetic example of a particular genre of New England social life—the productive party. They fit perfectly the Puritan ideal of sober mirth—of useful recreation. The general principle of raisings could be and was applied to a wide range of activities. Community woodcuttings or harvestings, for example, were relatively common. Usually not done at the homes of average farmers, these types of parties were most often held to benefit a local minister or a neighbour who was ill or experiencing hardship. Occasionally only men attended but usually women also did to prepare refreshments and to provide company after work was over. A woodcutting might turn into a tea party after the men finished the splitting and stacking.[3]

The concept of communal productive parties owed much to a general collectivist economic impulse that carried over from medieval

society to early modern England and parts of colonial America. Many
—perhaps a majority—of the first generation of New England towns
practiced a common-field system of agriculture whereby individuals
owned small strips or parcels of land that lay interspersed with those
of their fellow townsmen in large, common meadows. This type of
land distribution combined aspects of the medieval commune with
the emerging concept of individual land ownership—fee simple. And,
it imparted a measure of fairness by minimizing differences in the
quality of land assigned each townsman. This system of agriculture
also meant, however, that Puritan farmers usually worked side-by-
side in the fields with their fellows, not alone in some isolated
meadow. Additionally, early towns maintained common pastures,
wood-lots, and salt marshes.[4]

Common-field practices did not survive the 17th century, but a
few other forms of communal work did. Throughout the colonial
period, all able-bodied men owed the town several days work each
year on town highways. A few discharged their obligations by paying
money to hire someone, but most did the work themselves. Similarly,
towns met other needs through work groups; the maintenance of
fences around common town property, the creation and running of
grist mills, and so forth.[5] The communal impulse that suffused Puritan
society not surprisingly often carried over into work. Thus, for a
people who worked in groups and relaxed in groups, a combination
of the two activities in productive parties was more than desirable—it
seemed virtually natural.

In the 18th-century, as the Puritan ethos waned, many of the
more urbane young adults found raisings and other productive
parties too straight-laced and demure to be much fun. Nathaniel
Ames, a Harvard graduate living in Dedham, a mid-sized town near
Boston, thought them "very tedious scenes." Ames and others,
however, regarded one type of these parties as an exception: the
cornhusking. Probably because men could husk corn and socialize
with women at the same time, cornhuskings became associated with
great frivolity in the minds of adolescents and young adults. Indian
corn was the last grain of the year to be gathered in New England
and huskings turned into noisy harvest celebrations and parties.
Perhaps one could even search for sexual metaphors in the act of
husking itself. Whatever the physical or symbolic reasons, husking
became immensely popular at mid-18th century. Ames, the
sophisticate bored with raisings, described one in the 1760s. "Made a
husking entertainment," he wrote. "Possibly this leaf may last a
century and fall into the hands of some inquisitive person for whose

entertainment I will inform him that now there is a custom amongst us of making an entertainment at husking Indian corn whereto all the neighboring swains are invited and after the corn is finished they, like the Hottentots, give three cheers or huzzas, but cannot carry in the husks without a Rhum bottle. They feign great exertion, but do nothing until the Rhum enlivens them, when all is done in a thrice; then after a hearty meal about ten at night, they go to their pastimes."[6]

Women also held an array of productive parties to provide benefit from their group labor. Quilting, spinning, and sewing parties or "bees" were frequent. More tame—they customarily had no alcohol; smaller—usually attended by seven or eight women who did not bring their husbands; these bees reflected an austere vision of recreation for women. In their traditional forms they were prevalent among all classes and areas in the 17th century, but became increasingly associated with rural or small-town life in the 18th. The Revolutionary experience, however, made bees popular again among women from all classes and communities. Spinning bees in particular became a fixed part of a patriotic social life as women made cloth for men in the military.[7]

Bees were also capable of being adapted to more sophisticated circumstances. Ezra Stiles, a cosmopolitan minister in Newport and a future president of Yale College, described a pre-Revolutionary urban version of the spinning bee. No quiet, cooperative gathering of soft-spoken ladies, this "spinning match" was put on by "two Quakers, six Baptists, and 29 of my own society...we dined sixty people. My people sent in 4 lb. tea, 19 lb. coffee, loaf sugar, about 3 quarters of veal, 1 11/2 dozen wine, gammons, flour, bread, rice, *etc. etc.* In the course of the day, the spinners were visited by I judge six hundred spectators." Quite a bash. Stiles' Newport congregation staged what an earlier generation of women or what rural contemporaries might have called a spinning "frolic," a term that connotes much more frivolity and liveliness than its rural counterpart, the bee. The women staged the spinning match, however, for a traditional purpose: to produce all the cloth Stiles and his family were likely to need for a long time. They also made the match into a real party in order to have a good time—which they did. The women at the spinning match undoubtedly behaved themselves fairly well, but they might have appeared to be a raucous crowd to the farmers' wives of small-town New England.[8]

Teenage girls held quilting, spinning and sewing bees similar to the ones their mothers did. Often they helped each other ready things for their future life as a married woman. The most popular group activity for teenage girls in the warm weather, however, was the berrying party. Usually consisting of a small gathering of from three to seven girls, berrying parties were possible about two and one-half months of the year from early July to mid-September and often were all-day affairs. Widely held everywhere in the 17th century, berrying parties, as did bees, became more of a rural or small-town activity in the 18th century. Occasionally, however, a group of girls from a large town would take a trip out into the countryside to go berrying. Berrying parties usually were for girls; rarely did boys attend or have their own. For girls, the attraction of the berrying party was simple. It was productive, fun, virtuous and innocent of any negative connotations. Virtually no one would be prohibited from attending on moral grounds. It allowed young girls to be on their own for a brief time without the usual presence of adults. And, finally, young girls did not have many alternatives.[9]

The Pleasures of Civic Duty

In general, men had many more opportunities for socializing than women did; and in particular rural men had opportunities that rural women did not. By the late 17th century, a clear double-standard of conduct had emerged which judged men less harshly than women for a whole range of activities, cardplaying, drinking, and sex among them. Moreover, men could travel more readily, especially after dark, to take advantage of social opportunities that lay beyond the immediate neighborhood.[10] And, men had military and political obligations that furnished opportunities for social gatherings. Society regarded these parties also as being productive—as doing good for the commonweal.

Virtually all New England males between the ages of sixteen and sixty served in the militia. The number of militia-training days varied from time to time and among the differing colonies; threats to the peace usually occasioned more training days, times of tranquillity occasioned fewer. But, on average, in the 170 years between 1620 and 1790, local militiamen met six to eight times a year for drill exercises. Customarily held in April, May, September, and October, militia-training days often supplied the venue for a "fine toot," as one 17th-century soldier wrote in his diary. Obviously, if a military emergency lay at hand, the troops trained with serious purpose. But, if not, the formal aspects of training lasted only a few hours from mid-morning to early afternoon. The rest of the day and evening resembled aspects of a bachelor party.[11]

In the founding generation, this did not seem to be as true. Puritan militiamen from the 1620s through the 1680s regarded themselves as Christian soldiers doing battle for God. And, bloody battle often needed to be done thus underscoring the seriousness of the military meetings. Yet, even in these years, training days could be festive. An early historian of Stratford, Connecticut described an annual militia holiday the town celebrated beginning in 1654. A family affair, the entire community—old men, women, and children—gathered at 8:00 a.m. to watch the troops conduct exercises and parade in review. At mid-day, the women served a feast which included a special desert known as "training cake." In the afternoon, athletic contests of footracing, wrestling and "shooting at the mark" took place in front of a large audience. This military parade/town fair ended before sunset allowing both soldiers and their families to be home before dark. Little untoward behavior happened and training-day parties could be regarded as part of the same wholesome genre of social gathering as a barn raising. On the six or seven other days a year that Stratford's men trained, women and children did not attend, but the men brought lunches and also held contests.[12]

Problems of undue revelry began to arise at the end of King Phillip's War in 1676, when much of southern New England for the first time felt relatively free from Indian attack. In 1704, New England's wittiest and most perspicacious social commentator, Sarah Kemble Knight, characterized militia training as the "Olympiack games" and wrote that they were by far the biggest diversions in rural towns. Training days became the occasion for heavy drinking after perfunctory drill. By the middle of the afternoon, drunkenness and fighting often became problems. The soldiers did not go home before dark and they developed the habit of firing guns in the air as the meeting broke up. The problem of rambunctious militiamen became serious enough to warrant much attention in ministers' sermons. A collective jeremiad in 1719 accused the militia of making "war against the soul" instead of against military enemies.[13]

The French replaced natives as a threat to New England's security, but training day did not return to its ideal as a community holiday fit for the whole family or as a gathering of Christian warriors. Instead, it continued to descend into more of a boys-day-off party. During the wars with New France and in particular those of the 1740s and 1750s, militia companies were often away from their home areas for months at a time. Invariably, troops not under the watchful eyes of family and friends behaved with a great deal less restraint than when at home. And, extended military travel provoked a licentiousness that persisted after the troops returned; bad habits carried over to further exacerbate problems of wild behavior on training days. Parents complained about the ill effects the militia had on young men's character and conduct.[14]

In the 1750s a new social innovation made militia drill more of an explicit party—the training-day dance. Adding women to militia parties imparted some greater respectability to the evening activities, but it also gave rise to a new set of possibilities for bad conduct. Not even the grim emergency of the Revolution and calls for a renewal of earlier virtue could turn the clock back to the Christian warrior of the mid-17th century. In some of the most tense moments for the patriotic cause a "fine parcel of ladies" made sure the troops were "splendidly entertained."[15]

Similarly, election days in each colony were the occasion for a civic holiday. Massachusetts and New Hampshire held colony-wide elections for deputies to the General Assembly once a year in the spring; Connecticut and Rhode Island each held them twice a year in spring and fall. Much discussion preceded these elections although virtually no electioneering did. The day itself took on a festive atmosphere. Men gathered all day outside the meetinghouse where the ballots were to be cast. In particular elections provided diversion to rural freemen who took the day off to travel to the town center to socialize, discuss politics, and vote. A British official, Thomas Vernon, imprisoned in the remote farming town of Glocester, Rhode Island, was amazed by the excitement election day generated. "This being the day for the choice of deputies," he wrote, "we are told that there is a very great resort of people of all kinds and that it is a day of great frolicking. Our landlord and his three sons are gone having rigged themselves out in the best manner. I must observe that a man on horseback passed by with a very large bag full of cakes which are to be sold to the people."[16]

Unlike militia-training drills, however, election days never became unruly or associated with an ancillary range of social activities. Rather like church-related gatherings at the meetinghouse, election days retained their seriousness of purpose throughout all of colonial history. Refreshments always were available and these included beer and punch, but rowdiness was not tolerated.[17]

In addition to colony-wide election days, each town held town meetings which were local political holidays. In their founding years, towns met frequently, sometimes as often as once a month. Once the local population grew beyond several hundred people and once governing procedures became regularized, towns held fewer meetings; two or three per year was the norm for an established town in the 18th century. As they declined in number and increased in size, town meetings became more of a diversion from routine and took on more of the ambiance of a civic holiday. This was especially true for the annual election meeting which chose town officers for the ensuing year. By mid-18th century towns elected upwards from 50 people to office and some elected as many as 200. The sheer scope of the election meeting produced a social energy and hub-bub of activity.[18]

Only men could vote on election day or in town meetings; women and children, of course, did not attend. As a rough rule of thumb, approximately 50 per cent of adult males were admitted as freemen and entitled to vote although many fewer attended meetings. Nevertheless, New Englanders took governing seriously and the decorum of the meeting reflected this. Freemen dressed formally usually wearing what literally could be described as their "Sunday-go-to-meeting clothes." Always adjourned at least an hour before dark, election and town meetings offered occasions for quiet socializing of a conversational nature.[19] As young athletic men provided the spirit that sparked the ribaldry of training day, so did the wise fathers of the town provide the spirit that suffused election and town-meeting days with sobriety. They were a political parallel to the church meeting, but because they were fewer in number, elections and town meetings did convey more of the sense of a holiday. The Puritan ethos of duty and piety that failed to be strong enough to overcome the temptations of the training field, remained ensconced within the walls of the political and religious meeting hall. New Englanders were political creatures and they found much to enjoy in the give and take of a long day discussing everything from local fences to colony taxes to imperial shipping regulations. But, the election and town meetings never lost their essential Puritan purpose as civil versions of the congregational church meeting.

Public Punishments and Moral Theatre

A more grim type of civic gathering that was a combination of moral obligation and bizarre spectacle included men, women, and children in a gruesome community ritual—the witnessing of criminal punishments. These ranged from non-corporal public humiliation to whippings and mutilations to executions. From the first days of Plymouth through the Revolutionary era, magistrates and moralists felt that justice was best served and crime most effectively deterred if the authorities carried out all punishments in full view of the community. The English had long held similar public punishments, but Puritan New England created much more of a ritual to surround the physical acts. In many ways the whole drama resembled a sort of moral theatre. Sedate at first, punishments, in particular executions, took on a carnival atmosphere from the 1670s onwards. Advertised well in advance, they attracted large crowds: drums played, the participants marched in procession, and ministers gave long sermons replete with details and graphic language. The criminals, about to be punished for "black-mouthed oaths," "filthy drunkennesses," "vilest debauchery," and so forth were asked to play their part. Confessions provided the penultimate excitement before the final act took place.[20]

Executions often became the most talked-about event of the year and drew immense crowds. Both Governor William Bradford of Plymouth and Governor John Winthrop of Massachusetts thought John Billington's execution in 1630, the first one in New England's history, worthy of a long description in their journals. For James Morgan's in 1686, crowds began to gather in Boston a week ahead of the event. Some came at least 50 miles. On the Sunday before the hanging, two distinguished ministers preached sermons on the crime; and on the Thursday of the execution, Increase Mather preached a sermon to a crowd of 5,000, the largest theretofore ever gathered in New England. Vendors sold written broadsides which, like a theatre program, summarized the details of Morgan's crimes. Other particularly well-publicized ones included those of Esther Rogers in 1701 for murdering her children; the simultaneous executions of several pirates in Newport in 1723; and Hannah Ocuish's for murder in New London, Connecticut in 1786. As a general rule, the more grisly the crime, the larger the crowd at the execution. Although a majority of those hanged were men, women's executions drew larger audiences.[21]

Complete figures have not been compiled for all the executions in New England, but the lowest of estimates would suggest they averaged at least one a year in the late 17th and all of the 18th century. Prior to the 1670s, the number was fewer. Estimates of crowd size at them range from 3,000 to 6,000. And, unlike many of the harsher elements of early Puritanism, the spectacle of the public hanging did not fade in the late colonial period with the development of a more relaxed social ethos. In fact, executions increased in the years after 1750. Moreover, the rhetoric about criminality in the sermon literature of the late 18th century remained remarkably consistent with the language of the founding generation.[22] Public punishments as moral theatre combined the frivolity of mid-18th-century social gatherings with the more sombre aspects of the congregational gathering of the founding era.

Lesser punishments produced lesser drama than executions, but these, too, attracted crowds. Being more numerous, humiliations, whippings and mutilations were more a part of regular life. Diarists throughout the colonial and Revolutionary eras entered notations of seeing people "cropt and branded" or "whipped with rods." Authorities placed whipping posts, pillories, and stocks in prominent locations to facilitate public involvement. Students often went in groups to jeer criminals or pelt them with "every repulsive kind of garbage that could be collected." Nor did just rowdy young men take part. In the 1770s, 11-year-old Anna Winslow, the daughter of refined and wealthy parents, made trips with her friends to Boston's whipping post to watch sentences being carried out. A young Marblehead apprentice described the fate of Jeremiah Dexter "lately detected passing counterfeit dollars...[he] stood in the pillory in the presence of a great many spectators, many of whom were very liberal in bestowing rotten eggs...particularly Dr. Seth Hudson."[23]

As the 18th century wore on, magistrates became less inclined to punish people for some offenses such as idleness and fornication for which earlier Puritans had meted out harsh sentences. But with a large increase in population, enough thievery, drunkenness, and general all-around bad behavior existed to furnish a growing cast for center stage. And, of course, the Revolutionary practice of tarring and feathering loyalists or riding them on a rail, continued this longstanding practice of combining punishment, deterence, and entertainment.

Patriotism as Political Carnival

Another type of public spectacle in the 18th century more explicitly fused morality and ribaldry into an outdoor festival: the celebration of great historical events. Somewhat of a continuation of the Puritan tradition of thanksgivings, these political carnivals had none of the quiet, earnest sobriety associated with 17th-century feasting celebrations. Often they got out of control and ended in riot, fighting, and vandalism. The morning after, communities woke up with a hangover, sheepish faces, and a need to assess blame. Most associated with the larger towns and the lower ranks of the social structure, political carnivals took place in small towns as well and involved members of the elite, especially young ones.

New England celebrated only one of these festivals on a regular annual basis—Guy Fawkes Day on November 5. Held to commemorate the foiling of the so-called "Gunpowder Plot" when Catholic terrorists tried to blow up parliament in 1605, Guy Fawkes Day was celebrated in 17th-century towns with "bonfires, guns shot off and much revelry." By the beginning of the eighteenth, it took on much more of the ambiance of a 20th-century Halloween. People wore costumes, built floats to pull in parades, and feasted during the day: at night the celebration often degenerated into vandalism. As early as 1709, the day filled Samuel Sewall with fears over safety and public disorder. Originally endorsed by magistrates and ministers because it affirmed New England's vigorous Protestantism, anti-Catholicism, and English patriotism, Guy Fawkes Day increasingly became the subject of discussion and debate. A particularly riotous "Pope's Day" celebration invariably provoked calls for a return to Puritan traditions of restraint and sobriety. But not until the Revolution did any towns make a serious attempt to end all observance of the day. These attempts succeeded because the Revolutionaries wanted to avoid offending their Catholic French allies. Moreover, celebrating the glories of English parliament did not seem as patriotic in the 1770s as it had earlier. After the war, however, celebrations of Guy Fawkes Day began anew.[24]

Boston's Pope's Day celebration became infamous in the 1750s and 1760s. Regular commerce and business ceased. Huge groups of several thousand gathered in both the north and south ends of the city and marched towards the center in the early afternoon holding images of the Pope and Devil aloft. Much of the crowd had already consumed considerable alcohol before the march began. When the north-end and south-end crowds—now become mobs—met, they often tried to destroy each other's Popes. John Rowe, a merchant, described one of these scenes: "In the afternoon, they got the north-end Pope pulled to pieces...The south-end people brought out their Pope and went in triumph to the northward and at the Mill bridge a battle began between the people of both parts of the town. The north-end people having repaired their Pope but the south-end people got [won] the battle, many were hurt and bruised on both sides, and brought away the north-end Pope and burnt both of them at the gallows on the Neck. Several thousand people followed them, hallowing, *etc.*" This 1764 Guy Fawkes Day celebration provoked a particular outcry because a cart carrying the north-end Pope crushed and killed a young boy. Boston's riots, however, were only worse by degree than those in many other New England towns. Newport,

Rhode Island and New London, Connecticut became known for unusually wild ones; but small towns such as Newburyport and Marblehead, Massachusetts and even a few rural areas experienced recurrent serious disorder. Virtually all of New England celebrated Pope's Day to some degree.[25]

And, Guy Fawkes day was just the most raucous and regular of these political carnivals. From the 1680s, when a royal presence became apparent in New England, until the imperial crisis of the 1760s, the king's birthday was usually celebrated with toasts, parades, bonfires, fireworks, oxroasts, and general festivities. Special occasions also provided the moment for a good toot. When news reached Boston in September 1762 of a major naval victory in the French and Indian War, a day of thanksgiving was proclaimed. But, the party that ensued bore more resemblance to VE Day in 1945 than to a Puritan thanksgiving. A diarist described it as follows: "public rejoicing on account of the reduction of the Havannah. Sermon preached by Sewall, cadets mustered, bells rung, batteries fired, concerts of music, the town illuminated, bonfires, *etc*. Many loyal healths drunk, a vast quantity of liquor consumed, and General Winslow of Plymouth, so intoxicated as to jump on the table and break a great number of bowls, glasses, *etc*."[26]

In 1766, when the King's birthday began to lose its attractiveness as a public festival, another one began: the celebration of the fight against the Stamp Act. Although the act had been repealed in March, New England celebrated the event later, usually in May because the news had not reached the colonies until several weeks after the vote in Parliament. Throughout the Revolutionary era, most of New England held one of these political carnivals to celebrate the most glorious event in the pre-Revolutionary movement. Only gradually did July 4 and Independence Day overtake Stamp-Act celebrations as a day of patriotic festivity. Boston celebrated August 14 as a great holiday for four successive years, 1766 through 1769. On that date in 1765, 1,000 members of the newly formed Sons of Liberty destroyed the house of Peter Oliver, the distributor of the hated tax stamps in an effort to force him to resign his commission. For these four years, a gigantic parade of over three hundred chaises and coaches wended their way throughout the city in a day-long procession to commemorate the great Stamp Act riot/demonstration. This celebration, as did all of these carnivals, held the danger that the good times would get out of hand.[27]

Conclusion: Parties for the Common Good

On the surface, Guy Fawkes Day, public hangings, town meetings, militia drills, and houseraisings did not have much in common. Boisterous carnival, macabre spectacle, political convention, military exercise, and building party—they seem to run the gamut from the bloodthirsty to the bucolic. The differing surface manifestations, however, obscure a basic element common to all these activities: they were civic gatherings that produced something for the commonweal. All of them had a serious purpose: none were mere parties; none were examples of idle behavior whereby leisure or recreation became an end unto itself. All provided examples of how a people could gather together to do good for the community and have fun at the same time. Some of these gatherings remained more of a serious business and less of a party than others did: houseraisings took sweat and work; town meetings maintained a sober sense of decorum. Some became wild parties; as often as not, militia drills and Guy Fawkes Days got out of hand. But, houseraisings and town meetings had functions as parties; people looked forward to them as a chance to socialize and relax. And militia drill provided the community with needed security; Guy Fawkes Day affirmed New England's English and Protestant heritage. A day of patriotism, the wild and woolly Guy Fawkes celebration, despite all the problems it caused late in the colonial period, still satisfied Puritanism's basic test for appropriate leisure and recreation—it was useful.

Notes

[1] See Samuel Eliot Morison, *Builders of the Bay Colony* (Boston: Houghton Mifflin Co., 1930), 130, 131; Henry R., Stiles, *The Histories and Genealogies of Ancient Windsor, Connecticut*, 2 vols. (Hartford: Case, Lockwood, and Brainard Co., 1890), 433-35; and Alice Morse Earle, *The Sabbath in Puritan New England* (New York: Charles Scribners' Sons, 1891), 8, for general discussions of houseraisings. See the following two diaries for descriptions of houseraisings in the 1690s and 1770s respectively. Thomas Minor, *The Diary of Thomas Minor, Stonington, Connecticut* (New London, CT: Press of the Day, 1899), entries for 1690s, unpaginated; and James Parker, "Extracts from the Diary of James Parker of Shirley, Massachusetts," *New England Historical and Genealogical Register*, 69 (1915), entries for 1770s, 117-21.

[2] For the ceremonies see Morison, *Builders of The Bay Colony*, 131; Stiles, *Windsor*, I, 433; and Earle, *The Puritan Sabbath*, 8. John Ballantine,

"John Ballantine's Diary," in *Westfield and its Historic Influences, 1669-1919*, ed. John Hoyt Lockwood (Westfield, MA: privately 1922), 19 Feb. 1761, 1 Apr. 1761, 385-95.

[3]See a woodcutting described in Ebenezer Parkman, *The Diary of Ebenezer Parkman, 1703-1782*, ed. Francis G. Walett (Worcester, MA: The American Antiquarian Society, 1974), 11 Dec. 1750, 229.

[4]Many scholars have discussed these agricultural practices. For the most sophisticated studies of the transfer of English custom to the colonies see David Grayson Allen, *In English Ways: The Movement of Societies and the Transferal of English Local Law and Custom to Massachusetts Bay in the Seventeenth Century* (Chapel Hill, NC: University of North Carolina Press, 1981), 31-38, *passim*; Summer Chilton Powell, *Puritan Village: The Formation of a New England Town* (Middletown, CT: Wesleyan University, Press, 1963), 1-14; and Roy Akagi, *The Town Proprietors of the New England Colonies* (Philadelphia: University of Pennsylvania Press, 1924), 103-10.

[5]Bruce C. Daniels, "Economic Development in Colonial and Revolutionary Connecticut: An Overview," *William and Mary Quarterly* (hereafter cited as *W.M.Q.*), XXXVII (1980), 438-39; Thomas Lewis, Jr., "From Suffield to Saybrook: An Historical Geography of The Connecticut River Valley in Connecticut before 1800," (Ph.D., diss., Rutgers University, 1978), 124; and Isabel S. Mitchell, *Roads and Road-Making in Colonial Connecticut*, Connecticut Tercentenary Series, XIV (New Haven: CT Tercentenary Commission, 1933), 13-18. For the finest overall statement on communal economic patterns in a Puritan village see Frank Thistlethwaite, *Dorset Pilgrims: The Story of Westcountry Pilgrims Who Went to New England in the Seventeenth Century* (London: Barrie and Jenkins, 1989), 150-55.

[6]Charles Warren, *Jacobin and Junto: or Early American Politics as Viewed in the Diary of Dr. Nathaniel Ames* (Cambridge, MA: Harvard University Press, 1931), 29.

[7]Traditional—now regarded as old-fashioned—accounts of women's social activities in New England often discuss these bees. See for example, Catherine Fennelly, *Connecticut Women in the Revolutionary Era* (Chester, CT: Pequot Press, 1975), 37-46; and William Weeden, *Economic and Social History of New England, 1620-1789*, 2 vols. (New York: Hillary House Publishers, 1963), II, 730-33.

[8]Ezra Stiles, *The Literary Digest of Ezra Stiles*, 3 vols., ed. Franklin Bowditch Dexter (New York: Charles Scribners' Sons, 1901), I, 8-9.

[9]Weeden, *Economic and Social History*, II, 731-33. For charming descriptions of berrying parties see Elizabeth Porter Phelps, "Diary," in *Under a Colonial Rooftree: Fireside Chronicles of Early New England*, ed.

Arrin S. Huntington (Boston and New York: Houghton, Mifflin Co., 1891), 27-28.

[10]For the development of double-standards of conduct, see especially Nancy F. Cott, "Divorce and the Changing Status of Women in Eighteenth-Century Massachusetts, *W.M.Q.*," XXXIII (1976), 598-601; Mary Maples Dunn, "Saints and Sisters: Congregational and Quaker Women in the Early Colonial Period," *American Quarterly* (hereafter cited as *A.Q.*), XXX (1978), 584-90; and Roger Thompson; *Sex in Middlesex: Popular Moves in a Massachusetts County, 1649-1699* (Amherst, MA: The University of Massachusetts Press, 1986), 194-99.

[11]Stewart L. Gates, "Disorder and Social Organization: The Militia in Connecticut Public Life, 1660-1860" (Ph.D. diss., University of Connecticut, 1975), 17, 75; Richard Marcus, "The Militia of Colonial Connecticut, 1639-1775: An Institutional Study (Ph.D. diss., University of Colorado, 1965), 253-57; and Frances Manwaring Caulkins, *A History of New London, Connecticut* (New London: privately by the author, 1895), 406-07.

[12]For the concept of being a Christian soldier see John Ferling, "The New England Soldier: A Study in Changing Perceptions," *A.Q.*, 33 (1981), 31; and Ferling, *A Wilderness of Miseries: War and Warriors in Early America* (Westport, CT and London: Greenwood Press, 1980), 93-126. William Howard Wilcoxson, *History of Stratford Connecticut, 1639-1939* (Stratford, CT: Stratford Tercentenary Commission, 1939, 282-85.

[13]Sarah Kemble Knight, *The Journal of Madame Knight*, ed. Malcolm Frieberg (Boston: David R. Godine, 1972), 7 Oct. 1704, 20; Ferling, "The New England Soldier," 31-32; Wilcoxson, *History of Stratford*, 26; and Cotton Mather, et al., *A Testimony Against Evil Customs Given by Several Ministers* (Boston: B. Green, 1719), 4-5.

[14]Jabez Fitch, "The Diary of Jabez Fitch, Jr.," *Mayflower Descendant*, 2 parts (1899-1914), pt. 2, 43-49; L. Douglas Good, "Colonials at Play: Leisure in Newport, 1723," *Rhode Island History*, 33 (1974), 13; William Gregory, "A Scotchman's Journey in New England in 1771," ed. Mary Powell, *New England Magazine*, 12 (1895), 351; and Samuel Pierce, "Diary," in *The History of the Town of Dorchester, Massachusetts* (Boston: E. Clapp, Jr., 1859), 360.

[15]See Israel Litchfield, "Diary," in *The Litchfield Family in America*, ed. Wilford Litchfield (Southbridge, MA: privately by the editor, 1901), 325-26; and Ferling, *A Wilderness of Miseries*, 118-19, *passim*.

[16]Thomas Vernon, "The Diary of Thomas Vernon: A Loyalist," *Rhode Island Historical Tracts* 3 (Providence: Providence Press Co., 1881), 77-78.

[17]See Edward M. Cook, Jr., *The Fathers of the Towns: Leadership and Community Structure in Eighteenth-Century New England* (Baltimore and

London: The Johns Hopkins University Press, 1976), 1-10; Kenneth Lockridge, *A New England Town: The First Hundred Years* (New York: W.W. Norton and Co., 1970), 37-46; and Michael Zuckerman, *Peaceable Kingdoms: New England Towns in the Eighteenth Century* (New York: Alfred A. Knopf, 1970), 85-115, 172-76. Compare New England's elections to the raucous ones in Virginia described by Rhys Isaac, *The Transformation of Virginia, 1740-1790* (Chapel Hill, NC: The University of North Carolina Press, 1982), 88-93, 110-14; and Charles Sydnor, *Gentlemen Freeholders: Political Practices in Washington's Virginia* (Chapel Hill, NC: University of North Carolina Press, 1952), 21-34.

[18]Bruce C. Daniels, "Connecticut's Villages Become Mature Towns: The Complexity of Local Institutions, 1676-1776," *W.M.Q.* XXXIV (1977), 93-100; and Cook, *Fathers of the Towns*, Chap. I.

[19]See Daniels, *The Connecticut Town: Growth and Development, 1639-1790* (Middletown, CT: Wesleyan University Press, 1979), 77-93; and Daniels, *Dissent and Conformity on Narragansett Bay: The Colonial Rhode Island Town* (Middletown, CT: Wesleyan University Press, 1983), 98-101. See Vernon, "The Diary of Thomas Vernon," 77-78 for a description of formal dress.

[20]Ronald A. Bosco, "Lectures at the Pillory: The Early American Execution Sermon," *A.Q.*, XXX (1978), 158-60; and Edwin Powers, *Crime and Punishment in Early Massachusetts, 1620-1692: A Documentary History* (Boston: Beacon Press, l966), 1623-194.?

[21]Daniel E. Williams, "Behold a Tragic Scene Strangely Changed Into a Theatre of Mercy: The Structure and Significance of Criminal Conversion Narratives in Early New England," *A.Q.*, XXXVII (1986), 831-35; Good, "Colonials At Play," 14; Bosco, "Lectures at the Pillory," 158-70; and Powers, *Crime and Punishment*, 252-80.

[22]Bosco, "Lectures at the Pillory," 172-76; and Williams, "Behold a Tragic Scene," 827-31. Samuel Sewall notes executions throughout his diary. Sewall, *The Diary of Samuel Sewall*, 2 vols. ed. M. Halsey Thomas (New York: Farrar, Straus and Giroux, 1973), 1, 18, 22, 99, 100, 126, 153, 227, 292, 295, 310, 509.

[23]Fitch, "The Diary of Jabez Fitch," pt. 1, 40-42; Sewall, *The Diary of Samuel Sewall*, I, 572; Anna Green Winslow, *Diary of Anna Green Winslow, A Boston School Girl of 1771*, ed. Alice Morse Earle, (Boston and New York: Houghton, Mifflin Co., 1894), 111; and John Boyle, "Boyle's Journal of Occurrences in Boston," *New England Historical and Genealogical Register*, 84 (1930), 157.

[24]Thompson, *Sex in Middlesex*, 89; Sewall, *The Diary of Samuel Sewall*, II, 627; Caulkins, *History of New London*, 482; Boyle, "Boyle's Journal," 266; and James Barriskill, "The Newburyport Theatre in the

Eighteenth Century," *Essex Institute Historical Collections*, 91 (1955), 214-15.

[25]John Rowe, *Letters and Diary of John Rowe, Boston Merchant*, ed. Anne Rowe Cunningham (Boston: W.B. Clarke, 1903), 67-68; Barriskill, "Newburyport Theatre," 214-15; Caulkins, *History of New London*, 481-82; Good, "Colonials at Play," 13-14; and Boyle, "Boyle's Journal," 266.

[26]For the king's birthday celebrations see Raoul François Camus, "Military Music of Colonial Boston," in Barbara Lambert (ed.), *Music in Colonial Massachusetts, 1630-1820*, 2 vols. (Boston: The Colonial Society of Massachusetts, 1980, 1985), I, 76. For the Havannah celebration see Boyle," Boyle's Journal," 159.

[27]*Connecticut Courant*, 30 Mar. 1766 describes the first Stamp Act party in Connecticut. Boyle, "Boyle's Journal," 259-60, 266 describes annual Stamp Act parties in Boston.

NATIONAL PORTRAITS:
THE COLUMBIAN CELEBRATIONS OF 1792, 1892-93 AND 1992 AS CULTURAL MOMENTS

George E. Weddle

The Columbian celebrations of 1792, 1892-93 and 1992 offer portraits of American culture at particular moments of historical time. Such events occur with sufficient rarity that they provide unique opportunities to examine both cultural change and cultural continuity. Paying careful attention to how an event is celebrated— looking at what and who is included or excluded; examining the assumptions, rhetoric and symbolism surrounding the celebrations— gives at least some measure of the values, beliefs, practices and assumptions deemed most important by those groups with the power to define culture. How an event is commemorated matters. It matters who controls the definition of an event, what symbols they choose to emphasize and it matters who has a voice in deciding the terms upon which participation in the event is allowed.

In 1692 the anniversary of Columbus' voyage passed without recorded comment in the American colonies. It would have been remarkable indeed for the event to have been commemorated by the early English and Dutch colonists. In 1792, as the new nation began its voyage over uncharted republican seas, Columbus was recruited as a symbol of liberty and the rights of man. The principal celebration that year was held in New York (DeLancey 1-18). Smaller similar celebrations were held in Boston, Baltimore, Providence and Richmond. In New York the Society of St. Tammany or Columbian Order gathered at the "wigwam" for dinner and an address; toasts to liberty, emancipation and the rights of man were drunk and a monument to Columbus, liberty and the rights of man were unveiled (4-11).

For a new nation searching for self-identity, the use of the name and achievements of the man who had "discovered" the lands Americans now claimed seems natural. Columbus was bold, adventurous and fearless. He had taken his ships and sailed courageously toward the unknown. Thus he would seem to be the perfect symbol for the just launched republican ship of state, itself venturing into uncharted waters. But there is another significance to this celebration. The Society of St. Tammany was begun to counter an aristocratic association that arose about this time. The exact identity of that association is less important than is the fact that Columbus was appropriated as a symbol by a group espousing republican and enlightenment values in opposition to what they perceived to be an aristocratic association.

The appropriation of symbols for patriotic or ideological purposes was not new in 1792. It seems to be a part of the human need to define the world in which we live. Such appropriations of symbols for cultural, political or class purposes becomes even more necessary and pronounced in times of uncertainty or in times of conflict over cultural values and meanings. The Columbian celebration of 1892-93 is a perfect example of this phenomenon.

The Chicago World's Fair was a carefully composed, skillfully crafted, cultural portrait that reveals the cultural values and assumptions of those who wielded the brush. It also reveals the fears and uncertainties of a dominant class struggling to maintain its position in a period of rapid and bewildering change. The dramatic growth of industrial capitalism in the decades following the Civil War had elevated American capitalists to positions of great wealth and power. At the same time, the expansion of industry had led to increased immigration and to increased ethnic and class conflict. One of the ways this newly elevated cultural leadership justified its position was through the use of "civic ritual and patriotic symbolism" (Litwicki 50, 53).

Sensing the need to fortify their position and to "defend American culture from 'mongrelization'" elites both nationally and in Chicago "sought to educate and assimilate the outsiders to an American culture which they defined and controlled." To accomplish that task they turned to the use of "civic ritual in public celebrations" and to the celebration of patriotic symbols from a past that the new immigrants had not shared. Coupled to this celebration of American patriotic symbols were the evolutionary assumptions of late 19th century Americans. Races and nations each occupied a distinct position in an evolutionary hierarchy with the Anglo-Saxon (read American) at the top. Thus, a close linkage between the dominant evolutionary assumptions of the age and a restrictive definition of what being American meant were joined together at the fair (Litwicki 50).

The dedication, which took place in October of 1892, featured a massive parade through downtown Chicago. Over 80,000 marchers participated, including most of Chicago's ethnic groups who marched in parade with their benevolent and protective associations. The elites were willing and able to incorporate these groups but did so in terms that excluded most of the participants from the "American" culture being celebrated. Marching under the flag and under portraits of Washington, Lincoln and other long dead military and political leaders, the immigrant ethnic associations participated in defining America in terms that excluded them from participation in that culture. It was no accident that the flag and the Star Spangled Banner were prominently featured just as it was no accident that the Pledge of Allegiance was introduced as part of the national celebration. Immigrants could indeed become American if they pledged their loyalty and gave up foreign ways (Litwicki 53-54).[1]

The parade was a stirring spectacle that announced the beginning of a new age according to the *Chicago Tribune*. The fair signaled "the inauguration of the people's age.... the millennium of universal liberty and of the brotherhood of man" (*Chicago Tribune* 22 Oct. 1892: 10). The rhetoric by no means matched the reality. The "brother-hood of man" offered by those in power was conditioned on the acceptance of their superiority by those they deemed to be beneath them. For Black Americans, Native Americans and immigrants, it meant learning and accepting their assigned place in the hierarchy. Black and Native Americans did participate in the parade, but they did not participate on their own terms.

Black lodges of the Knights of Pythias marched in the parade but it was the "buffalo soldiers" of the Ninth Regiment that drew the attention of those on the reviewing stand. That was a role for which Blacks were suited. Further indicative of that attitude is the faint praise of a reporter for Frederick Douglass:

Remarkable for his discretion, good sense, and good citizenship, Mr. Douglass has never uttered a word too much in his life and has invariably called the attention of the colored people to the high energy and mentality of the white race, which they should imitate instead of trifling and jabbering. (*Chicago Tribune* 21 Oct. 1892: 5-6; Litwicki 54-55)

Native Americans were another group that needed to learn their proper place in American society. Dressed in their school uniforms, students from Carlisle Indian School marching in the parade drew applause from reviewers and the praise of reporters. The hope was that if all Indians had the benefit of Carlisle training then they might be fit for inclusion in American society. According to the *Chicago Tribune*, the Carlisle School was "the only place in America where good Indians really turned out" (*Chicago Tribune* 21 Oct. 1892: 5).

Although over 100,000 visitors were on hand for the Dedication on October 22, 1892, the common people of Chicago were not invited to the ceremonies. While the civic parade had emphasized patriotic themes and America, the oratory of the dedication ceremonies "was most notable for its paeans to progress." Henry Waterson, in his dedication address, claimed that "Since the advent of the Son of God, no event has had so great an influence upon human affairs as the discovery of the western hemisphere."[2] Chauncey Depew, when it came time for his oration, waxed eloquently:

> We celebrate the emancipation of man. The preparation was the work of almost countless centuries; the realization was the revelation of one. The cross on Calvary was hope; the cross raised on San Salvador was opportunity. But for the first, Columbus would never have sailed; but for the second, there could be no place for the planting, the nurture, and the expansion of civil and religious liberty. (*Magazine of American History* 463)

The dedication is itself culturally significant, but even more significant is the fair, which offers a telling portrait of the assumptions, hopes, dreams and fears of the leaders of the nation as they stood poised on the brink of the 20th century.

The Chicago World's Columbian Exposition was the most sophisticated attempt yet by American cultural and social leaders to define social reality (Rydell 39). It was to be a grand cultural and industrial extravaganza erected in the swamps of Jackson Park on the shores of Lake Michigan. In the minds of those who conceived and fought to bring it into existence, the fair would elevate Chicago to its rightful position as one of the leading cities of the world. It was also a means by which American cultural values could be defined and transmitted both to the world and to the lower sorts on these shores.

The fair was to be a demonstration of the progress of civilization on these shores since the arrival of Columbus in 1492. Progress, in the minds of the fair organizers, meant material progress which they equated with their own moral and social superiority. Progress also meant the evolutionary progress of races and cultures. Further adding credence to their presumptions were the efforts of the scientific community.

G. Brown Goode, assistant secretary of the Smithsonian was assigned the task of classifying the exhibits. He had a firm belief in the effects of heredity and believed that fairs such as the Chicago fair "both possessed great educational value as well as vast potential for creating the good citizenship necessary for advancing civilization" (Rydell 44). The fair was to show "the steps of progress of civilization and its arts in successive centuries, and in all lands up to the present time" (45). While Goode directed the classification of exhibits, Frederic Ward Putnam, head of Harvard's Peabody Museum of American Archeology and Ethnology, was hired to run department M which included the anthropological and ethnological exhibits. For purposes of classification, the Midway was also placed under department M. This had great consequences for the manner in which foreign cultures were received and assimilated by visitors to the fair. (55-68).

The anthropological and ethnological exhibits were the largest ever assembled. A special exhibit of Harvard's anthropology lab was provided, "including statues of the typical American man and woman." A Harvard undergraduate and a Radcliffe coed had been used as models for the statues, which were made available so visitors could have themselves measured and compared to them (Rydell 57; Flinn 53). So much anthropological material had been gathered that it could not be confined to one building with the consequence that the message of the evolutionary progress of races and cultures was spread throughout the fair. Nowhere was this more pronounced than on the Midway (Rydell 60-68).

A decision had been reached among the fair managers that the Midway would not just be devoted to cheap entertainment. It was also to be an educational experience. Part of that experience was the opportunity to see native Africans in the Dahomey Village, South Sea Islanders and various Native American tribes all going about their daily lives. China, having no official delegation at the fair, was also relegated to the Midway. Situated among the sword swallowers, Little Egypt, Fatima and other "Hootchie-cootchie dancers," and among the wild beasts and barkers and the giant Ferris Wheel, the native villages were reduced to sideshow attractions. The *New York Times* summed up the Midway quite well; "The late P.T. Barnum should have lived to see the day" (Rydell 61).

Julian Hawthorne, the son of Nathaniel, noted the evolutionary message of the Midway: "Roughly speaking, you have before you the civilized, the half-civilized and the savage worlds to choose from—or rather to take one after the other" (Rydell 64). Hubert Howe

Bancroft offered a word picture of the Midway as did Chauncey Depew. Depew's statement perhaps best reflects the cultural assumptions underlying the fair.

There was about the midway Plaisance a peculiar attraction for me. It represents the Asian and African and other forms of life native to the inhabitants of the globe. While it is of doubtful attractiveness for morality, it certainly emphasizes the value as well as the progress, of our civilization. (Bancroft; *New York Times* 19 June 1893: 5)

These exhibits were arranged according to the prevailing evolutionary assumptions regarding race and they helped reinforce American cultural values. As Bancroft wrote:

All the continents are here represented, and many nations of each continent, civilized, semi-civilized, and barbarous, from the Caucasian to the African black, with head the shape of a cocoa-nut and with barely enough clothing to serve for the wadding of a gun. (Rydell 62-68)[3]

Progress was the over-arching theme of the fair. As the above examples illustrate, the Social Darwinist and evolutionary assumptions of the organizers of the fair accorded each race and culture a particular place on this scale. Blacks were systematically excluded from the fair and, except for a handful of porters and janitors, they were completely absent from the White City. The only building to have blacks represented at all was the woman's building where there was a small display of Black women's "cultural contributions." Only one black woman was hired by the Board of Lady Mangers and she resigned because of the demeaning nature of the duties assigned her. Frederick Douglass was the only black American male to have an official role at the fair. He participated as the commissioner for Haiti.[4]

Some blacks demanded recognition and that a special day be set aside for them, as had been done for other groups. A Jubilee Day was finally established but it was promptly and emphatically boycotted by blacks. Whites were not excepted from being accorded their proper places. The fair was "for the Average People" for "the middling sort." It was not for the very rich or for the "helpless lot in the gutter," but was for the respectable middle. The "average people" were not left to form their own judgments, however. The numerous guide books and official histories issued in conjunction with the fair had a distinct didactic purpose. They reinforced the message of evolutionary progress, drew the reader's attention to the lessons that needed to be learned from the exhibits, and extolled American material, social and moral progress while denigrating other races and cultures.[5]

The racially tinged evolutionary assumptions were also given the status of science, thus further reinforcing such stereotypes in the minds of middle-class Americans. The exclusion of minorities and other races from the White City further added to this impression. Foreign cultures were relegated to the Midway while Native American exhibits were established both there and on a wooded island within the fair grounds. Flinn's *Official Guide* explains that:

This illustration of Indian and pioneer life is intended as a background to the Exposition, bringing out by comparison with greater force the advances made during the past four centuries, as shown in the great building devoted to the material and educational interests of man. (Flinn 54-55)

The clear message was that some had advanced further than others. But the theme of progress also echoed in other areas. There was progress in industry and technology, progress in the arts, in religion and for women. At the dedication ceremonies the previous fall, Mrs. Potter Palmer, president of the Board of Lady Managers, took note of the progress of women.

Even more important than the discovery of Columbus, which we are gathered together to celebrate, is the fact that the general government has just discovered women. (*Magazine of American History* 28, 461)

But there were also other notes sounded during the fair that were somewhat off-key.

Art was prominently featured both in exhibits and throughout the buildings of the White City. It was also prominently featured in the lagoons and waterways. Great concern and worry surrounded the artistic endeavors that were undertaken for the fair. It was a given that "no nation could be considered civilized and progressive whose aesthetic tastes and abilities did not match its industrial and technological achievements" (Badger 8). At all past world's fairs, Americans had been severely criticized for their lack of creativity and for the imitative quality of their artistic endeavors. No effort was spared to insure that this fair would be different. The nation and those who were in charge of the fair wanted to demonstrate to the world that the United States was ready to assume the leadership that was rightfully hers. But there was fear that Chicago and the fair would not be able to measure up to the standards of the world, and that the nation would be disgraced (Miller 17-22).

The fair also represents the imperialist ambitions of the nation. The State Department envisioned it as an opportunity to corner the trade of Latin America and to eliminate European influence from that area. European nations greatly resented our attempt to monopolize Latin markets and at first were inclined to boycott the fair. In the end they all came to the fair with the express intent of competing vigorously for those Latin markets (Cassell 109-24).

Another part of this imperialist vision was attempts by Chicago's business leaders to use the fair as a means to open trade with Latin nations. It was envisioned that the Illinois Central railroad would transport goods from Chicago to New Orleans where they would be shipped to Latin America. There was also an effort to develop Latin sources of raw materials for Chicago and the midwest. Arduously courting the representatives of Latin American nations proved to be of little avail. Little trade developed and few new markets were found (Cassell 109-24).

Frederick Jackson Turner announced the end of the frontier and the beginning of overseas expansion at the meeting of the American Historical Association held in conjunction with the fair. Progress could no longer be confined to these shores. It would be necessary for Americans to turn their eyes elsewhere in the future. Turner's thesis also contained an implicit message for the new immigrants. The frontier was responsible for molding the unique character of Americans. Having had no opportunity to live that frontier experience meant that the new immigrants could not develop those distinctly American character traits. Other means would have to be found to incorporate these new arrivals into American society (Rydell 47).

One of the most striking images is that of the White City gleaming brilliantly in the sunlight of the day and illuminated electrically by night amid miles of lagoons, streams and canals. But juxtaposed to this was the carnival atmosphere of the Midway with Little Egypt and the "hootchie cootchie" dancers, the Ferris Wheel, old Algiers, the Dahomey Village and Indian villages. Behind and all around these sites was the city of Chicago with its industrial filth and dirt, its stockyards, bordellos and gambling dens. In the last analysis the White City was facade, steel framework covered with a plaster of paris-like substance called staff. Most of it was whitewashed to present a neoclassical facade and, like a Hollywood set, all but one of the buildings were destroyed within a few years of the fair's closing (Badger 129-31; Burg 287-88).

Just as the White city was facade so, too, was the rhetoric of progress. Uncertainty and fear were present in equal measure. Only five years before the fair opened the Haymarket riots took place. Chicago and other cities had become overcrowded, filthy sewers overflowing with immigrants; immigrants who were to many middle-class Americans the dregs of the earth (Badger 31-39; Burg 273-75). Fear of radicalism, labor unrest and the loss of American values were all present at the fair, as was the fear of another financial crash. Even as the fair opened there were rumblings throughout the economy and by the time the fair closed, America was in the grips of one of its worst depressions. Thousands of poor, hungry, homeless and jobless men and women roamed the streets of Chicago. In the bitter winter of 1893-94 the abandoned White City became the refuge of vagrants and the homeless. In the face of economic collapse, faith in progress may have been slightly shaken, but the assumptions that had made the fair necessary and possible were still in command. The middle-class had their fair and now it was time to get on with the business of America (Badger 129-30; Burg 65-73).

Several contrasts and comparisons can be made between the fourth and fifth centennial celebrations. The most striking contrast is the lack of a world's fair in the United States to commemorate the event. This could easily be attributed to a lack of political will or the inability of the various parties to compromise and come to agreement. But it seems to me that it is symptomatic of more than competing personal and political agendas. What the lack of a fair suggests is a lack of vision and leadership. In many ways it is indicative of the deep divisions that exist within our society. What appears to be happening is a contest between an older culture whose assumptions and values are rooted in the past and a new cultural vision that is more open and inclusive, but which is still struggling to emerge and to fully define itself.

Ten years ago the Paris-based International Bureau of Expositions awarded twin world's fairs to Seville and Chicago to commemorate the quincentennial. According to its charter, the Chicago fair was to be a universal class fair, one which would include all nations. From the very beginning there were conflicts over the proposed Chicago fair. After several years of political posturing, finger pointing and argument, the Chicago fair collapsed. Central to this collapse was the issue of purpose. Secondary to this were the issues of who would pay for the fair and who would control it.

These are all important issues and the difference between how they were resolved in the 1890s and how they went unresolved now reveals a much different social and cultural reality. Of course, there were disagreements over the respective roles of the federal government, the state, the city and the civic and business leaders who organized the 1893 fair. Who should pay for it and who should have control over the fair were important areas of concern, but these were all worked out. They were worked out because those who wanted the fair to succeed all shared the same vision of themselves and their society (Cassell 230-44; Burg 43-61).

Both politically and economically, the 1893 event was easier to pull off. Those who controlled political and economic life shared the same assumptions and there was little room for dissent. There was wide agreement over the desirability of staging the fair. By a similar token there was wide agreement over the goals of the nation and over values that needed to be emphasized.

Unlike the proposed 1992 fair, the civic and business leaders of Chicago put up the money for the 1893 fair. They contributed millions of dollars of their personal wealth. In the 1890s, men like Cyrus McCormick, Pullman and Swift owned the businesses they ran. Their personal fortunes and their businesses were one and the same. They could use the profits from those businesses as they saw fit. Through subscriptions or through bonds issued under authority granted by the state of Illinois, the fair directors managed, in a very short time, to raise the needed money. Federal assistance was limited to $2.5 million in commemorative half-dollars, which were to be sold as souvenirs for double the face value. After some arm twisting and some concession on the part of fair organizers, the state of Illinois approved $5 million in bonding authority, with the clear understanding that the bonds had to be repaid (Badger 13-81; Burg 75-112; Cassell 230-44).

The proposed 1992 Chicago fair was estimated to cost $800 million. No governmental authority was willing to provide a share of the cost. Primarily because of the financial disaster of the New Orleans Fair, the proposed Chicago fair was never able to shake the image of losing financial proposition. Both the federal deficit and political divisions in Washington made significant federal help impossible. Even had federal aid been possible, it is unlikely that the Reagan administration would have assisted the Black Democratic mayor of Chicago in his efforts to find funding for the fair. The Bush administration clearly preferred private initiatives for funding the Quincentennial celebration. The state of Illinois refused to grant a $450 million loan requested by the Fair Authority. Instead, the legislature gave funds for one year's planning and study "with a mandate to come back next year with a detailed plan." This reluctance to commit funds was due to the failure of the New Orleans fair. It also reflected the political divisions within the state and the distrust downstate politicians have for Chicago. Chicago's mayor Harold G. Washington refused to saddle Chicago taxpayers with the cost. None of the civic and business leaders ever suggested that they would or could raise the needed funds privately.

Within Chicago, the political divisions were enough to kill the fair without any outside help. The once powerful Democratic machine was fragmented after the death of Mayor Richard Daley. Where once one man had directed city affairs, now there were numerous racial and ethnic factions contending for power and influence. Civic and business leaders no longer command the respect or wield the power they once did. Unlike the 1890s, business leaders work for the corporations they run and are responsible to a board of directors and to their stockholders.[6]

Chicago's business and civic leaders envisioned a lakefront site in the south Loop area for the proposed fair. They saw the fair as a way to bring attention and business to Chicago and as a way to refurbish a portion of the business district. Thomas G. Ayers, chairman of the Chicago Fair Authority, saw the fair as a "showcase for the city," much like 1893. In a *New York Times* interview he was quoted:

The '93 fair which was held 22 years after this city burned to the ground, changed the city from a farmers' and outfitters' city into a world-class city. It was a city of ideas, forward-looking, had vital leadership. I think Chicago has slipped and in many people's minds it's the dying capital of the Frost Belt. (*New York Times* 28 July 1984: 6)

The proposed fair was a real opportunity to change that image and put forward a vision for the 21st century. According to Ayers, "We're talking about something that will have an impact on the ideas and ideals of the world as we approach the 21st century." Unfortunately, few others seemed to share his vision. Some Chicago aldermen saw the positive benefits of the fair for Chicago, while others saw it as a means to achieve desired urban development. What they could never agree on was whose district should benefit from the redevelopment and the effects a fair might have on existing neighborhoods. Several sites were proposed, including an area on the south side. The Cabrini-Green housing development was offered as an alternative as was a location on the west side that had been devastated by the 1968 riots. One alderman proposed rehabilitating the South Works steel plant while others suggested that Lake Calumet on the far south side would be a proper place for the fair. That suggestion fell through when the aldermen conducting a new conference on the site became mired to their knees in mud.[7]

Unlike 1893, there did not appear to be any pressing national need or desire for a fair in 1992. The United States is not a nation on the threshold of world involvement as we were in 1893. Our place in the world is assured and there is no need to stake a claim to a position of leadership in the world. Indeed, we seem to be searching for ways to shift the financial, political and moral burden of world leadership onto the shoulders of others. In many respects the 1893 fair was a gigantic trade show. Business and industry displayed their wares throughout the buildings of the fair, while states vied with each other to insure that their products and industries were well represented.[8] Modern businesses don't need a fair to showcase their wares. Television is a more effective medium for selling products or gaining name recognition than any fair could ever hope to be. Television reaches millions of potential customers throughout the world with messages so subtle that people seldom realize they are being asked to buy the product. Unlike a face to face situation, the emphasis is not on the product but is on a feeling or an image. The image that is presented is much more important than the product being advertised, so money went to advertising rather than to a fair. *Adweek* claimed the Quincentenary was an Olympic-sized marketing opportunity for corporate America. It was also no accident that 500 years after Columbus' first voyage corporate America discovered Hispanics as a potential market.[9]

The collapse of Chicago's efforts to host a world's fair in 1992 was indicative of the deep social and political cleavages that still exist in Chicago. In some respects the Chicago situation mirrors the divisions within American society. While there was widespread agreement over the significance for America of the 1893 fair there were competing and conflicting views over the significance of the 500th anniversary. The Columbian Quincentenary became a battleground, both here and abroad. Voices were raised in protest as other visions of the meaning and significance of Columbus' voyage were put forth.[10]

Perhaps the most interesting comparison that can be made between 1893 and 1992 is that the 400th anniversary had almost nothing to do with Columbus, while for the 500th anniversary, much was made of the significance of Columbus and the meaning of his voyage for the modern world. The World's Columbian Exposition was not a celebration of Columbus and his exploits; Columbus was largely ignored. It was a celebration of the United States, of Chicago and of the 19th century and its magnificent progress. The Chicagoans who organized it meant it to be a celebration of their hometown, of their Victorian culture and of the confident century that was coming to a close.

A major difference today is that fewer people find anything to celebrate about Chicago or American culture and it appears that the general attitude at the close of the 20th century will be good riddance. This has not been a century of optimism characterized by a belief that utopia is right around the corner. If anything, the two decades preceding the Quincentenary were decades of cynicism, pessimism and greed. Many of those looking forward to the 21st century are looking forward to it with a sense of relief that the 20th century is finally drawing to a close.[11]

Notes

[1]For descriptions of the parade and marchers see "The Parade," *Chicago Tribune*, 21 Oct. 1892 and "The Procession," *Chicago Tribune*, 21 Oct. 1892.

[2]"On the Dedication," *Chicago Tribune*, 22 Oct. 1892, 10 quoted in Litwicki, "The Inauguration of the People's Age," 57.

[3]Contemporary indicators of the same assumptions can be found in W. Delano Eastlake, "Moral Life of the Japanese," *The Popular Science Monthly* 43 (1893) 327-48; "Freaks of Chinese Fancy at the Fair," *Chicago Tribune* 24 Sept. 1893, 33; "The Japanese Village," *Harper's Weekly* 1893; "The Johnson Family," *Harper's Weekly* 1893, a series of racist cartoons depicting a caricature of a black family visiting the fair. The series ran during much of that year. Quote is from Bancroft, *Book of the Fair*, 835. The same descriptive phrases can be found in *The Chicago Record's History of the World's Fair*. Chicago: Daily News Publishing, 1893, 235.

[4]Rydell, *All the World's a Fair*, 52-55; Ann Massa, "Black Women in the 'White City'," *Journal of American Studies* 8 (1974): 319-37; Elliott M. Rudwick and August Meier, "Black Man in the 'White City': Negroes and the Columbian Exposition, 1893" *Phylon* 26 (Winter 1965): 354-61; Jeanne Madeline Weimann, *The Fair Woman* (Chicago: Academy Press, 1981), 103-24.

[5]"The Jubilee Day Folly," *Indianapolis Freeman* (2 Sept. 1893); "The World in Miniature," *Indianapolis Freeman* (2 Sept. 1893); Rudwick and

Meier, "Black Man in the White City," 359-61; "A First Impression," *Cosmopolitan Magazine* 15 (1893): 536-37. Representative of this literature are Flinn, *Official Guide;* Bancroft, *The Book of the Fair;* and *The Chicago Record's History of the World's Fair.*

⁶*Chicago Tribune*, 3 May 1984, 1; 30 Apr. 1985; 21 May 1985; 14, 20 and 22 June 1985 and 6 July 1985 are among the many stories detailing the struggles within Chicago and Illinois to find some common ground regarding the fair.

⁷*New York Times*, 28 July 1984, 6; *Chicago Tribune*, 6 July 1984; 9 Aug. 1984; 17 Oct. 1984; 8 Nov. 1984; 22 Feb. 1985 and 15 Mar. 1985 provide representative stories of the battle over the site.

⁸Representative of the literature on state participation are E.C. Hovey, "Massachusetts at the World's Fair," *New England Quarterly* 9 (1893): 735-50; and Cassell, "Welcoming the World," 43-61.

⁹*Adweek* quoted in Montgomery, "Holy Columbus!," 26.

¹⁰Representative of the vast amounts of material on this aspect of the Quincentenary and of the various positions individuals and groups adopted can be found in the following: John Elson, "Good Guy or Dirty Word?," *Time* 136 (26 Nov. 1990): 79; James Muldoon, "The Columbus Quincentennial: Should Christians Celebrate It?," *America* 163 (27 Oct. 1990): 300-303; Charles W. Polzer, SJ, "Reflections on the Quincentenary," *America* 165 (16 Nov. 1991): 364-65; "AHA Endorses Quincentenary Statement," *AHA Perspectives* (Nov. 1991): 20; Molefi Kete Asante, "...And Then There Was Columbus," *Essence* 22 (Oct. 1991): 144; James N. Baker, "Quincentennial Fever," *Newsweek* 118 (Fall/Winter 1991): 79-80; Gregory Cerio, "Were the Spaniards That Cruel?," *Newsweek* 118 (Fall/Winter 1991): 48-51; Rae Corelli, "To Celebrate or Repent?," *Maclean's* 104 (5 Aug. 1991): 42-43; Paul Gray, "The Trouble with Columbus," *Time* 138 (7 Oct. 1991): 52-59; Suzan Shown Harjo, "I Won't Be Celebrating Columbus Day," *Newsweek* 188 (Fall/Winter 1991): 32; Jeffrey Hart, "Discovering Columbus," *National Review* 42 (15 Oct. 1990): 56-57; Charles Krauthammer, "Hail Columbus, Dead White Male," *Time* 137 (27 May 1991): 74; Hans Koning, "Don't Celebrate 1492— Mourn It," *New York Times* (14 Aug. 1990): A21; Mario Vargas Llosa, "Questions of Conquest: What Columbus Wrougt, and What He Did Not," *Harper's* 281 (Dec. 1990): 45-52; Martin E. Marty, "Discovering Columbus: A Quincentennial Reading," *Christian Century* 108 (20-27 Nov. 1991): 1105-07; Carl Mollins, "Goodbye Columbus!," *Maclean's* 104 (5 Aug. 1991): 36-37; David Neff, 'The Politics of Remembering," *Christianity Today* 35 (7 Oct. 1991): 28-29; Viveca Novak, "Quincentenary Quandry," *Common Cause* 17.1 (Jan./Feb. 1990): 5; Gerry O'Sullivan, "Goodbye, Columbus," *The Humanist* 51 (Sept./Oct. 1991): 46-47; Aric Press,

"Columbus Stay Home!," *Newsweek* 117 (24 June 1991): 54-55; Ernesto Sabato, "The 'Nina,' the 'Pinta,' and the Debate They Started," *World Press Review* 174 (Oct. 1991): 24-25. Reprinted from the liberal *El Pais* of Madrid; Kirkpatrick Sale, "What Columbus Discovered," *The Nation* 251 (22 Oct. 1990): 444-46; Sale, "Roll On, Columbus, Roll On," *The Nation* 253 (21 Oct 1991): 485-90; Raymond Sokolov, "Stop Knocking Columbus," *Newsweek* 118 (Fall/Winter 1991): 82; Harry F. Waters, "Rediscovering America," *Newsweek* 118 (7 Oct. 1991): 73-74; Garry Wills, "1492 vs. 1892 vs. 1992," *Time* 138 (7 Oct. 1991): 61. The list is by no means exhaustive and does not include the debates that took place within the academy nor does it fully reflect the concrete actions numerous groups undertook to stage alternative commemorations. It does reflect some of the diversity of opinion that surrounded the Quincentenary.

[11]The final two paragraphs draw heavily on the comments of Prof. John Teaford of Purdue University, for whose seminar in 19th- and 20th-century American history, this paper, in its original and somewhat extended form, was written.

Works Cited

"A First Impression." *Cosmopolitan Magazine* 15 (1893): 536-37.

"America Extends Hospitalities to the World." *Magazine of American History* 28 (Dec. 1892): 461, 463.

Badger, Reid. *The Great American Fair.* Chicago: Nelson Hall, 1979. 8, 13-81, 31-39, 129-31.

Bancroft, Hubert Howe. *The Book of the Fair.* Chicago: Bancroft Co., 1893.

Burg, David F. *Chicago's White City of 1893.* Lexington: The U of Kentucky UP, 1976. 43-61, 65-73, 75-112, 273-75, 287-88.

Cassell, Frank A. "The Columbian Exposition of 1893 and United States Diplomacy in Latin America." *Mid-America: An Historical Review* 67 (1948): 109-24.

____. "Welcoming the World: Illinois' Role in the World's Columbian Exposition." *Illinois Historical Journal* 79 (1986): 230-44.

Chicago Tribune 18 Apr. 1984, 1-2.

Chicago Tribune 12 May 1984, 13.

Chicago Tribune 19 May 1984, Sec 2, 3C.

Chicago Tribune 2 June 1984, 5.

Chicago Tribune 10 June 1984, 19.

Chicago Tribune 11 June 1984, Sec 2, 1C.

Chicago Tribune 14 June 1984, 35.

DeLancey, Edward F. "Columbian Celebration of 1792." *Magazine of American History* 29 (Jan. 1893): 1-18.

Flinn, John J. *Official Guide to the World's Columbian Exposition*. Chicago: Columbian Guide, 1893. 53, 54-55.

"In a Vast Umbrella." *Chicago Tribune* 21 Oct. 1892, 6.

"The Jubilee Day Folly." *Indianapolis Freeman* 2 Sept. 1893.

Litwicki, Ellen M. "The Inauguration of the People's Age: The Columbian Quadricentennial and American Culture." *The Maryland Historian* (1990): 50, 53-54.

Massa, Ann. "Black Women in the 'White City.'" *Journal of American Studies* 8 (1974): 319-37.

Miller, "The Columbian Exposition of 1893 and the American National Character." *Journal of American Culture* 10.2 (1989): 17-22.

Montgomery, Peter. "Holy Columbus!" *Common Cause Magazine* 15 (Nov./Dec. 1989): 24.

New York Times 28 July 1984, 6.

New York Times 13 Nov. 1984.

"None Can Compare With It." *New York Times* 19 June 1893, 5.

"On the Dedication." *Chicago Tribune* 22 Oct. 1892, 10.

"The Parade." *Chicago Tribune* 21 Oct. 1892.

Rudwick, Elliott M. and August Meier. "Black Man in the 'White City': Negroes and the Columbian Exposition, 1893." *Phylon* 26 (Winter 1965): 354-61.

Rydell, Robert W. *All the World's a Fair*. Chicago: U of Chicago UP, 1984. 39, 44-47, 52-68.

"Societies in Parade." *Chicago Tribune* 21 Oct. 1892, 5.

Wiemann, Jeanne Madeline. *The Fair Woman*. Chicago: Academy P, 1981. 103-24.

"The World in Miniature." *Indianapolis Freeman* 2 Sept. 1893.

"IT WAS EVERYTHING ELSE WE KNEW WASN'T": THE CIRCUS AND AMERICAN CULTURE

Doug A. Mishler

If ever there were a figure in American commercial entertainment who typified the stereotypical American traits of swagger, tenacity, and success, it was P.T. Barnum. He was the master of captivating the public imagination with his brand of astonishing exploits, bravado, and just plain humbug. He was the consummate showman of the quintessential American enterprise, the circus. With his facility for inflated rhetoric we might expect Barnum to have called the circus "the most exalted, fantastic, and stupendous form of entertainment, purveyor of the world's unparalleled wonders, transcending all other enterprises which wither in comparison." Bombastic as this might seem today, for the circus's golden age from 1870-1930 it probably was not an exaggeration.

During the decades of the late 19th and early 20th centuries the circus was preeminent among American commercial entertainments. Like burlesque, vaudeville, and minstrelsy, the circus was popular in the 19th century. Yet while these indoor amusements faded in the 20th century, due in large part to the arrival of the cinema, the circus persisted. And while outdoor entertainments such as fairs, pageants and carnivals were vibrant in the 19th century, their popularity was increasingly circumscribed by the early 20th century when amusement parks appeared. Of all America's cultural products, the circus was the enduring constant.

Besides its persistence, what made the circus preeminent was the breadth of its popularity. While fairs, pageants and other outdoor amusements consistently reached small-town America, their influence in urban areas diminished soon after the Civil War. Conversely, indoor entertainments like vaudeville really never played in rural areas (the cinema only reached rural Americans in the 1920s). The "big top," however, played in countless small communities from Monroe, Wisconsin, to Eureka, Nevada. And though some commentators maintain that the circus was only a rural phenomenon, New York, Boston, and Chicago were always enthusiastic about circus day.[1]

The circus was successful in so many locales because its appeal transcended race, gender, class and occupational distinctions. The circus audience's heterogeneity was manifest in Issac Avery's 1912 report that in Charlotte, North Carolina, "they came from all near-by towns and from distant places; and they appeared in silk hats, in celluloid collars, and in homespun clothes that marked the mountaineers." Men like Theodore Roosevelt, William Randolph Hearst Jr., and Calvin Coolidge enjoyed the clowns and acrobats circus as much, or more, than any Slavic laborer or Black sharecropper. Proper middle-class ladies commonly attended the circus as did Native Americans (Avery 34).[2] In some locales circus day was a type of holiday, schools and businesses closed and everyone went to the show. By the 1920s the circus held an almost mythic position in America. Modern artist and social critic Marsden Hartley stated in 1924 that the "one experience I long for each year...the one event which I regret missing above all others [if he was in Europe], it is the Greatest Show on Earth in Madison Square Garden." Indeed, during the 1930s with the creation of the New Deal WPA circus, the canvas fantasyland was presented as a cultural icon (Hartley 33).[3]

Whether in New York City or Peoria, Illinois, on some muddy lot or in Madison Square Garden, for 50 years nothing rivaled the circus's blend of bunkum, fantasy, and daring. It was a magic experience. As Richard Lingeman noted, it was "splendid and alien, a bacchanal of exotic impressions, beauty and sin and spectacle all intermingled." Booth Tarkington captured the effect of the bacchanal in his 1899 Novel *The Gentleman from Indiana*: "The bright sun of circus-day shone into Harkless's window, and he awoke to find himself smiling. For a little while he lay content, drowsily wondering why he smiled...drifting happily out of pleasant dreams into the consciousness of long-awaited delights that had come true"(Lingeman 309; Tarkington 115).[4]

Though the circus has been basically ignored by scholars, I believe it offers a unique vantage point for observing American society. The circus was more than a mere outdoor amusement, its enduring allure was linked to the turbulent and energizing forces that coursed through American culture. The fictional "Harkless" and millions of real Americans bonded with the circus in a manner unparalleled for other diversions—indoor or outdoor. "Circus day" existed as a defining event in people's lives. Discovering why that unique connection occurred enhances our knowledge of a dynamic 50-year chapter in American history.

Of all the elements which contributed to the circus's popularity, novelty was the most significant. Original and fresh presentations of unique features were the fundamental building-blocks of the circus. While thrills, humor, titilation and other components of the big top's appeal were important, novelty took precedence in shaping the public's connection to the circus. Indeed, the other elements were only significant if they were new—old thrills like old jokes quickly lost their attraction. Understanding why novelty was so important holds the key to comprehending the circus's social significance.

From the day in 1793 when John Ricketts entertained the weary President George Washington with "never before seen" equestrienne feats, uniqueness was integral to a circus's success. Barnum's presentation of Jumbo the elephant, "for the first time in America," in 1882, caused a sensation and solidified his circus's fame (while also adding a new word to the American lexicon). Besides human and animal acts, new technology and newer thrills were obligatory as exemplified by the Auto-Bolide (the automobile meteor), which stunned America in 1905 when it looped the loop with M'lle. de Tiers as its passenger, or Hugo Zacchini's blast-off from his cannon in the 1920s. Novelty was the life blood of the circus.[5]

The passion for novelty was betrayed in almost every description of the golden-age circus. Reporters would comment ad nauseam about the unique features of a show and about the "landslide of humanity" that ecstatically buried their town on circus day. The day began with the traditional "giant gratuitous street parade," which wound its way through the heart of the community. This procession was where the public first glimpsed exotic and marvelous creatures and where they witnessed prodigious demonstrations of human achievement. For many, the parade was almost as important an event as the circus itself. As a reporter in Appleton, Wisconsin, in 1916 noted, "the parade was a revelation and an innovation with its ever new displays." An 1873 Atlanta reporter stated that "the immense throng" appreciated the parade's "many novel and heretofore unseen specimens." It called the show a "great novelty" (*Appleton Evening Crescent; Atlanta Daily Herald*).

If the parade always caused a stir it was meant to. It was an ethereal advertisement of a show's unique features aimed at enticing the crowds into the big top. The people teased into a hunger to savor what they only tasted on the streets invariably flocked to the tent at show time. They often waited for hours in sun and rain to gain admission to the promised land. As one reporter stated in 1922, "The grounds were crowded early in the afternoon with fifteen

A Lithograph drawing of the sideshow, exotic people. Photo credit Circus World Museum, Baraboo, Wisconsin, and Ringling Bros. and Barnum & Bailey.

"M'lle de Tiers." Photo credit Circus World Museum, Baraboo, Wisconsin, and Ringling Bros. and Barnum & Bailey.

Crowds attending the circus. Photo credit Illinois State University, Special Collections.

A smoking wagon from a parade in Cleveland. Photo credit Illinois State University, Special Collections.

thousand people, thousands clamoring at the gate for admittance...most of the people held their ground standing for hours in the scorching sun. Several women and children, and some men, fainted under the strain."[6]

After the shows left town, they were commonly evaluated in what are called "afterblasts." Consistently, the primary consideration in these reviews was the freshness and creativity of the show. In 1911, the Eau Claire, Wisconsin, paper stated that the recent circus, "Delighted the public with its collection of marvels...all new acts...most of the artists making their first appearance in America." A show lacking new features would certainly garner negative reviews. In one 1879 critique from the gold-mining town of Virginia City, Nevada, the *Footlight* blazed, "We are indebted to the thing for complimentary tickets, but we nevertheless cannot praise it. (It contained) two or three horses...displaying more intelligence than their trainer, The performing Bison is an old ox wrapped up in a buffalo robe. Keep away! Stay Away. Don't encourage a pestilence in any form." The lions were old and "toothless," and many of the "new" acts had been seen before. The paper even went so far as to state that all who heard the circus band "suffered universal nausea."[7]

Circus advertisements prominently emphasized a show's new features and unique acts. Circus billers went through the countryside weeks before show day and pasted every fence, barn, storefront, and warehouse wall with lithographs and heralds which shamelessly aggrandized their show's "fantastic, never before seen" features. In one example, a hippopotamus was provocatively billed as a novelty of biblical proportion, the "blood sweating beast of the Holy Writ." Another lithograph extolled the unprecedented thrills "of a flight through space" seen in the loop the loop bicycling of "Volo the Volitant" and "the Great Ancilotti." The emphasis was always on "the world's last and greatest wonder" or "A Transcendently Amazing and Electrifying New Feature."[8]

The significance of novelty was also apparent in circus literature. In countless memoirs, stories, novels and poems, the allure of the circus was proportional to its unusual features. Alf Doten was a reporter, bon vivant, and circus devote in Virginia City, Nevada. He wrote in his journal of following circuses through the region's towns for days on end, watching the show over and over—savoring them. (Doten apparently went to every circus that played his area from 1865 to 1901.) He chronicled every aspect of a show from how crowded it was, to who attended, the number of people turned away, and, not infrequently, the near riot caused by those unluckily excluded. He was a connoisseur when it came to evaluating a circus's quality and, inevitably, his decision hinged on its novelty. On one occasion in 1869 he complained that the Castello show was "a damn big bilk" because there was "nothing new, except the elephant...the circus was poor—poor riders and tumblers...not a single new feature" (Doten, Vol. 2 1055).

Literary sources offered exquisite glimpses of the public perception of the canvas world. The literature describing the golden age highlighted the big top's appeal, thus books by authors such as Booth Tarkington, Thomas Wolfe, and Horatio Alger, gave novel attractions the most attention. In Alger's novel, for example, it was the circus's uniqueness which compelled the main character to run away and join up: "There was great excitement in Smyrna...strange wonders which were to be seen...this marvelous aggregation." The wonder and magnetism of novelty was best expressed by William Saroyan: "The circus was everything else we knew wasn't" (Alger 5; Saroyan 133-34).

Novelty came in many guises. It might simply be the fashionable or trendy new styles or perhaps the latest jokes and ideas from the urban centers which the rural populace encountered for the first time. In 1914 Hamlin Garland remembered how the circus "brought to our ears the latest band pieces and taught us the most popular songs. It furnished us with jokes" (Garland 136). It also brought uncommon physical achievements that stupefied the public, such as M'lle. Zazel "the human projectile" or Clyde Beatty's flamboyant and fiery wild animal act, or Madam Yucca's Samson-like lifting of a large draft horse. But perhaps the most compelling of all new features were the exotics—those never before seen beasts and people.[9]

The American public appeared to never tire of viewing the endless parade of exotic animals the circus brought before them. Even in cosmopolitan New York, people marveled at a circus's "strange new beasts" which no one had seen before. From white elephants to elephant seals or the "last Giraffe" ("when he is gone there are no more"), the diverse spectrum of colorations and species of the animal kingdom were menagerie staples. For Garland the big top was "a compendium of biologic research." In the 1930s, at a time when new species were more difficult to obtain, Frank "bring 'em back alive" Buck became a center-ring star solely because of his exploits in gathering exotic animals for the insatiable American consumer, such as Gargantua, the "world's most terrifying living creature...the largest and fiercest gorilla ever brought before the eyes of civilized man" (Garland 137).[10]

Buck's "World's most terrifying creature." Photo credit Circus World Museum, Baraboo, Wisconsin, and Ringling Bros. and Barnum & Bailey.

Side show group. Barnum and Bailey circus. Photo credit Illinois State University, Special Collections.

Bi-pedal creatures from exotic locales also fascinated circus goers. Hindus, Berbers, Asians and especially members of "lost" tribes constituted the heart of the side shows, spectaculars, and "ethnological congresses" during the late 19th and early 20th centuries. "Strange" humans were portrayed on one poster as coming two by two in Old Testament order to be presented to an entranced American audience. People were intrigued by the evolutionary and anthropological questions posed by such features as the "Giraffe-neck women" of Burma, and the King of the Zulus. Perhaps the most compelling of all were the "world's most weird human beings," the Ubangis, who toured with Ringling Brothers and Barnum & Bailey from 1930 to 1932. With their "alligator" features, created by placing wooden disks in their lips, they stunned and captivated the public. Ringmaster Fred Bradna recounted in his memoir, though he was repelled by their lack of hygiene and "civilized decency," they had an undeniable magnetism.[11]

Public interest so obligated circuses to exhibit exotics that if genuine "strange" people could not be obtained, no self-respecting show owner would think twice before fabricating them. Counterfeit circus exotica, more readily known as humbug, preceded P.T. Barnum's creation of the "Wildmen of Borneo" in the 1840s when he dressed up Long Island brothers, Hiram and Barney Davis, in animal skins and had them grunt. And, 40 years after the King of Humbug's death, humbug remained. The WPA circus in 1937 displayed "savage" African tribesmen, many of whom, purportedly, were discovered in Harlem. Humbug was a circus tradition that was best summed up by the mongoloid performer, "Zip" (William Jackson), presented as a "missing link" or simply as a "what is it" (labeled so by Barnum after a query by Charles Dickens). After more than 50 years as an exotic, Jackson reportedly made the deathbed confession, "Well, we fooled 'em for a long time, didn't we" (Bradna 242).[12]

The fact that deceit was common in circus features and tolerated by the public—in fact, enjoyed—and that the appellation "humbug" was synonymous with the circus long after Barnum passed from the scene, are indicative of the depth of popular interest in exotic people. Exotics had to be presented—legitimate or not. The demand was not just for curious aliens from strange lands, though, extraordinary human anomalies, "human prodigies," or freaks as they were commonly labeled, also captivated the public and drew them into the kidshow (sideshow).

Nowhere else but Barnum & Bailey's "Greatest Show on Earth" could the American public see Zip and the armless wonder Charles Tripp, or Chang and Eng the Siamese twins and Jo Jo, the Dog-Faced Boy. These featured attractions stimulated commotion whenever they appeared. As a reporter in 1873 Wheeling, West Virginia, pointed out, "whatever is monstrous in nature never fails to awaken human interest...go see these people before they leave the city." Like millions of other people, Carl Sandburg was simultaneously fascinated and troubled by the implicit contradiction of the freaks: "mistakes God had made (*Intelligencer,* Sandburg 189-93)."[13]

In a society increasingly confronted with conflict between race and class, where scientific and technologic change dissolved old certainties, where cultural fragmentation appeared imminent, many people were ill at ease. Like Henry Adams, they began to question the pace and direction of society. Novelty in the circus had a profound ameliorating effect. For many people the circus's unusual acts were a palliative, others found in novelty the reassurance of simpler times, and still more rediscovered their youth. The public embrace of the unique was part of the cultural response to the challenges then permeating American society.

As Hamlin Garland exhibited, the connection between the circus and its audience was built on fresh new features and new ideas. It was a rare unifying force in a society increasingly divided. To those feeling deprived culturally in the rural hinterlands, the spangled world brought the suggestion of what cosmopolitan life was all about. For a moment the people in Macomb, Illinois, could taste the fruits of city life. In much the same manner the canvas caravan offered a glimpse of the American dream to the recent immigrants toiling in the bleakness of the Bowery's tenements. The big top beguiled rural and urban audiences because it displayed the brightness, baubles and gaiety that were the purported results of the American system of self-interest and pecuniary gain. No where else could both farmer and foundryman experience such things.[14]

The circus was compelling for many Americans because it represented respite from societal turbulence. Many historians have focused their energies on the response to the societal turmoil that occurred at the turn of the century. Henry May emphasized the disquiet of a society facing the transition to a modern world, while T. Jackson Lears described a society with "no place of grace." For Roderick Nash these people were "the nervous generation." Robert Wiebe and Burton Bledstein portrayed the middle class as attempting to order a society seemingly out of control. Yet, in the big top, the audience found control and a place of grace.

From 1880 to 1940 the circus's unique blend of fantasy and reality made it a special haven. It projected a fantasy like the cinema but it was alive and immediate. It offered breathtaking daredevils and exotic wonder in addition to vaudeville's pretty girls and latest gags. More than Coney Island or carnivals, the circus's bacchanal of spectacle, fantasy, and exotica was considered wholesome and avidly consumed by all classes. It was an enchanted land far removed from the dilemmas of poverty, diminishing commodity prices or cut-throat capitalism. The people could lose themselves, at least for a little while, by laughing at the clown, marveling at the mid-air grace of Alfredo Codona, or contemplating Charles Tripp's struggle to overcome nature's fickle ways. The novel stunts of Volo, Ancilotti, and de Tiers signified more to the public than just escape from the confines of gravity. As the *New York Herald* stated in 1922, "The people...seek it each spring to find rest. They flee from jazz to the soothing notes of the calliope. Weary of lounge lizards and bonus Congressmen, they peer into the comparatively intelligent face of Zip the 'what is it.'" In 1932 psychologist Joseph Murphy explained that "the circus is a sort of psychic springboard that bounces us into an atmosphere where the worries and problems of our everyday lives are excluded (qtd. in *New York Herald*; Stephen)."[15]

While the circus represented a haven to many, other people perceived stepping into the big top as causing a realignment of time and space. The circus was a canvas time-machine transporting many customers back to their childhoods and rejuvenating them. As William Dean Howells, Thomas Wolfe and countless other writers have alluded to, by feasting on their popcorn and cotton candy, harried adults suddenly reemerged in their youth. In 1902 Howells described how the circus returned him to the delights of his youth. It offered "an old thrill of excitement, the vain hope of something prenatural and impossible...my heart rose at the sight of the tent." He remembered how the circus "rendered the summer fairer and brighter" (Howells 125-31).

Under the circus's unique spell, adults became children, once more carrying water to the elephants or peeking under the sidewall. Even a man expected to 'act his age' could not when it came to the circus. In 1926, Yale Professor William Phelps stated, "Heaven lay about me in my infancy and it took a circular shape...It was authentic bliss, a delirium of delight. And now that I am over sixty I find I still love the circus." Perhaps an Alexandria, Louisiana, newspaper in

1937 expressed it best when it noted: "Tomorrow the fountain of perpetual youth comes to town...there has never been an entertainment devised that will roll back the years...and return boyhood's happy days as can a circus" (Phelps; *Daily Town Talk*).

To create such a potent temporal distortion, the circus had to offer more than just nostalgia. To succeed it had to contain novelty since it was the crucial element that had always forged the bond between child and circus. A child-like sense of wonder had to be recreated to make the adult's visit regenerative. Traditional acts might work for a moment of two, but their dearth of innovation would soon shatter the crucial psychic connection. Without new features the show would be just a "damn big bilk."

Perhaps what was most fundamental about the appeal of novelty in the circus was that it was controlled. New ideas or objects, whether the automobile, the cannon act, or an alien race, were always safely consumed under the canvas. At a time when modern America mutated with breathtaking and seemingly unbounded rapidity, the big top offered manageable change. As noted, Henry Adams was shaken by the implications of societal transfiguration presented by the dynamo in 1893—his world seemed to lose its center. Many less articulate Americans felt a similar dislocation. The times seemed to move too quickly, challenges to the Anglo-Saxon roots of American culture appeared unending and inexorable.[15]

The canvas world, however, was a liferaft on a sea of change. In the circus change came in more palatable, bite-sized pieces. While outside the automobile might be a perplexing symbol of social transfiguration, in the hands of the circus it became an entertaining agent of man. Octave Mirbeau stated that with the automobile life had become an "endless race track," and "Everywhere life is rushing insanely like a cavalry charge." Yet under the big top that same auto with M'lle. de Tiers aboard was catapulted through the air under human direction. It performed as planned in a system of ordered and predictable stunts. Feats such as this demonstrated humanity's control over technology. While the psychic disturbance of seeing a woman propelled through space in the Auto-Bolide might be great, it was controlled and non-threatening to all in the house (save M'lle. de Tiers) (qtd. in Kern 113).

At a time when the urban centers were being inundated by immigrants, the circus presented cultural pluralism more simply and benignly. The assimilation of new people into America caused a sense of cultural fragmentation at the turn of the century; nativism and eugenics were symptomatic of the response against rapid societal upheaval. It might be understood, therefore, why the circus would be attractive by presenting alien people piecemeal to the American public. They could be understood with more equanimity in the sawdust arena where there was no competition for jobs, no social threat to traditional values.[17]

Self-control and control over the personal environment were also manifest in the circus. Wild animal trainers such as Beatty, or tiger trainer Mabel Stark, exhibited a powerful control over their environment where any loss of control might mean injury or death. The wirewalkers and aerialists demonstrated considerable personal control. Their acts required perfect symmetry between body and mind. Architect Irving Pond noted in 1924 that their "final accomplishment involves travail of spirit and a discipline of mind and body almost beyond belief...technical perfection in their execution, and spiritual qualities...beyond the demands of any and all other arts" (Pond 28, 34).

Finally, in an era of technological and social dynamism, the spangled fantasy symbolized simpler times. The big top came to represent the innocence and even romance of America before the dislocations of modern life. Garland wrote in 1914 of the circus "filing our minds with the color of romance." And Howells admitted that if the circus no longer seemed as grand as in his youth "the fault was in me...It was I who had shrunk and dwindled." Visiting the circus rekindled fond memories of long past simple pleasures. As the *Baltimore Sun* summarized in 1934, "the circus is one institution which remains reassuringly constant...the winds of change and faction are blowing strong throughout the world, but under the big top a man stares at much the same splendors and death-defying feats that he used to." That "reassuring constant" represented an era of shared values and principles, before the details of everyday life became seemingly so involved and problematic. For this reason the circus would be included in the cultural nationalism of the New Deal. It exemplified what Michael Kammen has recently labeled as "democratic traditionalism." For many people the circus was equated with a simple, stable, and happier day (Garland 130; *Baltimore Sun*; Kammen 299-301).

Novelty and the circus were synonymous. Extraordinary achievements, exotic creatures and cultures, people with anomalous physical appearances, all these were integral in the big top's unique appeal. In large measure the circus's essential magnetism lay in its pleasing and reassuring message which ameliorated societal strain and disquiet; a message composed of a variety of fresh and unusual features.

Beyond the cotton candy, the ethereal performance of trapeze performer Lillian Leitzel, the monstrous elephant, and the boy sneaking in under the tent, there was more to the American circus. Between 1880 and 1940 the circus was not just a cheap amusement like Coney Island's Dreamland or the carnival, it was an extraordinary event. John Waldorf fondly remembered the circus day of his youth in Virginia City, "what used to get a rise out of me was something better than candy and presents...No not christmas...It was the coming of the circus." For Marsden Hartley the appeal transcended the earthly realm: "If there really is to be a Heaven hereafter, then let me go straight by the pelican air service to that division of it set apart for the circus...I can join that splendid horde all turning and springing and flying...and merge myself in the fine pattern which these superior artists make." P.T. Barnum, James A. Bailey, and the Ringling Brothers infused the circus with bunkum, brilliance, and often outrageous fabrication, which inspired in the public an unequalled sense of wonder, and made circus day a vital cultural symbol (Waldorf 69; Hartley 88).

Notes

[1]Two excellent studies of the social role of the cinema and its audience are Larry May's and Charles Musser, *High-Class Moving Pictures: Lyman H. Howe and the Forgotten Era of Travelling Exhibition, 1880-1920*, (Princeton: Princeton University Press, 1991).

Traditionally Barnum & Bailey, and then later Ringling Brothers and Barnum & Bailey, opened in New York for six to eight weeks.

The premise of circus being only rural is presented in the following:

Brooks McNamara, *Step Right Up*, (Garden City, New York: Doubleday and Co. Inc., 1976).

William Slout, *Theater in a Tent: The Development of Provincial Entertainment*, (Bowling Green, Ohio: Bowling Green University Press, 1972).

Robert Bogdan, *Freak Show:Presenting Human Oddities for Amusement and Profit*, (Chicago: University of Chicago Press, 1988).

[2]These men were all part of the Saints and Sinners Club which was devoted to advancing the circus in New York. Coolidge went to the circus even as president, as noted in Betty Bell's memoir *Circus: A Girl's Own Story of Life Under the Big Top*, (New York: Brewer, Warren & Putnam Inc., 1931), 82-90.

The Virginia City *Territorial Enterprise* reported on August 27, 1879 that when some of the Paiute Indians realized they did not have enough money to gain admittance to the circus they were "most disconsolate beings."

[3]The Eureka, Nevada *Sentinel* on March 9, 1878 informed businesses three months ahead of time about a circus's impending visit so they could "arrange their business affairs," to close the day of the show.

The WPA created circus units in several areas between 1937 and 1939. The most important of these was the New York City Federal Theater Project show which had its own tent, its own elephant, and played before hundreds of thousands of children during the depression.

The circus became part of the search for a "useable past."

[4]Also the same type of rhetoric is seen in many memoirs, such as Dixie Willson, *Where the World Folds Up at Night*, (New York: D. Appleton & Co., 1932), 10: "It seems impossible now, to conceive that life might have gone on without the circus."

[5]For specific history of the circus since 1870 the latest chronological work is John Culhane's *The American Circus*, (New York: Henry Holt and Co., 1990). A more detailed analysis of the significance of these events has not been written.

[6]Lacrosse, Wisconsin, no paper title, August 3, 1922, no page number. Clipping located in GT-file Circus World Museum.

A similar quote is located in the memoir of Issac Avery, *Idle Comments*, 33: "Fourteen thousand people saw the afternoon performance...It rained in a torrent and ten thousand were drenched while waiting for tickets, but they seemed not to care `wet in a cozy, complete way.'"

[7]Eau Claire, Wisconsin; (N.p.) GT-file CWM.

Virginia City *Footlight*, August 25-26, 1879. In its discussion of the Chiarini circus the paper also stated sarcastically that it was amazing that Mr. Chiarini, dead for four years, did not rise out of his grave to smite the people using his name.

[8]The best work on circus advertising is Chapie Fox and Tom Parkinson, *Billers, Banners, and Bombast*, (Boulder, Colorado: Pruett Publishing Co., 1985).

[9]Zazel exploded (literally) on the American scene in 1880 when she was shot from a cannon (using a spring) and hurled forty feet through the air, and caught by her partner hanging from a trapeze. Beatty's career stretched from the 1920s to 1960s. Ms. Yucca was a phenomenon from the 1880s to 1910s, and a darling of Bernarr McFadden and the physical culturists.

[10]Buck was a star of the Ringling show in the late 1930s even though he really had no act, he just posed with animals he had captured.

Gargantua quote from Ringling poster from 1938.

This attitude of the honor of gathering unknown animals for public consumption is the central theme of Allen Chaffee's novel *Sully Joins the Circus*, (New York: The Century Company, 1926). A youth drops out of Harvard to capture wild animals.

The two big draws of the 1930s were the unusual animals Gargantua (an acid scarred Gorilla) and Goliath (an elephant seal).

[11]This poster from 1884-1885, located at CWM.

The most detailed analysis done on ethnographic congresses is Bluford Adams's Dissertation recently completed at the University of Virginia.

Fred Bradna, *The Big Top: My Forty Years with The Greatest Show on Earth*, (New York: Simon and Schuster, 1952), 243-251. His account is illuminating both for what it says about the public desire for exotic people, as well as what it discloses about the racism and Anglo-superiority of the 1920s and 1930s.

[12]The WPA account is from anecdotes found in documents at George Mason University, and at Illinois State University's Special Collections.

[13]The public was fascinated by the everyday lives of the freaks, such as how Charles Tripp could write with his feet (since he was born without arms). In one brochure it exclaimed that Tripp wrote "with a clear hand." Located in Hertzberg Collection of the San Antonio Public Library.

Here Sandburg recounts his reaction to freaks that include Chang and Eng, but also typical circus freaks: giants, fat ladies and dwarfs. He notes meeting someone like Tripp who worte his name with a pen between his toes a feat that effected Sandburg deeply: "It was the prettiest my name had ever been written…I was near crying" (193).

[14]Albert Mclean, in *American Vaudeville as Ritual*, suggests that there were 'new folk' in the city, consisting of new immigrants and lower middle-class, who found in vaudeville the promises of America's success myth, and displays of pecuniary extravagance. A similar thesis has been presented by Larry May in *Screening Out the Past*.

[15]Codona was the most dashing hero of the circus's golden age, and the most accomplished aerialist of all time. He performed from the early 1920s until a fall ended his career in 1933. Many clowns in vaudeville and the movies started out in the circus, one example being Red Skelton.

[16]Tom Lutz has recently suggested that the social dislocation of the era was responsible for the pervasive malady neurasthenia. Tom Lutz, *American Nervousness, 1903: An Anecdotal History*, (Ithaca, New York: Cornell University Press, 1991).

[17]A recent work on American attitudes about anti-foreign sentiment and the sterilization campaigns: Philip Reilly, *The Surgical Solution*, (Baltimore: Johns Hopkins University Press, 1991).

Works Cited

Alger, Horatio. *The Young Acrobat of The Great North American Circus.* New York: American Publishers, 1889.

Allen, Robert C. *Horrible Prettiness: Burlesque and American Culture.* Chapel Hill: U of North Carolina UP, 1991.

Appleton Evening Crescent 1916. (Appleton, WI) Clipping K file at Circus World Museum, Baraboo, WI.

Atlanta Daily Herald 3 Dec. 1873: 4. Atlanta K file, Circus World Museum, Baraboo, WI.

Avery, Isaac. *Idle Comments.* Charlotte, NC: Stone Publishing, 1912: 34.

The Baltimore Sun 14 May 1934. Gt-file, Circus World Museum, Baraboo, WI.

Bledstein, Burton. *The Culture of Professionalism.* New York: Norton and Co., 1976.

Bradna, Fred. *The Big Top: My Forty Years with The Greatest Show on Earth.* New York: Simon and Schuster, 1952.

Daily Town Talk (Alexandria, Louisiana) 10 Sept. 1937. n.p. Gt clipping file, Circus World Museum, Baraboo, WI.

Doten, Alfred. *The Journals of Alf Doten.* Vols. II and III. Ed. Walter Von Tillburg Clark. Reno, NV: U of Nevada P, 1973.

Garland, Hamlin. 1914. *A Son of the Middle Border.* New York: Macmillan, 1918.

Hartley, Marsden. "The Greatest Show on Earth: An Appreciation of the Circus from One of Its Grown-up Admirers. *Vanity Fair.* Vol. 22.6 (Aug. 1924): 33.

Howells, William Dean. "A Circus in the Suburbs." *Literature and Life.* New York: Harper and Brothers, 1902.

Intelligencer 6 Apr. 1873. n.p. Clipping file of Wheeling, West Virginia, Circus World Museum, Baraboo, WI.

Kammen, Michael. *Mystic Chords of Memory: The Transformation of Tradition in American Culture.* New York: Alfred A. Knopf, 1991.

Kern, Stephen. *The Culture of Time and Space 1880-1918.* Cambridge, MA: Harvard UP, 1983.

Lears, T. Jackson. *No Place of Grace.* New York: Pantheon, 1981.

Levine, Lawrence. *The Unpredictable Past: Explorations in American Cultural History.* New York: Oxford UP, 1933. Chs. 9-13.

Lingeman, Richard. *Small Town America: A Narrative History.* New York: C.P. Putnam's Sons, 1980.

May, Henry. *The End of American Innocence.* New York: Alfred A. Knopf, 1959.

McLean, Albert. *American Vaudeville as Ritual*. Lexington: U of Kentucky UP, 1965.

Nash, Roderick. *The Nervous Generation*. New York: Rand McNally Co., 1970.

New York Herald 29 Mar. 1922. Qtd. from Sells-Floto Circus Program, 1923.

Phelps, William. *New York Evening Telegraph* 13 Sept. 1926. Chindahl File C, Box 6, Circus World Museum, Baraboo, WI.

Pond, Irving. *A Day Under the Big Top: A Study of Life and Art*. Chicago: Chicago Literary Club, 1924.

Sandburg, Carl. *Always the Young Strangers*. New York: Harcourt Brace, 1952.

Saroyan, William. "The Circus." *My Name is Aram*. 1937. New York: Harcourt Brace, 1941.

Stephen, Isabel. "Why We Go to The Circus." *Philadelphia Public Ledger* Gt Clipping File, Circus World Museum, Baraboo, WI.

Tarkington, Booth. *The Gentleman from Indiana*. New York: Grosset & Dunlap, 1899.

Waldorf, John Taylor. *A Kid on the Comstock*. Berkeley: U of California, Friends of the Bancroft Library, 1968.

Wiebe, Robert. *The Search for Order*. New York: Hill and Wang, 1967.

Wolfe, Thomas. "Circus at Dawn." *The Complete Short Stories of Thomas Wolfe*. Ed. Francis Skipp. New York: Charles Scribner's Sons, 1987.

THE MENACE OF THE WILD WEST SHOWS

Susan F. Clark

For over 30 years, from approximately 1883 to 1915, Buffalo Bill's Wild West Exhibition enjoyed a place as the "National Entertainment." Though the ownership and title of the show changed several times, the basic content remained essentially the same: cowboys performed feats of skill and daring, Indians attacked peaceful settlers, and great battle scenes depicted the bravery of the conquering U.S. Cavalry in the face of brutal savagery. These images of the West, patronized largely by East Coast and European audiences, were accepted as "authentic" and "genuine." It has only been in recent years that the myths surrounding the characters and events that made up the very stuff and substance of the Wild West Exhibition have been scrutinized with any intention of rectifying earlier misconceptions. In both Arthur Kopit's play, *Indians*, and Robert Altman's subsequent film adaptation, *Buffalo Bill and the Indians; or, Sitting Bull's History Lesson*, Buffalo Bill is portrayed as a muddled and misguided showman, interested more in his own self-aggrandizement than in the truth or message of his Exhibition. True as this may be, the implication that Buffalo Bill acted out of any deliberate intention to mislead, or with any malice towards the Indians, fails to consider the Wild West Exhibition as a product of the moral, political and scientific views held in the late 19th century. What can be shown is that William Cody was an astute assessor of contemporary thought and opinion, and that he fashioned his Exhibitions to reinforce and coincide with the existing standards of the time. As the concerns of the nation changed and evolved, parallel adjustments were made in the episodes shown in the Wild West Exhibition. The fact that these myths and legends continue to survive and influence our lives speaks eloquently of their magnetic and pervasive qualities.

It is undeniable that Buffalo Bill and his partner Nate Salsbury went to great lengths to portray "realistically" the episodes of the West. Not only were real cowboys, real Indians and real heroes (not the least of whom was Buffalo Bill) employed to impersonate themselves in actual events, but genuine props, such as the

145

Deadwood Stagecoach and Indian tepees, and real horses, elks and buffaloes were also utilized to create a picture of "reality." Perhaps the most extensive preparation for any of the Wild West Exhibitions was the planning and execution of effects for Steel Mackaye's "Drama of Civilization." Opening in New York's old Madison Square Garden on November 25, 1886, the drama was divided into four "epochs," each one introduced by an orator who would explain what was about to be seen. Matt Morgan painted four semi-circular panoramic drops, each measuring 40 feet high by 150 feet long. A special grid and winch system was installed to maneuver these backgrounds easily, and the realism of the panoramas was viewed with amazement:

...Mr. Morgan puts in mountains whole, and the chief criticism made by the finical art critics is, that his valleys are larger than the original.—The artist is swung in a chair scaffold, yesterday, away up in the roof of the Garden. At this dizzy height, he was painting the top of a California redwood tree. He limned a crow on one of the topmost boughs at such an airy pinnacle that the bird took fright, and almost fell into the middle distance. Then Mr. Morgan caught a rope, swung down the tree a little, painted a knot hole and put a chipmunk in it. Then he swung up again into the air and covered the top of Pike's Peak with eternal whitewash. After that he turned to painting a cyclone—so natural, that he had to hold his hat on with one hand, while he employed a brush with the other. (Brasmer 145)

A steam line was installed in a special trench dug under Twenty-Seventh Street so that truckloads of dried leaves could be blown across the arena during the prairie cyclone scene. According to at least one report, over $60,000 was spent in creating the effects for the production, at a time when the average yearly income for an office worker was approximately $450. In short, it is hardly surprising that the thousands of people who saw the "Drama of Civilization" were convinced that they were seeing a "true" picture of American progress. Because the characters, the action and the scenery were so vividly created with such verisimilitude, it is little wonder that the subliminal "message" of the drama itself was never questioned.

"The Drama of Civilization" consisted of four "epochs," each showing America's progress in civilizing the untamed wilderness. "The Primeval Forest," the first scenario, showed Indian and other forms of natural life before the discovery of the continent by Columbus. After showing the Indian's attack on a group of grazing elks, the scene shifted to a pow-wow and war dance in the Indian camp, which was interrupted by a wild band of Pawnees, and ended in a wild massacre of Indians killing Indians. The second scenario, "The Prairie," opened with Buffalo Bill charging on a herd of wild buffaloes, followed by peaceful settlers bedding down for the night in the open prairie. This scene was disrupted by a raging prairie fire, which sent animals, settlers and nearby Indians scattering in a wildly dramatic flight. The third epoch exhibited a cattle ranch where the cowboys, happily content lassoing steers and riding wild mustangs, were attacked suddenly and senselessly by a band of savage Indians. The massacre of the cowboys was abbreviated only by the arrival of another band of cowboys, who proceeded to decimate the barbaric Indians. The fourth, and originally the final, scene showed a mining camp, the Pony Express and the Deadwood Stagecoach under assault by bandits and Indians. At the end of the scene, the mining camp itself was totally destroyed by a cyclone, which threw bodies into the air and flattened the encampment. Later on in the season, another scene was added to the show, which was to be the climactic finale of the Wild West for many years to come. "Custer's Last Stand" was portrayed, showing General Custer hopelessly outnumbered and under attack by hordes of marauding Indians. As his men fell around him, Custer valiantly remained seated on his horse in the center, until finally he is defeated by the multitudes of Indians. After his defeat, Buffalo Bill arrived on the scene, and the words "TOO LATE" appeared projected above him.

Whether the message was consciously appreciated or not, "The Drama of Civilization" made a clear statement that there were two major blockades standing in the way of progress. The Indian and nature were linked together as the only malevolent forces capable of stopping or destroying the white man's attempts to conquer the frontier. No other obstacles intruded on the happy rowdiness of the cowboys or the peacefulness of the emigrants. In simplistic terms, the white man, who represented all that was "good" in civilization, was pitted against the wild and barbaric elements that symbolized those "dark" factors that must be vanquished before civilization can be complete. Both on a physical and spiritual level, these incomprehensible and uncontrollable "evil forces" must be defeated or overcome in order to insure the survival of mankind. In the Mackaye drama, the settling of the frontier achieved archetypal dimensions, and subduing the savage opposing forces became a moral obligation if the safety of the nation and its future generations were to be insured.

Contrary to the enticements of the advertisements and Buffalo Bill's claims that his show was "educational," audiences did not gather to become informed about the history of their country. Newspaper reporters such as Ned Buntline, and others more reputable, had been writing stories and features on the settling of the West and the Indian wars for several years. Dime novels had helped to popularize the characters and events, while greatly exaggerating the facts. Buffalo Bill himself capitalized on episodes such as his "duel with Yellow Hand" by quickly reproducing the action on stage in the form of a melodrama. But by 1890, the peak year of Buffalo Bill's Wild West Exhibition, the frontier days were all but over. One year after "The Drama of Civilization" opened, the Dawes Allotment Act was passed, allotting acreage to individual Indian families and claiming the remainder as U.S. property. Just a few years later, the Battle at Wounded Knee marked the official end of the Indian wars. It is significant that the Wild West Exhibition's period of greatest popularity came when the issue was all but decided. Once it became clear who the "victors" really were, the nation stood ready to proclaim them heroes.

The settling of the West had long been a driving preoccupation of the American people. Some scholars argue that it is the single most influential factor in the determination of our political and social fabric (see Slotkin). In his famous paper, "The Significance of the Frontier in American History" (1890), Frederick Jackson Turner concluded that "the significance of the West lay not only in having provided the United States with an empire on its doorstep, and room for the natural expansion of the Anglo-Saxon race; its significance lay also in the social and cultural effects which the actual process of filling this area had on the American people" (qtd. in Cohen 30). Famous politicians and celebrities such as Andrew Jackson and Daniel Boone had idealized the image of the self-made man and the concept of rugged individualism. Horace Greeley's advice to "Go west, young man, and grow up with the country" was given credence as a likely formula for success. The wide open spaces of the west were an agrarian dream to those urban dwellers suffering the effects of over-crowded cities and a failing economy. As state after state was added to the union, national pride grew seemingly in proportion to the size of the country. Other countries sought to add to their colonies; the United States needed to go no further than its own continent to prove its strength.

Yet the conquering of the West had ramifications other than the bolstering of American pride and individuality. As an examination of

Buffalo Bill's Exhibition so vividly highlights, the process of gaining the land could only be accomplished by the necessary removal, or subjugation, of the Indians. The act of mass extermination was calmly accepted and even actively cheered by the majority. Audience members showed overwhelming approval of the soldiers, settlers and cowboys of the Wild West; Indians, including the great Chief Sitting Bull, were hissed and booed during their moments on the stage. Without a word being spoken between the adversaries, it was clear to the audience who the "good guys" and the "bad guys" were.

Many stories and legends surround Buffalo Bill's relationships with the Indians, and most of them indicate a feeling of mutual respect between the two. Many sources contend that had Cody been allowed to complete his mission to speak with Sitting Bull, the chief might not have been shot and the Battle of Wounded Knee could have been avoided. Luther Standing Bear, the Indian interpreter for some of Cody's European tours, writes with the highest respect and admiration for "the Colonel" (Standing Bear—several chapters on Wild West tours). Even Black Elk, who was accidentally abandoned in England as the rest of the show left for home, felt no rancor that some attempt had not been made to locate him before the company set sail (Neihardt 190-91). Many Buffalo Bill historians point out that Cody allowed the Indians to show their war dances and tribal rituals without distortion, and that Sitting Bull was allowed several moments alone on stage in "heroic posture." And, perhaps the most persuasive evidence of all, there was never any shortage of Indians willing to appear in one of Buffalo Bill's "shows."

Nevertheless, no matter how many indications there are regarding Buffalo Bill's friendship for the Indian and their regard for him, there is no denying the fact that the Wild West Exhibition did little, if anything, towards raising the image of the Indian in the public's esteem. Every scene involving them ended in their defeat at the white man's hands, usually justified because the Indian attack was clearly "unprovoked." Even in the portrayal of Custer's Last Stand, in which the Indians overcome the white man, their victory is sullied by the clear understanding that they did not play fairly. The message of Custer is that if the Indians are allowed to outnumber the white man, he will be rendered defenseless. Cody carefully avoided portraying any scenes, and there certainly were many that could have been shown, that revealed the U.S. Cavalry attacking unsuspecting and unarmed Indians. Buffalo Bill did not even go so far as John Clum, who earlier toured with a "Wild Apaches Show," in showing "the Indians at home, engaged in social games, and as happy and contented as any white man" (Ryan 153). The Indian Village that existed alongside the Wild West Arena was a portrayal of Indian life; but it also provided cheap accommodations for the Indians, who slept on the straw covered ground through the winter and were assigned to eat at a table separate from the rest of the company in the mess hall (Standing Bear 132-50).

Since the time of the earliest settlers, the image of the Indian had been both horrifying and tantalizing to Americans. Early captivity myths emphasized the conflict between dark and light, Christianity and heathenism, in the context of sexual assault and murderous barbarianism. Although the first tales were born of actual captures and rescues, the captivity narratives soon became a vehicle for religious and political sermonizing.

...between 1682 and 1716 captivities were the only narratives about the frontier published in America. The captivity psychology made only one relationship between white and Indian conceivable—that of captive to captor, helpless good to active evil. Captivity psychology left only two responses open to the Puritans, passive submission or violent retribution. Since submission meant defeat and possible extermination, New England opted for total war, for the extirpation or imprisonment on reservations of the native population. (Slotkin 145)

By the 18th century, another viewpoint was considered and some novels portrayed the Indian instead as the "Noble Savage," although his nobility never denied the possibility that his untamed spirit might break lose in violence. Despite these views, up until the 1830's most American intellectuals regarded the Indians as having the potential for attaining equality with the white man through the process of education and social interaction. This attitude caused A.P.K. Safford, the Territorial Governor of the Southwest, to grant permission to John Clum's appeal to tour the "effete East" with his Apaches:

I concur heartily in the undertaking and believe it will be conducive to great good. Your Apaches never appreciate the immensity of our domain, the enterprise and culture of our people, and the advantages of peace, until they have mingled with and learned civilized people by actual contact, and practical association. (Ryan 149)

It is ironic to note the Indian response to such "actual contact" with "enterprise" and "culture." In a speech delivered at the Fourth

Annual Conference of the Society of American Indians, held at Madison, Wisconsin on October, 1914, Chauncey Yellow Robe described the "Menace of the Wild West Show."

Some time ago, Judge Sells, the United States Commissioner of Indian Affairs, said: "Let us save the American Indian from the curse of whiskey." I believe these words hold the key to the Indian problem of to-day, but how can we save the American Indian if the Indian Bureau is permitting special privileges in favor of the wild-west Indian shows, moving-picture concerns, and fair associations for commercializing the Indian? This is the greatest hindrance, injustice and detriment to the present progress of the American Indians toward civilization... The Indians should be protected from the curse of the wild-west show schemes, wherein the Indians have been led to the white man's poison cup and have become drunkards. (Yellow Robe 224-25)

By the middle of the 19th century, influenced perhaps by the Gold Rush and the completion of the transcontinental railway, the desire to conquer the western frontier escalated. Almost as if to justify the mass slaughter and denigration of the Indians that was taking place, "scientific" investigations sought to prove that racial inferiority was both inherent and inevitable. This pre-Darwinian concept maintained that man was not descended from a single source (i.e. the Judaeo/Christian Adam and Eve), but that polygenesis allowed for the creation of separate, and not equal, human races (Horseman 152). The inferior races included all who were not of Caucasian origin. Both scientific and political journals accepted the "evidence" of differences in racial skull sizes and formation, as well as considering the perceived failure to accomplish integration with mainstream America as proof that neither the Negro nor the Indian would ever be capable of the intellectual achievements of the white man. As the two largest non-Caucasian minority groups in the country, the Negro and the Indian were often compared and contrasted to each other.

The doctrine of the Unity of Race, so long believed by the world, is ascertained to be false. We are not all descended from one pair of human beings. This fact is now as well established in the scientific world as that a horse cannot produce a cat or a lion or a mouse. The negro till the end of time will still be a negro, and the Indian still an Indian. Cultivation and association with the superior race produce only injury to the inferior one. Their part in this mysterious world drama has been played, and, like the individual, the race must cease to exist. (Horsman 152)

Translated into political doctrine, this type of "scientific" research became one of the major rationalizations for the continuation of slavery in the South, and the obliteration of the Indian in the West. Further expanded, it provided the justification for the removal of the Mexicans from the Pacific Coast and Texas. Near the turn of the century, as the term "Caucasian" became further delineated to mean "Anglo-Saxon," this attitude resurfaced in the form of open hostility towards the thousands of European immigrants seeking new homes in the United States.

Given these views, a part of the American psyche, consciously or not, it is hardly surprising that few objections were raised to Buffalo Bill's advertisements promising to show the "wild dusky warriors" giving their "weird war dances." Nor could it be expected that audiences would do anything but respond enthusiastically to the recreation of events showing the superiority of the white man, and guaranteeing his future success. A poster for Buffalo Bill's Wild West in 1898 showed a South American Gaucho, a Mexican Vaquero, a Cossack, an American Indian, an Arab and an American Cowboy riding side by side with the promise to exhibit the "Wild Rivalries of Savage, Barbarous & Civilized Races" (Rennert). American audiences had little difficulty in comprehending which of the figures represented the "civilized races." There is evidence that Buffalo Bill planned to capitalize on racist sentiments in another type of show as well. In a show called "Black America," Cody hoped to present an exposition on the history of American slavery.

The show will be composed of one thousand Negroes who will every day present, in tableaux and human panorama, the entire history of American slavery. These tableaux will represent the Negro as a savage, as a slave, a soldier and a citizen. The best Negro talent in the U.S. will be employed in this great show and everyone knows that the colored man is strictly in it when it comes to entertainment.

Mr. Cody said,"Negro humor and melody will in this show reach the acme of perfection, as we have engaged a large company of the most celebrated opera and jubilee singers and each and every member of the aggregation will possess musical talent, so that the grand chorus of one thousand voices will be a thrilling performance." Imagine one thousand Negroes, in varied costumes, parading and singing in one great wave of melody, those old plantation songs. Scenes descriptive of the ante-war period will be presented, showing the plantation with cotton pickers at work and the various other phases of plantation life, even the auction block and the whipping post will be faithfully shown. (Yost 264)

Despite the fact that Cody's plan failed, which may have been solely due to poor management as Salsbury was sickly at the time, the original concept reveals a very stereotyped image of the Negro as a musical and comic entertainer. The reporter commenting on Cody's description of the show displays his bias by focusing on the promised enactments of plantation life, with the whipping post and the auction block, potent symbols of subjugation, particularly mentioned. Unlike the Indians, however, the Negro's position in society after the Civil War improved slightly as more and more Americans became convinced that the former slaves could benefit by education and learning.

...*The Nation* and other magazines contrasted the treacherous character of the Indian with the Negro's genial temperament. Words and phrases such as "fiendishness," "brutal torture," and the killing of innocent whites by "hearth and home," frequently occurred in recountings of Indian actions on the frontier. Some people speculated that greater sympathy existed for blacks because they were more necessary than the Indian to society, especially in the South. Besides, in the South blacks and whites lived in close contact and it was claimed that natural human sympathies developed. In contrast, Indians were isolated from all but a fraction of white Americans, who only knew about them from news accounts, stories and magazine articles. Negroes seemed to be making more progress than Indians, partly because they were trying more. (Wilson 73)

Other attempts Buffalo Bill made to satiate the public interest in seeing their nationalistic dreams and aspirations vilified were more successful. Fortified by its demonstration of strength in having "tamed the untameable" on its own continent, the United States began to look further afield for new wildernesses. In a rapid succession of events, the country quickly became involved in Cuba and the Phillipines, spurred by an enthusiasm to share "the American way" and, not uncoincidentally, prove the assertion of American power and dominance. The year after the Spanish-American War, Cody added "The Battle of San Juan Hill" to the program, employing sixteen of Teddy Roosevelt's "Rough Riders." Pageants displaying Cubans, Fillipinos and Hawaiians were added to represent the "new islands." In response to a growing awareness of European unrest, the theme of military preparedness became an important aspect of American life. In the same way that many private lodges and organizations such as the Knights of Columbus and the Knights of Pythias had begun to sponsor drill teams, so, too did Buffalo Bill add military and artillery exhibitions as integral parts of the performances. The theme of the show expanded far beyond the original confines of the Wild West, although these elements always remained a part of the show. As the frontiers of the United States widened, Buffalo Bill correspondingly turned his attention to the concerns of the nation.

Not solely because of Buffalo Bill, but certainly assisted by his recreations, the Frontier Myth and its corresponding symbols have become an indelible part of our national culture. The western movie, which Buffalo Bill helped to foster in its infancy, also did much to reinforce the images of cowboys and Indians that influence contemporary thought and policy. Phrases such as "The Last Stand," "Indian Country," and "the Lone Ranger" all conjure up preconceived notions that "do not require an explanatory program." As Richard Slotkin points out in his most recent book, comprehension of these myths and their origins is essential to understanding a culture's moral and ethical values.

These metaphors not only define a situation for us, they prescribe our response to that situation...Myth is invoked as a means of deriving usable values from history, and of putting those values beyond the reach of critical demystification. Its primary appeal is to ritualized emotions, established beliefs, habitual associations, memory, nostalgia. Its representations are symbolic and metaphoric, depending for their force on an intuitive recognition and acceptance of the symbol by the audience. (Slotkin 18-19)

Despite the post-world war recognition of the inevitable horrors and consequences of racial extermination and grandiose imperialism, outbreaks such as the Vietnamese War were discussed and negotiated using the same terminology and mental attitude exploited by the Wild West Exhibition. Richard Slotkin uses this as evidence that the Frontier and its brutal realities have shaped the American consciousness to its present violent state. Whether "credit" for this can go to Buffalo Bill or not is a matter for debate. Violence, the superiority of the white man and pride in American civilization were all constant themes of the Wild West Exhibition. Though a healthy cynicism towards these attitudes has altered the potency of their appeal, it is undeniable that the myths and legends perpetrated by Buffalo Bill's Wild West Exhibition continue to shape the forms of American dreams.

Works Cited

Brasmer, William. "The Wild West Exhibition and *The Drama of Civilization.*" *Western Popular Theatre.* Eds. Mayer and Richards. London: Methuen & Co, 1977.145.

Cohen, Bronwen J. "Nativism and Western Myth: The Influence of Nativist Ideas on the American Self-Image." *Journal of American Studies* 8:1 (Apr. 1974): 30.

Horsman, Reginald. "Scientific Racism and the American Indian in the Mid-Nineteenth Century." *American Quarterly* May 1975: 152, 164.

Neihardt, John G. *Black Elk Speaks.* New York: William Morrow & Co., 1932.190-91.

Rennert, Jack. *100 Posters of Buffalo Bill's Wild West.* New York: Darien House Poster Art Library, 1976. Poster #66.

Ryan, Pat. "Wild Apaches in the Effete West: A Theatrical Adventure of John P. Clum." *Theatre Survey* 6.2 (Nov. 1965): 149, 153.

Slotkin, Richard. *The Fatal Environment: The Myth of the Frontier in the Age of Industrialization 1800-1890.* New York: Atheneum, 1985. 18-19, 145.

Standing Bear, Luther. *My People, the Sioux.* Lincoln: U of Nebraska P, 1975. 132-50.

Wilson, Charles R. "Racial Reservations: Indians and Blacks in American Magazines, 1865-1900." *Journal of Popular Culture* Summer 1976: 73.

Yellow Robe, Chauncey. "The Menace of the Wild West Show." *Quarterly Journal of the Society of American Indians* July-Sept. 1914: 224-25.

Yost, Nellie Snyder. *Buffalo Bill.* Chicago: The Swallow P, 1979. 264.

SUMMER AND WINTER FESTIVALS IN THOMPSON, MANITOBA

Michael T. Marsden

The Royal Bank of Canada devoted a special issue of its perennially well-written monthly *letter* to "The Community Festival Idea," as they called it. The author had specific goals in mind for such celebrations:

The festival should strengthen interest in more than mundane things. It should help us to improve the quality of our lives.

...The festival must pay attention to the fitness of things and show respect for the beliefs and customs of the community. (October 1985: 1, 4)

This newsletter was most timely, for it marked what others such as Sheldon Smith have noted as a "world wide trend toward festival celebrations" which could be interpreted as "retribalization" related to "the redefinition of ethnic identity in a post-colonial world" (93).

Studies of any such emerging community festivals must, of course, focus on the nature of the particular community, for the community is, as Conrad Arensberg and Solon Kimball note, "a main link, perhaps a major determinant, in the connections between culture and society" (ix). They add that "Communities seem to be basic units of organization and transmission within a society and its culture" (15).

It would seem reasonable to suggest that one of the least studied areas of human celebration, the community festival, might provide a significant window into the culture of a community. It may well provide us with a narrative about the community's cultural essence.

It is with these thoughts in mind that I would like to turn to my field work in Thompson, Manitoba in the summer of 1984 and the winter of 1985. After consideration of various field study options, I decided to focus on the province of Manitoba, reasoning that a more detailed study of the popular entertainment forms within a specific geographic region would be preferable to a more superficial sampling

157

King Miner Statue at the Recreation Center in Thompson, Manitoba. (Photo by Michael T. Marsden.)

over a greater area. The decision turned out to be a fortunate one because the regional focus revealed cultural textures I was unaware of from prior field experiences.

In planning my research that summer, I chose to visit the town of Thompson, Manitoba because it was the community farthest north of Winnipeg which was hosting a festival during my period of travel. I had little background information about the community until after arriving there in mid-July to study their "Nickel Days" festivities. I soon learned that Thompson was a recent community, founded in 1957 because of a large nickel strike in the vicinity. Thompson is a totally planned community which resulted from a joint venture of the provincial government and the Inco Corporation (International Nickel Company of Canada, Limited), a British-American mining corporation. The community was named in honor of Dr. John F. Thompson who was Inco's Chairman of the Board (Fraser 1985).

In 1983, Thompson's population was 13,877, with over half of the residents under 25 years of age and over 80 percent under 40 (Kuz vii). According to informants, the population of Thompson was as high as 25,000 or 26,000 in the early years when it was a boom town.[1] But the recession of the early 1970s reduced the population to its present level. Thompson is a family-centered community, but it is also a highly mobile one. Only in recent years has the population begun to stabilize, with even some former residents returning.

Thompson was isolated in the late 1950s and early 1960s since the only way in or out was by train or by plane. A year-round road had not been built, though a winter road across frozen lakes and fields had been constructed to move equipment and supplies into the community in the early years. Several residents told me of having to travel a good distance to even listen to a radio broadcast since signals from the southern part of Manitoba did not carry as far as Thompson. But it was a new beginning, a new life for many. Thompson is a city where people have come who might have had a past they would prefer to forget. But in Thompson, like many American frontier towns, people become what they are, not what they were.

Thompson is also an ethnically diverse community. In addition to the native Cree Indians, the community is made up of Irish, Welsh, East Indians, Portuguese, and Hungarians, among other nationalities. It is a community with two indoor shopping malls across the street from each other, a large indoor Recreation Center featuring two ice arenas and a curling rink, and a large pool complex. It is a community where seaplanes are common and where newness and northness are omnipresent qualities. It has become the hub of activity for the area north of the 53rd parallel.

Nickel Days is organized and run each July by the Nickel Days Board of Directors and is a self-sustaining community effort to provide family-centered entertainment in mid-summer. The featured events are the King Miner competitions which were established to celebrate the mining industry which supports the community and to display the skill and stamina of the community's best local miners. All of the competitions are taken from activities which are performed as everyday work activities in the mines. Included are stoper drilling, jack leg drilling, crib building, log sawing, ladder climbing, slusher mucking, steel packing, muck-machine mucking, and fire fighting. In addition to receiving cash prizes, the winners are heralded as the best professional miners in the community. The competitions, which are administered by the United Steelworkers of America, Local 6166, are clearly intended to place the major industry of the region in a most positive light and to raise its workers to heroic stature. In the process, work activities become meaningful play activities as well.

Although the Nickel Days festivities do feature multi-ethnic presentations, the King Miner competition is strongly mainstream culture. The cost of running the festival is estimated to be around $100,000, and not surprisingly, Inco Limited is a large contributor since it is the largest employer in the area.[2] The union contract even calls for the Monday following Nickel Days to be a holiday.

The Nickel Days festival also brings in a carnival and musical entertainment for the public. When I visited in the summer of 1984, the musical entertainment consisted of a young magician, a rock group called Free Ride who played Beatles tunes, and a male/female singing duet performing quasi-country music. These entertainers were enthusiastically welcomed by the crowds as valuable diversions. Foot races were organized for all age groups. The 6- to 12-month-old ten-meter crawl was unusual and not very successful; the 9- to 15-month toddle was delightful. Perhaps the most innovative field event was a "Mom's Boot Toss" in which the wives were encouraged to imagine themselves mad at their husbands and then toss a fireman's boot at their imaginary husbands. The event seemed to reveal more than was intended about gender relations in the community.

One of the ice arenas was turned into a display area for community organizations from the Knights of Columbus, who were promoting the visit of the Pope to Winnipeg that September, to the Multi-Ethnic Center which was trying to bring attention to efforts to promote an awareness and appreciation of the ethnic diversity of

King Miner Competition as part of Nickel Days in Thompson, Manitoba, 1984. (Photograph by Michael T. Marsden.)

the community. They sponsored a variety of ethnic dance presentations which included East Indian and Irish music and dancing. Also included in the festivities were a game of Trivial Pursuit being broadcast live over the local CBC station and casino gambling. A humorous bathtub race was featured on the last day of the festival.

A major regional softball tournament was scheduled for an area adjacent to the festival on the same weekend that Nickel Days was held. This provided further evidence that Nickel Days, while certainly a family-oriented festival, was clearly male-centered. The values and attitudes represented by the various activities were largely those associated with male culture. Additionally, the competitions were glorifications of male prowess and stamina. Nickel Days is an opportunity for the community to gather and celebrate the skills which provide them with a living and lifestyle. The King Miner statue at the entrance to the Recreation Center is a non-ambiguous statement of the significance of these male rites of summer in Thompson.

Each winter since 1971 the Thompson Kinsmen have sponsored the Kinsmen Winter Carnival in Thompson and celebrated the frontier skills which both native and immigrant trappers perfected in order to survive in the northern wilderness. The festival in 1985 was held in early February and I elected to return to Thompson to study the festival as a major seasonal rite of passage. According to many of the residents, the people up north depend upon each other a great deal and create their own entertainment forms out of necessity. This mid-winter festival is no exception. The Kinsmen Winter Carnival has taken on added significance in the last few years because it is the first of a series of festivals at which the same contestants compete on a circuit. So in many ways it is a friendly trial run for festivals such as the La Pas Northern Manitoba Trappers' Festival which is held the following week and which is the second oldest festival in Canada.

The patented icon for the Kinsmen Winter Festival is Rudy the Raven. The raven is one of the few birds to remain in Thompson during the long, hard winter, and so it is an appropriate choice as a symbol for the festival. The Kinsmen have created an anthropomorphic Rudy who visits schools and to whom the children respond most positively. Needless to say, Rudy is omnipresent throughout the festival. The City Center Mall in Thompson had a display of Rudy art work which had been commissioned from the community's school children. The Kinsmen even market Rudy puppets and Rudy dolls, using the latter as a major prize in a treasure hunt during the festival.

The Kinsmen Winter Festival is a cooperative effort between the area's band Indians and the Kinsmen. The Kinsmen request applications from various bands for the naming of a venerable Indian trapper to serve as the honorary Okimow of the North for the festival. The title, which means big chief, is given each year to a senior Indian Trapper who "has proven his mastery of the skills needed to live in the tough northern environment. The person also must have made a significant contribution to his people" (*Winnipeg Free Press*). Trapper Charlie Queskekapow of the Norway House Indian band was the 1985 honorary Okimow. The King Okimow competition involves 16 events and tests the survival skills of the competitors in events from lumbering to moose calling and flour packing.

The festival provides an interesting marriage of native and non-native competitors engaged in essential indigenous skill activities, thus providing the opportunity for an appreciation of native culture. But, as in the case of Nickel Days, work activities are presented as competitive play events.

The festivities began on Friday evening with opening ceremonies at the outdoor Snow Stage where the skill competitions were to begin the next day. Inside the Recreation Center, costumed children skated around the ice arena in a mid-winter Halloween costume competition which provided clear evidence of the family-centered nature of the festival. As was the case for Nickel Days, casino gambling was available for adults in another section of the Recreation Center.

Throughout the weekend, children's events were scheduled from jam pail curing to youth hockey and even sleigh rides. But events of a more general audience nature were also hosted including wrist wrestling and a beard growing competition. An interesting aspect of the beard growing judging was that it was done by women, an almost singular instance of female control in what was essentially a male-oriented celebration.

The King Okimow competition included a snowshoe race, various lumbering skill competitions, trap-setting, fire building, tea and banook bread making, rope climbing, squaw wrestling, moose and goose calling, flour packing, and fish eating. Each competitive event was timed and the King Okimow was determined by the total points accumulated. Trapper-cattleman Walter Koshel of Carrot River Valley was named the 1985 Okimow of the North.

Additional events for the public were scheduled throughout the festival and included a senior dog-team race and a junior dog-team race, a dog pull where the winner pulled more than 20 times his weight (*Winnipeg Free Press*), concerts, a dance in the evenings, and even helicopter rides. Two of the more unusual events were the tobacco spitting competition, which was open to men and women, and the brewing and serving of moose nose soup in the open air. I am not certain if the moose nose soup was a joke at naive festivalgoers' expense or if it was a sharing of a regional delicacy as claimed. Barre Toelken discusses the ambiguity of moose nose among the Indians of Canada and the Pacific Northwest in his *The Dynamics of Folklore* (202-06).

An effort was made to balance the survival skills competitions with events of a more general interest so that the weekend became a true celebration for the community. Preliminary jigging contests, with an emphasis on northern variations, were held at a number of the local bars; the finalists were presented and judged on the last day of the festival at the Recreation Center. Ice sculptures were also encouraged and judged through the community, although that year's severe winter cut down on the number of entries. The Kinsmen made efforts to meet the entertainment needs of Thompson's many constituencies.

These brief descriptions of Thompson's two major annual festivals are intended to illustrate both the continuities and the discontinuities between the two festivals which were created to serve the entertainment needs of a totally new population in a hostile environment. While both festivals serve to display patterns of work and to transform them into play, the Kinsmen Winter Carnival makes a much more direct effort to involve native Indian culture in its design. The Nickel Days Festival focuses much more upon the multi-cultural nature of the non-Indian population. This distinction becomes particularly meaningful when it is realized that, according to one informant, when Thompson had a population of 25,000, only 3 to 5 percent were Indians; but when the population decreased to less than 15,000, the Indians comprised almost 25 percent (Sterritt).

The organization of the two festivals differs significantly. While the Nickel Days Festival is run by an elected board of directors representing various community groups, the Kinsmen Winter Carnival is the sole product of one organization. Thus the Kinsmen Winter Carnival has a tighter structure and can be more focused in its efforts to enlighten as well as entertain visitors with indigenous cultural patterns.

There are many unanswered questions about the social and cultural significance of these two major festivals in Thompson. What, for example, has been the overall effect of the dominance of Inco

Kinsmen Winter Carnival "Okimow of the North," Thompson, Manitoba, 1985, Moose Calling Competition. (Photo by Michael T. Marsden.)

Limited in the community upon the popular entertainment forms which are generated within that environment to meet community needs?

How integrated are the native people into these popular entertainment forms, especially those which feature Indian culture? Other than by donning colorful native attire from fur hats to embroidered deerskin jackets, gloves and boots, how have the non-Indians adapted to the Indian ways which surround them?

Do these festivals really serve to bring the various subgroups within the society together and to further better understanding between the groups? Or do they serve to reinforce the differences, with only an occasional pause to contemplate the cultural variety. In his study of Midwestern festivals, Sheldon Smith notes that:

What we say about ourselves when we celebrate ourselves may be much more accurate than what we say in self-criticism. Our festivals, unlike earlier "folk" festivals, celebrate our contemporary pluralism. These are celebrations that show us to have matured to the point where we can enjoy one another's differences. (92)

While Smith considers such Midwestern expressions of cultural pluralism to be "unconscious representations" (91), the cultural pluralism within the Thompson summer and winter festivals has for the most part been consciously placed there. Yet a basic ambiguity remains in the celebratory messages projected by these festivals. Perhaps this ambiguity is exemplified effectively in the personality of Mr. Cecil Smith, whom I met on the last day of the Kinsmen Winter Carnival. Mr. Smith, who was the Master of Ceremonies for the King Okimow Contest, came to the area in 1947 as an employee of the Hudson Bay Company. He later became a trapper and fur buyer, and then a provincial employee which required him to travel all over the north. He married a Cree Indian woman and in 1971 was elected a Member of Parliament from the Thompson riding, a post he served in until 1979. For Mr. Smith, the progress which the mining industry brought with it was important; for many of the people who came north this was "their last hope." Many proved hardy and survived; others left. But this is the law of the frontier, and Mr. Smith values such progress and feels that the Indians profited from it too. Preferring not to concern himself, at least publically, with the negative influences of civilization, such as the use of various grocery shelf products to create potent and dangerous "high's" for indigent Indians who live on the outskirts of the community, Mr. Smith is opposed to

Kinsmen Winter Carnival, "Okimow of the North," competitors/sponsors, Thompson, Manitoba, 1985. (Photo by Michael T. Marsden.)

beer gardens at the community festivals because they do not project the right image. For Mr. Smith the pioneer, Thompson is a community where thousands have adapted to the environment and now call it home. They even have a sizable population over the age of 40 for the first time in the community's history. But during my visit, a rumor that a local Indian trapper who had the registered trap lines around the Thompson area was unhappy with a local community youth trapping project which infringed upon his territory hinted loudly at unspoken tensions which the festivals have not resolved.

While there would appear to be significant correspondences between Midwestern community festivals and those in the central Canadian provinces, a great deal more research needs to be done to provide valid cross-cultural analyses. Community studies must provide the background for any such analyses of specific entertainment forms. And these community studies may take unusual forms, such as the one pioneered by an outstanding Ohio junior high school instructor, Mr. William Young, who has each of his students "adopt" a small Canadian community, roughly equivalent in size to their hometown of Clyde, Ohio. The students then correspond with other students in their adopted town. The results of such contacts have included audio as well as videotapes in which the Canadian and American students share the "essence" of their communities with each other.

Fortunately for my research, one of Mr. Young's students adopted Thompson and the results are intriguing. Among the many responses from Thompson school children she received were the following:

I'm from Jamaica and I am used to warm weather so I find it very cold here. My friends who have lived hear (sic) all there (sic) lives are used to it. I've lived here for 9 years and I'm still not used to it.　　　　—first student

Thompson isn't a bad place to live if you like cold weather and a lot of snow.... If your father's looking for work Inco's hiring on men now. In the summer we went camping and we met some people from Ohio (sic) I don't know if you know them or not they had a dog that understood how to count.　　　　—second student

There is a mine called Inco. It's fun in the summer time. We have a fair called Nickel Days.　　　　—third student

If you think we live in igloos then your (sic) wrong. A lot of people have asked us if we live in igloos. They were from the States. That (sic) so stupid.

—fourth student

Well, Thompson's not that big and not that small. The population here is 75% Indian and 25% white people. I'm among the white people.

I was born here so I can't say I hate the place. Actually, I wouldn't live anywhere else. Everybody sticks together here, but if you say the wrong thing to the wrong person watch out! But that rarely happens.

The biggest hang outs (sic) here are the pool halls. There (sic) 2 of them and I only go in 1 the other one is strictly for Indians. The shows and uptown is also popular to hang around here.

If you really want something good tell the truth about Thompson on weekends you can find 10, 20, Indians past (sic) out uptown along the side walks cold weather or no cold weather.

—fifth student

Festivals may well reveal to us more about the community sponsoring them than those celebrating realize. But we need to find confirmation for these "revelations" in other sources in order to develop a complete socio-cultural understanding of a community. And while crossing the border may necessitate learning a few new dialects, the cultural narratives of community festivals speak clearly and directly to those who would listen, whether they are in Michigan or Manitoba.

Notes

[1]There are stories about how some early miners came to Thompson and did not even last a full shift. The average stay in the early days was said to be 11 days. The provincial government guaranteed roundtrip travel fares for those workers who would go north and give it a try. Apparently, many went north just for the trip and had little or no intention of staying.

[2]Estimates received from informants about the percentage of the work force in Thompson employed by Inco ranged from 14 percent to 40 percent.

Works Cited

Arensberg, Conrad M. and Solon T. Kimball. *Culture and Community*. New York: Harcourt, Brace & World, Inc., 1965.

Fraser, Hugh S. *A Journey North: The Great Thompson Nickel Discovery*. Thompson, Manitoba: Inco Limited, Manitoba Division, 1985.

Kuz, Tony J. *"Thompson 1983: A Demographic, Economic and Social Analysis."* Municipal Planning Branch.

The Royal Bank of Canada Monthly Letter: "The Community Festival Idea." Oct. 1985: 1, 4.

Smith, Sheldon. "The Re-Establishment of Community: The Emerging Festival System of the American Midwest." *Journal of American Culture* (Fall 1985): 93.

Sterritt, Ada. Interview at *The Thompson Citizen* in Thompson, Manitoba, 8 Feb. 1985.

Toelken, Barre. *The Dynamics of Folklore*. New York: Houghton Mifflin Company, 1979.

Winnipeg Free Press 2 Nov. 1985: 2.

TWO NORTHWESTERN OHIO
BEAUTY PAGEANTS:
A STUDY IN MIDDLE AMERICA'S
CULTURAL RITUALS

Michael T. Marsden

More than a decade ago I began to study beauty pageants as a participant/observer in the role of a pageant judge. And I began to reexamine some of the cultural assumptions about beauty pageants and their functions in our contemporary society. My field research focused on two local Northwestern, Ohio pageants, Henry County's Miss Tomato Beauty Pageant and West Unity's Miss West Unity Beauty Pageant. While I have collected data on the more formal Miss Ohio franchised scholarship pageants, the focus here is on the local pageants because my research indicates that they more directly reflect local community values and attitudes.

The 1981 pageant was the 23rd such pageant held at the Henry County Fairgrounds in Napoleon, Ohio. The first Tomato Festival and Miss Tomato Beauty Pageant was held in 1950. Although there were some years in the 1950s when it was not held, the Miss Tomato Beauty Pageant has been held annually since 1960. Since there are 16 townships in Henry County, each township is expected to sponsor at least one candidate; if there is more than one candidate from a particular township, a preliminary competition is held to determine who represents the township at the Miss Tomato Beauty Pageant. Preparation for the pageant begins in early June and concludes on the first weekend in August when the Miss Tomato Beauty Pageant marks the beginning of the annual Henry County Fair. The number of county businesses who sponsor the pageant varies from between 50 to 100 each year; but the financing of the pageant is an all-county effort, and thus a cohesive element.

While the name of the pageant does cause some amusement among the non-residents of Henry County, it is quite appropriate given the importance of the tomato plant in the economy of rural Henry County.

THE HENRY COUNTY FAIR BOARD

proudly presents
the

22nd ANNUAL TOMATO FESTIVAL

"HENRY COUNTY - HOME OF CHAMPIONS"

SATURDAY, AUGUST 15, 1981   7:00 P.M.

HENRY COUNTY FAIRGROUNDS

The fact that the Miss Tomato Beauty Pageant is a scholarship pageant is important to the community. A scholarship of $500 was presented to the winner, with a $300 scholarship offered to the first runner-up, a $250 scholarship to the second runner-up, and a $125 scholarship to the third runner-up. These scholarships are emphasized in the publicity before and after the contest and are provided by the county businesses and through funds raised in the community at large.

It is the position of the pageant's organizers and promoters that such beauty pageants are educational opportunities for contestants. They argue that they are providing the young women with lessons in poise, posture, make-up, public speaking, etc.—in short, an intensive finishing school experience. According to a former director of the pageant, the Miss Tomato Beauty Pageant's primary purpose is to get 17- to 19-year-old young women who are reluctant to change and develop, to change and develop. Pageant promoters have had to come to terms personally with the negative impact beauty pageants can have upon participants. Their reasoning is that since some young women have physical and personal qualities which are valued by our society, these qualities should be understood to be talents which can and should be recognized and evaluated by society, just as is the case with other talents in sports, science, etc. Simply put, beauty pageants provide the opportunity for young women to excel in the area of physical aesthetics. But it is also important, according to pageant promoters and directors, to understand that one of the primary gains of participating in beauty pageants is the opportunity to build up one's self-confidence by testing one's abilities.

The Miss Tomato Pageant day begins with a series of three-minute, individual interviews with the contestants conducted by the five judges. Each judge is provided with biographical sketches on the contestants in advance of the interviews, and these sketches provide a framework for the interviews which cover topics from personal goals to current events.

These interviews are followed by a large luncheon involving the judges, the contestants, Festival and Pageant sponsors, and Festival and Pageant Committee members. After appropriate opening remarks, the visiting queen (or possible queens) is (are) asked to say a few words of encouragement to the contestants. For the 1982 Pageant, the reigning Miss Ohio was in attendance. The luncheon is followed by a long break of about four hours during which the contestants are given ample opportunity to prepare themselves and their wardrobes for the evening's events.

At about 6:00 PM the judges and contestants regroup for a parade into the Henry County Fairgrounds where the beauty pageant will take place. A police escort is provided for the visiting queen and the judges to the Fairgrounds. The parade which initiates the Henry County Fair, as well as the Tomato Festival and the Miss Tomato Pageant, is a county-wide celebration of the past year's accomplishments.

The 1981 parade is worthy of a rather detailed description since it was given the theme of "Henry County—Home of Champions." The parade prominently featured various successful athletic teams. Some of the championship teams and individuals displayed included: the 1981 Napoleon High School state championship basketball team; the 1981 All-Ohio Lutheran state basketball champions, the St. John's Eagles: the 1981 Kalida High School championship basketball team; the 1980-81 Holgate High School winning girls basketball team; the 1981 Patrick Henry High School baseball team; Mr. Mike Hartman, the state wrestling champion from Patrick Henry High School; the Patrick Henry High School track team who were NWOAL champs; the 1981 Napoleon High School cross-country team who were state runners-up; Napoleon's undefeated Little League baseball team, the Twins, who were league and tourney champs; the 1980 state championship Napoleon High School water polo team; Renisa Young, a tennis player from Napoleon High School who participated in the state tournament; and members of the 1980 Liberty Center High School football team who were in the state playoffs. Despite the marching bands, the occasional female athlete, and the various religious and community floats, the Tomato Festival Parade was a dramatic ode to maleness, a male version of the debutante's ball. This display of male victors, asking for and receiving community approval for their achievements, served as a prelude to the display and judging of ideal femaleness in Henry County, Ohio.

To refer to a local beauty pageant as a cultural ritual is not to suggest in any way that the pageant or its sponsors should be treated uncritically. Rather, the phrase is intended to describe the process by which people who are concerned about their community gather to celebrate their human harvest and praise their collective success.

The 1981 Miss Tomato Pageant consisted of a series of initial introductions as the contestants passed the parade reviewing stand in their convertibles during the parade, and appeared in an evening gown competition and a swimsuit competition. The reigning Miss Tomato was asked to comment on her year as the Tomato Queen,

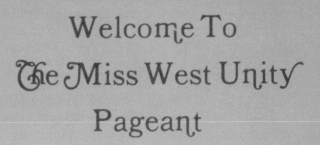

Welcome To
The Miss West Unity
Pageant

This Year's Theme

"Fairyland Fantasy"

Thursday, June 24, 1982
7:30 P.M.

Hilltop High School
Gymnasium

West Unity, Ohio

and the reigning Miss Ohio sang several numbers. One element of the process worthy of special mention is the fact that when the contestants first introduced themselves at the microphone in their evening gowns, they acknowledged their parentage to all assembled. Thus, they were announcing the beginning of the harvest in human terms, just as the county fair which surrounded them was announcing its harvest in agricultural terms.

What quickly became apparent was that the Miss Tomato Pageant, like many of its counterpart beauty pageants in the Midwest, has little to do with voyeurism and sexism and a great deal to do with the development and implementation of a popular aesthetic of beauty operative in the culture which is translated and evaluated by the judges, and then transmitted through the dramaturgy of the pageant to the younger generations for initiation and to the older generations for confirmation. This is not to suggest that sexist elements are not present in pageants such as the Miss Tomato Pageant, for they are.

But for the most part, the pageant is a process of aesthetic agenda-setting which the citizens of Henry County become involved in each year as they subtly redefine the qualities of ideal womanhood by displaying and evaluating the "best" of what they have raised up to challenge earlier articulations of the standards. This process is not perceived as being in any way demeaning or vulgar. Rather, it is presented as a respectful acting out of community standards and values in human form, perhaps even human art form if one accepts the argument that people can use their bodies as art forms.

In adjacent Williams County of Ohio the small community of West Unity sponsors a Miss West Unity Beauty Pageant as the annual kickoff to its Egg-N-Fest each year in late June. The Egg-N-Fest and the Miss West Unity Beauty Pageant were started in 1972 by the Chamber of Commerce as an attempt to keep the people in town for the first weekend of summer and to give the community a sense of coherence. Although there are two large egg processing plants in town and a significant number of the residents of the area make their living working in them, the focus of the pageant is less upon the symbol of the egg and more upon the festivities marking the coming of summer. Perhaps it can be perceived as a late Easter for this community at the top of Northwestern Ohio.

The 1982 Miss West Unity Pageant which I judged was the eleventh such pageant. The Miss West Unity Pageant and the Egg-N-Fest not only provide coherence for the residents, they also serve as homecoming events to draw back former residents. As in the case of the sponsors and promoters of the Miss Tomato Pageant, the sponsors and promoters of the Miss West Unity Pageant perceive the Pageant as an educational process which can instill self-confidence in the contestants and nurture talent. One major difference between the Miss West Unity Pageant and the Miss Tomato Pageant is the talent component. Whereas the Miss Tomato Pageant does not have a talent segment because it is held outside in the Henry Country Fairgrounds, the Miss West Unity Pageant has a fully choreographed and orchestrated opening number involving all of the contestants as well as a full talent competition. Each contestant either arranges for a commercial sponsor for herself or is provided with one by the Pageant organizers. This commercial identification is most important and it is emphasized in the Pageant's narration and the official program.

As in the case of the Miss Tomato Pageant, contestants in the Miss West Unity Pageant are involved in lengthy rehearsals for the pageant. But in the case of the Miss West Unity contestants, the rehearsals are spread out over an eight to nine week period because they involve the opening production number as well as the other aspects of the pageant. The organizers of the Miss West Unity Beauty Pageant are quite clear on their perceptions of the educational value of their enterprise. It is their position that the Pageant functions as a "good leveler" and that it allows a cross section of young women to compete. Contestants are instructed in walking smoothly, speaking into a microphone, developing their talent, being creative with costuming, and working as a team with the other contestants. In addition to serving as an educational experience for the contestants, the Pageant serves as a major opportunity for women in the community to put their skills of choreography, hair styling, costuming, stage designing, and organization to community use. In their own words, the Miss West Unity Beauty Pageant has "brought many talented women out from under their dishes and diapers."

The Pageant actually begins when they hold a contest earlier in the year to choose a theme for the Pageant and Egg-N-Fest. This theme, which in 1982 was "Fairyland Fantasy," then controls the major production number for the Pageant. The Pageant is usually held on a Thursday evening and marks the official beginning of the Egg-N-Fest over which the new Miss West Unity will reign. The judges' interviews are held about an hour before the pageant begins. After the opening number, the Mayor of West Unity welcomes the audience. This welcome is followed immediately by the swimsuit competition. For the first Miss West Unity Beauty Pageant in 1972, the organizers decided on shorts and blouses instead of swimsuits for the contestants because they thought that a swimsuit competition would be considered offensive by the community. However, they were criticized for not having the swimsuit competition, and so each year they poll the contestants about whether they have any objections to the swimsuit competition. They have had a swimsuit competition each year. The talent competition follows immediately upon the swimsuit competition. After a 15-minute intermission, the evening gown competition is held. During the 1982 Pageant, as the final judges' voting was being tallied, the Master of Ceremonies invited all of the eight former Miss West Unity Queens in attendance to join him on stage. He then asked them what they had been doing since they gave up their crowns, and the responses formed a continuing narrative of success. As an apparently unplanned event utilized to fill in vacant time, the display of former Miss West Unity Queens served to validate the whole process.

The total community involvement in the process is obvious to even the most casual observer. It was clear through the judges' interviews with the contestants that they enjoyed living in West Unity and that they had a good sense of place, of where they are and where they belong. The community, in search of a reason to pull themselves together at the beginning of each summer season, has developed a popular and meaningful ritual which celebrates the values of the community and calls special attention to them through the Miss West Unity Beauty Pageant contestants whose successes result from their community work and pride. The process is one where traditional womanhood is not only upheld, but glorified. In addition to receiving a mini-finishing school education, as was discussed above, the contestants claim to be able to get to know well a number of other young women whom they have only known casually. Female bonding apparently does occur between contestants, between former contestants and current contestants, between current contestants and the Pageant organizers, and between the contestants and the women of the community at large. And, of course, the numerous small children in attendance at this Pageant are being influenced for future participation, either as direct participants or as support persons.

As is the case with the Miss Tomato Beauty Pageant, the contestants in the Miss West Unity Beauty Pageant publicly announce their parentage when they introduce themselves at the beginning of the program. The close-knit community involvement in the Pageant is effectively demonstrated by the fact that the 1982 Miss

West Unity was the younger sister of the 1973 Miss West Unity. Pageant organizers perceive the Pageant to be a community celebration of community standards and values. And they believe that, in addition to instilling self-confidence and nurturing talent in the contestants, they are providing a major social function which serves as a cohesive factor for the West Unity community, past, present and future.

Beauty pageants operate on a variety of levels, and may be more or less reflective of their communities depending upon the particular sponsoring agencies and their relative amount of control over the pageants. The regional Miss Ohio Scholarship Pageants, for example, do not reflect the attitudes and values of the specific communities hosting the competitions as much as they do those of the state organization which regulates them. Nevertheless, there remains a consistency to the aesthetic codes employed in the competitions despite different levels and complexities of operation. For example, in the community-based beauty pageants the swimsuit competitions are not erotic. The contestants are judged on the criteria of balance, proportion, appropriateness of swimsuit, etc., and those aspects of the competition which might be judged by some to be erotic are negatively evaluated in the judging process. It should be kept in mind that these pageants are evaluating daughters, sisters, and neighbors; it is primarily when the audience becomes distanced from the individuals in the competition, something which is most difficult in a local pageant, that the process becomes impersonal and dehumanized.

In his study *The Feast Of Fools: A Theological Essay on Festivity and Fantasy* (1969) Harvey Cox claims that "Festivity and fantasy are not only worthwhile in themselves, they are absolutely vital to human life. They enable man to relate himself to the past and the future..." (7). He adds that, "Ritual is social fantasy" (71). For the residents of Henry County and West Unity, Ohio, their beauty pageants and attendant festivals are significant social fantasies in which their communal values are related to their past rural American traditions and their present social systems. These beauty pageants are celebrations of femaleness as defined by their respective communities.

Community-based beauty pageants are like popular story narratives, formulaic with their conventional and inventional elements. And they are essentially emotional, not intellectual articulations. But at all levels of competition, there is an attempt to keep them personal, to provide family and community information about the contestants—to humanize them and thus the process. The contestants are not examples of abstract body art, they are ideal daughters.

It is important to emphasize that community-based beauty pageants are dramatic events. What marks a winning contestant is her ability to play the role of the ideal American Daughter for her particular constituency. The contestants are costuming themselves, performing talent, etc., not for themselves nor for members of their generation, but for the judges and the other representatives or members of their parents' generation. The cultural ritual I referred to above is a ritual of cultural attitudes and values which contestants have learned to dramatize most effectively through beauty competitions, thus proving that beauty can be art.

Work Cited

Cox, Harvey. *The Feasts of Fools: A Theological Essay on Festivity and Fantasy.* New York: Harper and Row, 1969.

NEW ORLEANS' BOURBON STREET: THE EVOLUTION OF AN ENTERTAINMENT DISTRICT

Les Wade

As the most famous thoroughfare in New Orleans, Bourbon Street has been frequented by such notables as Walt Whitman, Oscar Wilde, Sarah Bernhardt, and William Faulkner. The street has also hosted lesser lights, including Tee Tee Red, Candi Bar, and Rebecca de Winter, alias, the "Bride of Satan." Distinguished almost from its inception by an antic disposition, Bourbon Street has through its past appealed alternately to the highest and lowest of aesthetic sensibilities, drawing divas, poets, artists, jazz musicians, and exotic dancers alike. Regarded today as the South's leading adult playground, Bourbon Street is synonymous with "carnival" and "license" (an image that belies the corridor's rigorous civic oversight).[1] If the history of theatre is at its most fundamental level a chronicle of control and regulation, born of the most basic question—how and where does a community go to play, Bourbon Street offers the cultural historian a most rich and provocative text. Like Shakespeare's Bankside, New York's Great White Way, even Minneapolis' Hennepin Street, Bourbon Street exemplifies the emergence and construction of a liminoid space,[2] a site culturally marked and designated for ludic activity. In short, Bourbon Street has found its identity as an entertainment district, with an emphatic, longstanding, and often suspect regard for the performing body.

Roland Barthes was one of the first and most vocal advocates of an urban semiotics, an approach evidenced in his now famous essay on the Eiffel Tower (Barthes 3-18).[3] Giving prominent attention to the site and civic positioning of theatrical activity, recent scholarship in theatre studies has followed this type of inquiry with notable and sometimes fascinating results. Marvin Carlson's *Places of Performance* provides a general introduction to spatial semiotics and a "global" interpretation of the physical theatre and its civic locale (Carlson 1-13). Steven Mullaney's *The Place of the Stage* likewise examines theatre in its geographical context, presenting a detailed and highly insightful reading of performance activity and its control/dispersion in Elizabethan London.[4] Focusing upon Bourbon Street's preeminence in New Orleans' performance history, this essay also understands the city as a social text, a cultural artifact. Such an analysis not only bears upon Bourbon Street's specific systems of signification but draws attention to the forces and pressures affecting New Orleans' social formations at large. Bourbon Street's service as a ludic space must therefore be viewed as evidence of more fundamental cultural contestations; one must recognize the street's participation and complicity in the "ongoing production, negotiation, and delimitation of social meanings and social selves" (Mullaney xi). In this light, Bourbon Street exists as a textual byproduct of social process. The corridor exposes the community's "utilization" of theatre; it moreover reveals the civic operations that inform the authorization, control, and signification of "play."

Although Bourbon Street is most readily recognized as America's striptease capital, its "legitimate" theatre history is extensive, colorful, and often surprising. On this street, James O'Neill once played his Count of Monte Cristo; Lugné-Poë lectured on the evolving modern drama of Europe; and Thorton Wilder for a time rented the apartment now occupied by former Congresswoman Lindy Boggs. Bourbon Street's emergence is, of course, intimately connected to the origin and wider development of New Orleans, and the corridor's theatrical history thus speaks to the economic, political, and demographic forces that gave rise to the community itself. In fact, the excavation of Bourbon Street as a sign connoting theatrical entertainment goes back to 1718, the date of New Orleans' founding, when Governor Jean-Baptiste Bienville authorized the adoption of an "ideal" city plan—geometric and rational in design—with four major thoroughfares running parallel to the Mississippi River (Chase 22).

With fortified ramparts defining the boundaries of the city (swamps and marshlands beyond), New Orleans was prevented from sprawling outward but rather grew inward, creating a dense and highly articulated city center—the area known today as the Vieux Carré. Through the ensuing decades, each of the city's four major streets assumed a distinct personality and a recognizable civic function. Decatur Street, closest to the river, became a labor zone befitting the river economy. Chartres, the next street over, evolved as a commercial zone, once the city's primary mercantile district. The third thoroughfare, Royal Street, established itself as a banking and financial center, later acquiring a cultivated reputation for its dealers of antiques and *objets d'art*. Finally, the innermost of the principal

Former site of the French Opera House—now the Bourbon Inn. (Photo by Les Wade.)

arteries, Bourbon Street, in the words of one local historian, "provided light relief."[5]

Throughout its colonial history and well into the 19th century, Bourbon Street sustained a respectable residential population, and perhaps the street's want of an informing governmental or commercial interest, along with its marginal position in the city's municipal design, explains in part the development that followed, that is, the emergence of Bourbon Street as the city's avenue of "mirth and revelry."[6] Although New Orleanians had long staged pageants and assorted spectacles in private residences, no theatres had been built by 1791 when the first troupe of professional players visited the city. This lack was remedied by 1792 when a residence on St. Peter's Street, a half block off Bourbon (now the site of Pat O'Briens), was converted into a performing space. Two other theatres soon appeared: the Théâtre d'Orleans (1809), located on Bourbon Street, and the Théâtre de Saint Philip (1810), situated between Bourbon and Royal.[7] Significantly, we note that the city's first theatres were located either on Bourbon Street itself or one of its immediate cross-streets. This initial clustering suggests the nascent outline of a ludic zone, with performance spaces deployed in satellite fashion around the city's more dominant institutional sectors.

The preferred entertainment of the time was French opera, which the Creole aristocrats cherished as a requisite component of civilized society, and in the first half of the 19th-century New Orleans claimed the title as the America's foremost opera city. As evidence, the great diva Adeline Patti performed her world debut in New Orleans; leading European troupes commonly inaugurated their American tours in the Crescent City. In fact, New Orleans gave birth to the country's first professional resident company.[8] Bourbon Street proved the home to this burgeoning opera scene, which peaked in 1858 with the building of the sumptuous French Opera House. Designed by the Parisian born architect Henry Gallier, Jr., the lavishly adorned edifice accommodated an audience of 2,000 and was considered the finest opera facility in the country. New Orleans historian Harnett T. Kane confirms that "Old Bourbon was the opera street of New Orleans" and notes that a number of ancillary businesses—of wig makers, costumers, etc.—appeared on the corridor, along with rooming houses catering to players, musicians, dancers, and technicians (Kane 241). Although Bourbon Street experienced noticeable diversification in the 19th century, witnessed in its range of commercial activities—from stationery shops to Chinese laundries to mortuaries, the thoroughfare was clearly distinguished and enlivened by its theatrical activity, known accordingly as "the Broadway" of New Orleans (*Frank Leslie's Illustrated Newspaper* 357).

Other forces were however at work upon 19th century Bourbon Street which would contain its influence and undermine its honorable status. In short, New Orleans' theatrical history exhibits a cultural powerplay between the city's French and Anglo-American populations, one that renegotiated the street's social function, recontextualizing both its entertainment fare and future. Following the influx of American settlers brought by Louisiana's accession to the United States, New Orleans virtually divided into two cities—the long established French Quarter, or Vieux Carré, and the new American sector that developed opposite the Quarter, south of Canal Street, which grew "uptown," developing into the Central Business and Garden districts (Stanforth 7). With French opera securely established on Bourbon Street, Anglo-American citizens desired more familiar forms of entertainment and supported the building of

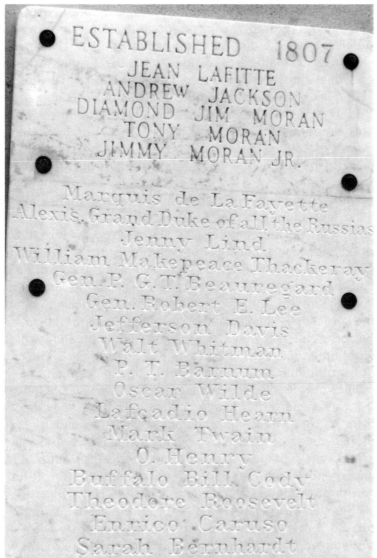

Marker outside the Old Absinthe House bar. (Photo by Les Wade.)

new theatres, such as the American Theatre and the St. Charles Theatre (both located in American neighborhoods), where "straight" dramas were performed in English (Fossier 470). As a consequence, we note a polarity in New Orleans' theatrical life coinciding with the city's geographical and cultural division. From the Anglo-American perspective, which developed into the hegemonic force during the 19th century, the theatre of Bourbon street was regarded as exotic, sophisticated, yet most importantly, foreign. It is significant that, as

New Orleans entered the 20th century, most movie houses and vaudeville chains (promoting representations of Anglo-American ideology) were located in the American sector, south of Canal, while Bourbon Street remained associated with the French artform. Bourbon Street thus accrued connotations of Latin cultivation, as well as Latin laxity, decadence and hedonism—qualities opposed to the Protestant ethos. Quite simply, as Anglo-American interests grew dominant, Bourbon Street was inscribed as a site of "difference," authorized as the purveyor of an "alternative" performance, and it is thus not surprising that the opera should pave the way for the cabaret.

The rather prideful contention that New Orleans has always revered the "joys of the flesh and blood" (Shea 10) performer takes a different light when one considers the city's regard for prostitution. While opera was highly influential in Bourbon Street's 19th-century development, the flesh trade in the early 20th century helped define Bourbon Street as we know it today, a sidewalk carnival profiteering on the female form. In figurative terms, the street's genealogy evinces an ironic succession—the diva and hooker engender the stripper.[9]

It has been said that New Orleans was "born in sin and spent the next two hundred years living up to it" ("Women…" 12). The city's history of prostitution perhaps validates such a perception, for few municipalities have treated the oldest profession with such tolerance. Though locals speak of the famed "casket girls" (maidenly émigrés brought to the New World under the auspices of the Church) as the city's first generation of wives and mothers, the earliest female settlers were by and large prostitutes expelled from Parisian jails. Attracted by the city's seaport commerce and general laissez-faire attitude, prostitutes throughout the 19th century flocked to New Orleans, and by 1850 the city was regarded as the prostitute capital of America (Johnson 235). Their numbers were so great that in 1857 city officials attempted (in vain) to license their ranks (Kane 261). It was during this time New Orleans consolidated its image as a "good time town," home to saloons, gambling, and all orders of illicit pleasure.

At the close of the last century, New Orleans' reputed "sporting life" was perhaps at its zenith. The city counted over 80 gambling houses, 800 bars and saloons, and prostitution, though illegal, was widespread and flourishing (New Orleans Vignette 29). Brothels, or "crib houses," proliferated throughout the western side of the Vieux Carré (opposite the river), extending eastwards to and including Bourbon (Plan… 13). The thoroughfare's marginality is again apparent, with Bourbon Street serving as a line of demarcation, in effect, containing the brothel trade, separating the less respectable areas of the Quarter from the highly commercialized and better established corridors of Royal and Chartres.

The demographics of prostitution in New Orleans, however, took a radical turn in 1897, when the city authorities, led by alderman Sidney Story, attempted to regulate the trade by ordaining a legalized brothel district on the outskirts of the Quarter proper (chiefly along Basin Street). Named in derision of the august alderman, "Storyville" proved the only authorized redlight district in the country.[10] In its heyday Storyville employed over 2,000 prostitutes. This period stands as one of the more colorful and most studied eras of New Orleans history, frequently depicted in literature and film, having given rise to such legends as brothel proprietress Lulu White, entrepreneur Tom Anderson, who published a Bluebook directory for the city's visitors that listed prostitutes by their body type and erotic specialty, and even Louis Armstrong, who practiced his jazz style in brothel parlors. In Storyville, sex was not only merchandized but theatricalized. Select houses offered erotic presentations for their customers, most notably that of Emma Johnson, a reportedly tyrranical madame, who mounted sex "circuses" on a dais-like platform, staging variable enactments of sexual possibility (Johnson 246). While serving the rudimentary economics of the prostitution trade, Storyville, it is important to note, generated a complementary entertainment industry, one not only impacting the rise of jazz but the stage presentation of the female nude, the feature that would prove the keynote of Bourbon Street cabaret theatre.

The years immediately following World War I witnessed a significant dislocation in the social strata of the Vieux Carre and a realignment of its entertainment establishment. Importantly, the vitality of the New Orleans opera scene had been on the wane since the early years of the new century, and Bourbon Street's most famous landmark, the French Opera House, had experienced considerable duress (Kane 257). Damaged by the hurricane of 1915, the structure demanded expensive repairs, taxing the theatre's already precarious fiscal situation (costs for "rat-proofing" had depleted the theatre's financial reserves). In essence, the plight of the French Opera House is symptomatic of Bourbon Street's more general decline as an entertainment center; theatres south of Canal, in the American sector, hosted the major touring shows and provided vaudeville offerings, while Storyville's Basin Street for the last two decades had sustained the city's "nightlife." Moreover, what remained

(Photo by Les Wade.)

of Bourbon Street's repute as an opera center was dealt a deathblow in 1919, when the French Opera House was razed by fire. In the morning paper, local writer Lafcadio Hearn expressed the doleful sentiment of New Orleanians at large when he wrote: "the heart of the French Quarter stopped beating last night" (qtd. in Stanforth 29). Signifying the expiration of its most dominant institutional presence, the destruction of the opera house, for all intents and purposes, closed a chapter in the history of Bourbon Street, drawing to an end the corridor's long-lived partnership with the high arts.

Although opera houses and brothels may seem an incongruous match, Bourbon Street in part owes its ascent as a mecca of erotic entertainment to the demise of its opera scene; a second event however also figures heavily in Bourbon's transformation—the closing of Storyville. At the behest of Navy authorities, who viewed the district as a health risk to servicemen, Mayor Martin Berman (after voicing vociferous opposition) in 1917 abrogated Storyville's legal status, causing an immediate dispersion of the prostitution trade. Many prostitutes simply moved their business from Basin Street, at

(Photo by Les Wade.)

the very edge of the Quarter, back into the areas of the Vieux Carré where their enterprise had formerly flourished. In short order, Bourbon Street assumed Basin Street's "fun duties," emerging as the home of Dixieland jazz and, importantly, the site for sexual consumerism.

In his analysis of Renaissance theatre, Stephen Greenblatt exposes how hegemonic controls moved the practice of exorcism from the legitimate order of the church to the liminal arena of stage; this, however, did not undermine the appeal of the ritual but simply changed the site of its performance, inadvertently investing the public theatre with a more radical and subversive power (Greenblatt 101-23). A similar transference is evident in post World War I New Orleans, with civic officials attempting to suppress the illicit "entertainment" of Storyville, only to find it later reconstituted and resituated. The relative coincidence of Storyville's closing and the razing of the French Opera House invites the conclusion that the opera's loss was the flesh trade's gain, that is, Bourbon Street's demise as an opera center created an urban vacuum which the erotic entertainment industry easily assumed. In brief, the authorities expelled Storyville's subversive potential from Basin Street only to have it cross the Quarter and relocate on Bourbon Street, an acknowledged theatre zone in need of charismatic infusion.

The interim between the two world wars gave rise to Bourbon Street's station as the heart of the New Orleans nightlife. Prostitution held a continued and often obtrusive presence, earning the street the nickname "harlot's row" (Navard 59). To many New Orleanians, however, especially the monied and powerful with financial interests in the Central Business District and residences Uptown, the fate of Bourbon Street was of little concern. This was before the call for architectural preservation, and the historic value of the French Quarter was ill-appreciated; the sector was widely considered a "slum" (Bacon). Associated with French indolence and indulgence, the old Quarter was thus viewed with indifference if not disdain by a prominent sector of the population, accorded little significance in the city's commercial and cultural well-being. This position of "otherness" in the geographical and social text of the city in part accounts for the street's ensuing attraction for liminal activity—not only that of prostitutes but artists, students, and bohemians at large.

Drawn by the social and moral openness of the Vieux Carré, along with its quaint (if dilapidating) beauty and inexpensive housing, a large number of writers moved to the city during the 1920s. In fact, New Orleans of this era experienced something of a literary Renaissance,[11] evidenced in its active coterie of writers and the local publication of *The Double Dealer*, an avant-garde literary magazine among the first to publish the work of Ernest Hemingway. With authors such as Sherwood Anderson, William Faulkner, John dos Passos, and Oliver LaFarge, the Vieux Carré witnessed an exceptional creative climate. Anderson even sent a call for artists to leave the industrial cities of the North and Midwest and to relocate in the Quarter, a place he believed offered what "American wants and needs." Anderson wrote:

There is something left in the people here that makes them like one another, that leads to constant outbursts of the spirit of play, that keeps them from being too confoundedly serious about death and the ballot and reform and other less important things in life. (Anderson 3)

Bourbon Street, significantly, was home and playground for many of these artists.[12] Anderson himself resided on Bourbon Street. Faulkner and his clique regularly met at Joe Cassio's grocery (700 block of

Bourbon) where bootleg liquor was openly dispensed. Faulkner furthermore, upon receiving news that his novel *Mosquitoes* had been accepted for publication, held a celebratory dinner at Galatoire's, one of Bourbon Street's most renowned and venerated restaurants. During these years, the face of Bourbon began to show subtle signs of change as it assumed both a new population and social function. No longer the street of grand opera, the corridor emerged as a site of counterhegemonic energy, harboring the disaffected and the decadent.

After the disbandment of Storyville, a number of new nightspots begin to appear on Bourbon Street. Opened in 1925 Maxime's proved one of the most popular clubs of the period, offering music and the discreet service of alcohol ("Bourbon's Babe"). The club LaLune opened soon thereafter in the 800 block and also established itself as a local favorite (it would later be the home of Pete Fountain's jazz club). The second edition of the famous Absinthe Bar further appeared at this time, maintaining the trade of its forbear after it had been closed for liquor violations (prohibition statutes were enforced on an arbitrary and often intermittent basis). The repeal of the 21st amendment in 1933 brought a surge to Bourbon Street's nightlife activity, witnessed in new clubs such as the New Silver Slipper, the Shim Sham, and the Café de l'Opéra. Importantly, this period marks the rise of a significant feature of the Bourbon Street entertainment scene—the floor show. Accompanied by big band ensembles, the floor show highlighted the dancing (and sometimes singing) of beautiful starlets and chorus lines. These acts were not particularly lurid or titillating, yet they helped set a precedent for the more risque acts that would follow with the coming of World War II. It was during the war years, in fact, that Bourbon street assumed the image and identity we know today (Kolb 64). Catering to the large numbers of servicemen passing through the city—and their desire for prurient entertainment—Bourbon Street nightclubs welcomed and accommodated the GI, maximizing their profits with increasingly brazen displays of erotic spectacle. Music became ancillary; the floorshow translated to the stripshow. The 24-hour "honky tonk" street had been born.

The war years spurred tremendous economic growth in New Orleans, and the city entered the postwar era robust, flourishing, and perhaps a bit self-conscious with its newfound status as the population and business center of the South.[13] Relinquishing its image as a sleepy, luxuriant old world city, New Orleans pushed forward, with modern expressways, new public infrastructure, a far-reaching suburbia, and booming industries. The military complex had used New Orleans extensively as a transit and shipping center, and the city's riverfront activity carried on after wartime with little diminishment. As a port, New Orleans ranked second in tonnage handled, only behind New York. The waterfront capacity was extended to over 150 wharves (20 miles), leading to the creation of a free trade zone in 1947. New Orleans at this time capitalized on its proximity to Central and South America, emerging as the air hub of the Americas. The military use of synthetic rubber, moreover, helped stimulate the region's petrochemical industry, which developed along the Mississippi River northward to Baton Rouge, causing the area to be known as the "American Ruhr" (it is today known as "cancer alley"). Cheap transportation, labor, and power rendered New Orleans a transit, manufacturing, and financial center, and, coupled with the election of reform minded mayor Chep Morrison, who envisioned a progressive direction for city government, New Orleans entered a dimension hitherto unexperienced, emerging as a powerful player in the region's (and country's) commercial and cultural well-being.

New Orleans' postwar economic boom brought Bourbon Street to its maturation as an adult entertainment center, and the period from 1945 to 1962 may be considered the "glory days" of the thoroughfare (A Plan...). New Orleans' unprecedented status as transportation center and player in large-scale corporate enterprise increased the visibility of the city and spawned an influx of visitors that sustained the nightlife industry that had formerly catered to servicemen. Now seen as a "glittering expanse of nightclubs and saloons," the street during these years supported a sizeable number of stripclubs, most with suggestive and provocative names—for example, the Silver Frolics, the ShoBar, the Poodle Patio, the Hotsy-Totsy, Chez Paree, and, not forgetting tradition, the Old French Opera House (Kane 12). Local writer and newspaperman Robert O'Roark likened the transformed Bourbon Street to New York's 42nd Street and Broadway and noted the change with some regret: "The once quiet little holes-in-the-wall now have neon signs and barkers extolling the charms of the dozen—count 'em—goosepimpled dames who writhe, bump, and grind inside" (O'Roark 31). This was the Bourbon Street of international fame, the Bourbon Street of Blaze Star, renowned stripper and former mistress to then governor Earl Long, whose act "the Heat Wave" earned her over a $1,000 dollars a week (Star and Perry 102). Bourbon Street at this point consolidated its reputation as an adult playland, and the city openly touted the variety and "lustiness" of its entertainments. With its

(Photo by Les Wade.)

offering of over 75 acts in a five-block stretch, Bourbon Street represented the heaviest concentration of burlesque in the country ("Strippers..." 66).

Although the post-war stripclub scene has played a dominant role in fashioning the Bourbon Street mythos of today, its iconography and performance conventions seem relatively tame, even quaint, to a contemporary eye. As a rule, the stripclubs of this era attracted their customers with showcases filled with life-sized photographs of the strippers and with garish marquees announcing the number, name, and nature of the acts. Vying for acclaim and financial reward, strippers attempted to individualize their performances by contextualizing their nudity in unusual scenarios and by assuming provocative stage-names. The following sample suggests the range of aliases and their billings:

Alouette LeBlanc	World's Greatest Tassel Dancer
Tee Tee Red	The Daring Dazzling Redhead
Galatea	The Statue Brought to Life by Love
Candi Bar	The Texas Darling
Tootsie Roll	Famed International Exotic
Renee Lamont	The Girl in the Red Velvet Swing
Saloma	The Turkish Delight
Sandi Kofaux	The Fire Ball

The striptease itself more often than not proved more "tease" than anything else. Alcohol Beverage Control codes enforced tight restrictions on the boundaries of performance and degrees of nudity permitted; convention called for the dancer to strip to her pasties and G-string—further exposure was disallowed. Titled "The Pillow of Love," the act of Lilly Christine, the highly popular Cat Girl, typified the striptease performance of this time (Griffin 56). Dressed in a G-string and transparent black negligee, the Cat Girl danced alluringly before her audience, using two pillows for concealment. After singing "Would You Like to Put Your Head on My Pillow," she punctuated the conclusion of her act by tossing the pillows into the crowd and quickly crossing offstage. More titillation than anything else, the performances practiced in these clubs finally depended less on the disclosure of private parts than the public provocation of the male imagination.

While Bourbon Street's stripjoints and jazz clubs experienced tremendous popularity, the 1950s also bore witness to Bourbon Street's more seamy and duplicitous underside. Indeed, the phenomenon of striptease appears rather benign considering the more nefarious activities that flourished in the stripclub environment. Tourbooks of this time often cautioned the visitor to the very real dangers of the "scene" and the possibility of victimization. Most clubs during this era supported the practice of B-drinking, where a "hostess" would manipulate a customer through sexual insinuation, leading him to run up an expensive bar tab (while she herself drank a watered down mixture of vanilla extract) (Griffin 54). Prostitution was pervasive and occurrences of a tourist being drugged (by a "Mickey Finn") and "rolled" were commonplace. In actuality, Bourbon Street's ill-repute during these years stemmed as much from its vice activities as its erotic performance. Characterized by extremely dim lighting and an abundance of con-artists, the Bourbon Street stripclub was home to gambling, prostitution, narcotics, and other sundry forms of exploitation directed toward the "easy mark." The clubs become appropriately known as "strip and clip" joints.

Highlighting the erotogenic disposition of Bourbon Street, Oliver Evans in 1959 wrote:

In no other neighborhood anywhere in the world, so far as I know, is the importance of sexual desire acknowledged so universally, nor its presence felt so profoundly—not even in places dedicated almost exclusively to its satisfaction, like the notorious Barrio Chino in Barcelona or the San Pauli district in Hamburg. (Evans 80)

By the late 1950s Bourbon Street erotica had achieved national notoriety, which, considering the general tenor of the period, underscores certain ironies. The 1950s are most often regarded as a decade of trenchant conservatism, marked by the Eisenhower years, the paranoia of McCarthyism, and the wholesale adoption of the consumer ethic. This national disposition in some measure, however, can be seen as contributing to and authorizing Bourbon Street's license as purveyor of erotic performance. Bourbon Street, in short, was tolerated, even valued as a zone of permissiveness, a commissioned site of excess, venting and thus containing the possible radicality of uninhibited sexuality. The comment of one visitor to post-war New Orleans, who remarked that "Bourbon Street puts on a show that tends to make New York and Chicago seem repressed" (Bass 40), supports the notion that Bourbon Street was, in face of the country's general conservatism and sexual prudishness, acting as a recognized and clearly delineated zone of erogenous play, something of a repository for the suppressed national libido. This perception is at least in part validated by the fact that Bourbon Street lost much of its lustre and sense of "naughtiness" during the more liberal decade of the 1960s when candid sexuality became mainstream.

In recent years it has become clear that Bourbon Street's appeal and function have experienced significant change, and to a great degree the street of today lives off of its reputed "former glory." During the 1950s the street reached its height of activity, the apex of its renown, and seized a potent though perhaps dubious position in the national consciousness. This was the Bourbon Street of jazz and strip clubs; Bourbon today exists more as a simulacrum, a reflection or reenactment of its one-time vitality and power. As consequence, the corridor of contemporary times functions not so much as a libidinous zone but as an historical landmark. The signs and symbology of the street are suspiciously self-reflexive, indicating less the site of burlesque performance than the glorification of the site itself. It might be said that today's street simply stages its own fabled identity, reconstituting its images and icons for the ever important tourist dollar.

From the 1960s to the present, Bourbon Street, in image and reality, has experienced a noted decline, one that intimately informs the renegotiation of the street's civic service. The status of Bourbon Street in many ways parallels the profile of the city at large, which, despite its promising entry into the postwar era, found itself unable to overcome the chronic problems of parochialism, poverty, unemployment, and fiscal mismanagement. New Orleans seemed to recede from the horizon of the New South, passed over by industry and investment for cities such as Houston and Atlanta.

In these years a number of factors have worked to alter the complexion of the Bourbon Street corridor. In the early 1960s, the fervent reform efforts of D.A. Jim Garrison targeted the stripclub scene, resulting in a code of ethics (accepted by club managers) that included the disallowance of prostitution, improper illumination, and barker misconduct ("Bourbon..."). The seeming repression of the club scene, however, coincided with forces external to the club environment which liberalized and transformed the more general ambience of the thoroughfare. In the late 1960s and early 1970s, the Quarter experienced an influx of counterculture groups—hippies, bikers, Processareans, Hare Krishnas, etc.—that threatened and alienated business operators and tourists alike (Smith). This period saw Bourbon Street assume a demeanor nearer to that of a carnival midway than a nightclub or theatre precinct. Housing T-shirt shops, peep shows, wax museums, and sidewalk concessionaires, Bourbon Street reduced itself to an unseemly degree of "tackiness."

This era also evinces the precipitous decline of the striptease. From nearly three dozen clubs in its heyday, the number of Bourbon Street stripclubs had fallen to fewer than ten in 1970 ("Strip..."). No longer holding the allure it once commanded, the stripshow exists at present as something of an anachronism, affording a trip through nostalgia, rendered quaint, even innocuous in light of the media's sexual frankness and the ready accessibility of hardcore pornography (available at a much cheaper rate). Bourbon Street has long carried a sullied reputation, but for many the street of contemporary times— with the comings and goings of adult bookstores, porno arcades, and massage parlors, has lost the old-time, nostalgic taint of sin and given over to obscenity and "sleaze."

Though the future of Bourbon Street can of course only be surmised, there are certain indicators that suggest that the thoroughfare, despite its tawdriness, will retain an indispensible civic function and may even experience a new degree of theatrical vitality. Given that tourism has supplanted the port commerce as the city's chief source of income, city officials have regarded Bourbon Street with renewed interest. Indeed, in rather metonymic fashion, the street, for the visitor, often represents New Orleans itself. As innumerable tourbooks attest, a trip to New Orleans is not complete without a visit to storied Bourbon Street. Consequently, civic officials have for several years made attempts to revitalize the corridor, to upgrade its image and boost its economy. Such efforts, however, have begged the question as to what direction Bourbon Street should in fact take. What are the appropriate features of the thoroughfare? To what extent should city fathers orchestrate, design, or prescribe Bourbon Street's demeanor?

Seen in the subtle (and sometimes not so subtle) deployment of bureaucratic regulations, an informing public policy is at work that seeks the recreation of Bourbon Street's historic fame. For example, a moratorium on liquor licenses prevents any new club from opening on Bourbon Street that does not provide live entertainment. Tellingly, the entertainment preferred by city officials is jazz, which is of course both in keeping with the street's heritage and attractive to those tourists seeking "authentic" New Orleans experience. Tax breaks are even offered to clubs willing to schedule jazz bands as their predominant fare (Donze).

Along with specific statutes relating to pornographic content, civic regulation has moreover controlled the proliferation of peep shows and adult bookstores through zoning and landuse ordinances. The chief instrument of regulation—the Vieux Carré Commission— has given the heart of Bourbon Street (from the 200 to the 700 block) a unique designation as the "Vieux Carré Entertainment District," with ordinances specific to the businesses and operations permitted within this precinct (Vieux Carré Commission). Not only does the Vieux Carré Commission inform the street's commercial activity, it also prescribes its physical appearance and demeanor. Significantly, the color of paint used on business exteriors must be in keeping with the "traditional" palette of the Quarter; shutters, hinges, even doorknobs must also aim at historical accuracy. In essence, the Vieux Carré Commission seeks the preservation of the Quarter's architectural integrity and distinctive heritage. Yet, this begs the obvious question as to what goes for "history" and whose version of history should be given legitimacy.

Even though one observes attempts to suppress the street's overall "sleaze" and to reduce the street's affront to the tourist sensibility, the stripclub is not isolated for censure. This is largely due to the incalculable service it provides. The Bourbon Street stripclub is not valued so much for the entertainment or performance it offers but for its mere existence. Quite simply, the club serves as an historical reminder, validating the street's legacy as home to jazz and erotic spectacle. The clubs are thus not targeted for exclusion, rather they are controlled through contextual forces—VCC guidelines, Alcohol Beverage Control regulations, health codes, etc.—and thus made less threatening, less salacious, yet still potent to the vacationer as a sign of sin, a sign of Bourbon Street's inglorious past and infamy.

In sum, what one witnesses in more recent years is a movement to reconstitute Bourbon Street, to fashion it according to the dictates of businessmen, civic officials, and the tourist industry, providing the visitor something of a lifesize diorama of New Orleans' colorful and often checkered history. Such efforts have all the more clearly marked Bourbon Street as a theatrical zone. With a keen eye to the vacation and convention dollar, city leaders have effectively rendered Bourbon Street a civic theatre—the street as theatre—a grand environmental spectacle catering to the pedestrian viewer. A modern, profane version of the medieval cycle drama, Bourbon Street functions as a theatricalized marketplace, where the city hustles business and promotes its image to a national audience.

To conclude, the history of Bourbon Street offers valuable illumination as to how a community sanctions and positions its entertainment arenas. It perhaps more importantly shows how illicit performance, in the instance of striptease, can be coopted by and finally made to serve the interests of the hegemonic order. Once a thoroughfare of marginality, in both population and cultural function, Bourbon Street has been drawn to the center, granted a position of preeminence in the city's mythology and self-representation. In negotiation of the Louisiana Purchase, Napoleon's emissary Tallyrand exhibited a keen degree of salesmanship and declared that "without New Orleans Western America is valueless" (qtd. by Chase). Given the modern New Orleans of tourbooks, conventions, and workaday vacationers, the city without a Bourbon Street might find itself similarly wanting. No longer so beleaguered by charges of immorality or indecency, the street has shed its image as a public menace and now stands as a New Orleans signature, a civic asset, as indispensible to the city's vaunted cultural uniqueness as Mardi Gras, shrimp creole, mausoleums, and streetcars.

Notes

[1]See Samuel Kinser, *Carnival American Style* (Chicago: the University of Chicago Press, 1990). Kinser's text is perhaps the most comprehensive work on New Orleans culture and its forms of representation. Kinser confirms the city's association with the carnivalesque—he examines in particularly the phenomenon of Mardi Gras; he, however, also notes that the carnival experience is a highly regulated and monitored event.

[2]Victor Turner has brought the concept of liminality to high prolife in performance studies. Turner recounts how the liminal process often involves

spatial differentiation, where ludic activity is set off, physically removed from the normative order and assigned a ritually potent locale. See the example of the Ndembu of Ambiz in Victor Turner, *The Ritual Process* (Ithaca: Cornell University Press, 1969) 100.

[3]For an overview of urban semiotics and examples of its application, see *The City and the Sign*, ed. M. Gottdiener and Alexandros Ph. Lagopoulos (New York: Columbia University Press, 1986).

[4]Steven Mullaney, *The Place of the Stage* (Chicago: the University of Chicago Press, 1988). Citing the work of Stephen Greenblatt, Mullaney's preface argues for a cultural poetics and outlines his own understanding of the city as text. See vii-xii.

[5]Sarah Searight, *New Orleans* (New York: Stein and Day, 1973) 198. Searight offers a highly informative account of the city's early development. For further historical background see Charles Dufour, "The People of New Orleans," *The Past as Prelude: New Orleans 1718-1968* (New Orleans: Pelican Publishing Co., 1968) 20-41).

[6]For a fuller discussion of New Orleans' early theatrical history, with emphasis upon how Bourbon Street served to designate French culture, see my article "Le théâtre français de la Nouvelle-Orléans: les origines du burlesque de la rue Bourbon," in *L'Annuaire théâtral: Revue québécoise d'études théâtrals* 12 (automne 1992): 7-30.

[7]Mathe Allain and Adele Cornay St. Martin, "French Theatre in Louisiana," *Ethnic Theatre in the United States*, ed. Maxine Seller (Westport, CT: Greenwood Press, 1978) 139. This essay provides the most current and extensive survey on New Orleans' early theatrical activity. For further discussion of the city's theatre history see also Oliver Evans, New Orleans (New York: Macmillan, 1959) 51-52; Henry Arnold Kmen, "The Music of New Orleans: The Glamor Period, 1800-1840 (New Orleans: Pelican Publishing Co., 1957) 467-484.

[8]Deirdre Stanforth, *Romantic New Orleans* (New York: Viking Press, 1977) 29. This text gives a detailed survey of the rise of opera in New Orleans. For more information see Kmen, "The Music of New Orleans."

[9]Selections relating to the history of prostitution in New Orleans and Bourbon Street's 20th-century evolution have been translated in my essay, "Le théâtre français de la Nouvelle-Orléans: les origines du burlesque de la rue Bourbon."

[10]For the most complete examination of Storyville, see Al Rose, *Storyville* (Tuscaloosa: University of Alabama Press, 1974).

[11]For an overview of this period, see Stella Pitts, "The Quarter in the Twenties," *Times Picayune Dixie Magazine* 26 November 1982: n.p.

[12]The following information is drawn from the pamphlet by W. Kenneth Holditch, *A Literary Tour of the French Quarter* (New Orleans: n.p., 1974) 1-3.

[13]Pierce F. Lewis, *The Making of an Urban Landscape*. Cambridge: Ballinger Pub. Co., 1976) 32. This text expertly examines and documents New Orleans' growth and development in the years following World War II.

Works Cited

Newspaper articles found in the Vertical Files of the New Orleans Historic Collection, the Tulane University Louisiana Collection, and the Hill Memorial Library of Louisiana State University.

Amoss, Jim. "William Faulkner and Other Famous Creoles." *Lagniappe* 6-12 Mar. 1976: 3.

Bacon, Joe. "Living in the Quarter." *New Orleans Magazine* Aug. 1982: n.p.

Barthes, Roland. "The Eiffel Tower." *The Eiffel Tower and Other Mythologies*. Trans. Richard Howard. New York: Hill and Wang, 1979. 3-18.

Bass, Hamilton. "Boom Town, Dream Town." *Holiday* Feb. 1948: 40.

"Bourbon Street: Amused over Crackdown." *Baton Rouge Morning Advocate* 12 Aug. 1962: n.p.

"Bourbon's Babe." *New Orleans Times Picayune* 30 Aug. 1987: n.p.

Carlson, Marvin. *Places of Performance: The Semiotics of Theatre Architecture*. Ithaca: Cornell UP, 1989. 2.

Chase, H. Van R. "The Personalities of New Orleans, Louisiana." Address before the Members' Council of the Association of Commerce, New Orleans, 5 Dec. 1935: 9.

Chase, John. *Frenchmen, Desire, Good Children, and Other Streets of New Orleans*. New Orleans: Robert L. Crager & Co., 1949. 22.

Donze, Frank. "Bourbon Street Tax Cut Puts Jazz in Its Place. *New Orleans Times Picayune/States Item* 27 Sept. 1985: n.p.

Evans, Oliver. New Orleans. New York: Macmillan, 1959. 51-52, 80.

Fossier, Albert. *New Orleans: The Glamor Period 1800-1840*. New Orleans: Pelican, 1957. 467-84, 470.

Frank Leslie's Illustrated Newspaper 22 Aug. 1868: 357.

Greenblatt, Stephen. "Shakespeare and the Exorcists." *After Strange Texts*. Eds. Gregory Jay and David Miller. Tuscaloosa: U of Alabama P, 1985. 101-23.

Griffin, Thomas. "The French Quarter." *Holiday* Mar. 1957: 54, 56.

Johnson, Phil. "Good Time Town." *The Past as Prelude*. New Orleans: Pelican, 1968. 235, 246.

Kane, Harnett T. *Queen New Orleans*. New York: William Morrow & Co., 1949. 12, 241, 257, 261.

Kolb, Carolyn. *New Orleans*. Garden City, NY: Doubleday, 1972. 64.

Mullaney, Steven. *The Place of the Stage*. Chicago: The U of Chicago P, 1988. vii-xii.

Narvard, Andrew J. *Basin Street: Its Rise and Fall*. New Orleans: Harmanson, 1952. 59.

New Orleans Vignette. New Orleans: Vignete, 1977-78: 29.

O'Roark, Robert. "O'Roark Says." *New Orleans State Times* 31 Mar. 1948: n.p.

A Plan for Revitalization: Bourbon Street. New Orleans: Marks, Lewis, Torre and Associates, 1977. 13, 15.

Shea, Al. "Nitetime Beat." *Go: The Authentic Guide to New Orleans* Sept. 1983: 10.

Smith, Charles C. "Street Legal in New Babylon." *New Orleans Magazine* Aug. 1981: n.p.

Stanforth, Deirdre. *Romantic New Orleans*. New York: Viking P, 1977. 7, 29.

Star, Blaze and Huey Perry. *Blaze Star*. New York: Praegger, 1974. 102.

"Strip Is a Dying Art in New Orleans." *Baton Rouge State Times*. 13 July 1970: n.p.

"Strippers Beat a Wrap." *Life* 4 Apr. 1960: 66.

Vieux Carré Commission. Vieux Carré Commission Guidelines 1968: xx.

"Women Who Shocked America." *Stag* Aug. 1955: 12.

ALTERNATIVE THEATRES IN KENTUCKY

Marilyn Casto

To most people, a theatre constitutes a fully enclosed space of wood, stone, and concrete. Other concepts have found audiences. From the early 19th century into the 20th century, audiences for tent shows and Chautauqua sat beneath canvas roofs. In the late 19th century, park pavilions and roof gardens permitted patrons to commune with nature while viewing a play. Amphitheatres contain the popular outdoor dramas of this century.

All these alternative theatres maintained structural references to conventional playhouses, despite wide variation in construction materials. The basic auditorium layout of stage and house remained the same.

None of these innovative theatrical forms competed directly with conventional theatres and opera houses. In the first place, they were confined to the summer season. Most early theatres went dark in the summer, because heat made enclosed populated spaces unbearable. Furthermore, the target audience sometimes differed from that of permanent theatres. Rural residents who attended tent shows might never darken the door of an opera house.

Outdoor Theatres

Permanent outdoor theatres fall into three categories. The first began during the late 19th century as adjuncts to parks or as roof gardens. Early in the 20th century, a back-to-nature movement took a more intellectual approach to outdoor playhouses. Later in the 20th century, historical dramas in outdoor amphitheatres began to draw large crowds. Kentucky has had examples of all types.

Before air-conditioning, outside gatherings held more appeal in the summer than enclosed theatres. Traditionally, theatres went dark during the hot months, but by the latter part of the 19th century, entrepreneurs had hit on the idea of pleasure gardens, beer gardens, and roof-top theatres. Summer theatres generally closed when the regular fall theatrical season opened (*Courier-Journal* 19 July 1879; Dimmick 70).

203

Following European precedent, New York led the way in establishment of roof gardens in America. Madison Square Garden and the Casino were among the best known (Johnson 16). The Casino (1882) offered the first roof garden (Van Hoogstraten 15). In a discussion of a local esplanade (The Auditorium), a Louisville newspaper cited the Casino as a model worthy of emulation (*Courier-Journal* 10 June 1900). According to the reporter, the esplanade at ground level operated exactly like a roof garden without the city pollution. In 1893 there was some discussion concerning use of the Louisville Commerce Building's roof for summer theatre (*Courier-Journal* 16 July 1893). Roof-top theatres were short-lived. By the 1920s the spread of air-conditioning and the greater height of buildings and correspondingly windy conditions spelled the end (Johnson 186).

Such facilities leaned heavily to vaudeville, a frothier fare better suited to its surroundings than legitimate drama. Around the turn of the century, Kentucky had its share of outdoor entertainment sites.

Lexington's Woodland Park Auditorium, sometimes known as the Auditorium Theatre, was a frame structure of board and batten siding broken by numerous semicircular arches. These arches were used for two small louvered windows on the upper front facade, for a large central window, and for entrances below. Across the front was a hipped roof entrance. Above that the short square end towers flanked a lower central portion containing the large semicircular window flanked by plain rectangular windows. In appearance, the building, a product of the late 1880s, seems a curious blend of Gothic influence (the vertical siding) and a hint of early Modern (the arches) (*Lexington Transcript* 19 July 1887; Ranck 56).

The Lexington Chautauqua owned Woodland Park until the city purchased it in 1904 as its first public park. At that point the city fully enclosed the auditorium (Waller, *The Velvet* 12-18; *Lexington Transcript* 8, 10, 17, 1877; *Lexington Herald* 1 Oct. 1905.)

A variety of activities occupied the stage from time to time. These included John Philip Sousa, Otis Skinner, and Irene Castle in *Dances and Fashions of 1923* together with the Moscow Artists' Ensemble (Bowmar).

Phoenix Hill Park offered Louisvillians a hall at which speeches and occasional vaudeville were given (*Courier-Journal* 1 Aug. 1897). Phoenix Hill actually was a brewery, later extended into a beer garden, incorporating a large hall, a pavilion, skating rink, bandstand, and bowling alley (Creason 49).

Gottfried Muller (Miller), a German builder who operated taverns and sold real estate in Louisville at various times, built the brewery in 1865 with Philip Zang and Philip Schillinger (Hammon 156-63). He located the speaking hall on top of the building. A covered beer garden adjoined it.

In the years around 1900 it became a popular entertainment spot, but prohibition killed the brewery and with it, the park amenities. In 1938 the wreckers demolished Phoenix Hill.

Fontaine Ferry Park in Louisville was developed as a summer garden about 1887. Within the park was a music pavilion surrounded by a sand-covered area and rustic seats for about 400 people, a skating rink, scenic railway, and other amusements (*Courier-Journal* 5 Aug. 1894, 4 Aug. 1907).

Within a few years, the owners built a theatre for vaudeville (*Courier-Journal* 2 May 1909, 4 Aug. 1907). J.D. Hopkins, the manager of Hopkin's Theatre announced in 1903 that he and A.C. Stuevers of St. Louis intended to construct a summer theatre in a local park. The Hopkins Pavilion Theatre presented vaudeville acts. Reflecting the coming trend in entertainment, the park also erected a structure for movies (*Courier-Journal* 18 Aug. 1903; 18 July 1906; 5, 18 Aug. 1907; 2 May 1909).

The theatre was redecorated in 1909 and enclosed in 1921. Hinged panels replaced the latticed sides of the theatre to cut down on light and still permit ventilation (*Courier-Journal* 15 May 1921, 8 May 1921).

In the quest for diversified entertainment, the late 19th-century summer theatre entrepreneurs built into single complexes parks, music pavilions, bicycling paths, theatres, and promenades. During the summer months, a family could be sure of finding some type of wholesome amusement at these attractions.

The best known of these facilities in Louisville, the Auditorium, opened in 1889 (*Courier-Journal* 15 May 1904). An amphitheatre (1886) used for fireworks and spectacular performances, such as *The Last Days of Pompeii* or *Americus*, sat next to the Auditorium building (*Courier-Journal* 20 May 1894; *The City* 120). In the center of the amphitheatre, multi-colored lights shaded 15 feet streams of water from a fountain (*Courier-Journal* 10 June 1900). An esplanade, between the fountain and the building, where patrons could sit with their drinks or stroll and socialize, formed part of the facility. Red, white, blue, and orange lights outlined this area (*Courier-Journal* 10 June 1900). Customers might while away the time between acts admiring the fountain and the decorative foliage.

The music of a band gave further incentive to linger. Other features of the grounds included a deer park, an artificial lake, a music stand, and a bicycle path (*Illustrated* 85).

Captain William F. Norton, having acquired about 3,000 folding chairs and a collection of scenery, acted with what must have seemed to him to be perfect logic, and constructed a facility to hold his new possessions (*Courier-Journal* 7 May 1904). James B. Camp originated the Auditorium idea and worked with Norton to complete the facility, later acting as manager (*Courier-Journal* 15 May 1904). The pair had brought Edwin Booth and Lawrence Barrett to Louisville for a series of performances in the old Exposition building. Since that structure lacked scenery and seats, Norton and Camp bought some scenery which Tom Keene had left at the Exposition structure. Later they decided to construct a permanent summer theatre (*Courier-Journal* 15 May 1904).

Norton, an eccentric and interesting individual, carried out his theatrical activities under the name Daniel Quilp, the unpleasant character in Dicken's *Old Curiosity Shop* (Johnson 531). Having diverged from the staid banking career of his father, Norton chose a nom de guerre to avoid embarrassing the family (Gatton viii). The name seems an odd choice, but Norton explained that he preferred a pseudonym unlikely to be adopted by anyone else.

He opened his amphitheatre with Edwin Booth and Lawrence Barrett in a week of Shakespearean repertoire (*Courier-Journal* 23 Sept. 1889). One of the stories about Booth originated with his Hamlet role at the Auditorium. Supposedly, during the "To be or not to be" speech, he looked down at the footlight trough and unthinkingly read off the sign written across the back—"Do not spit in the trough" (*Courier-Journal* 15 May 1904).

In later years, summer opera drew crowds. The John C. Duff Opera Company and the Fay Opera Company both staged performances in Louisville (*Courier-Journal* 16 July 1893). Other prominent performers included Ellen Terry, Henry Irving, Sarah Bernhardt, Madame Schumann-Heink, and Lillian Russell. In its brief life, the Auditorium hosted concerts, lectures, and political speeches. The latter included Theodore Roosevelt. Henry Stanley, the African explorer of "Dr. Livingstone, I presume" fame spoke at the Auditorium. The hall was used for exhibitions and balls at various times. In 1904 the structure closed with a last performance by John Philip Sousa (*Courier-Journal* 15 May 1904, 6 Feb. 1897, 2 Mar. 1897, 24 Apr. 1904).

A frame building with vertical siding, it was garnished by gables, a pediment, and balustrades. A hipped roof punctuated in the center of the front and sides by large ornament-filled gables sheltered the entrance. Above the roof line rose a pediment with decorative tympanum.

When the facility was sold in 1904 the advertisements gave the dimensions of the building as 122 feet wide and 180 feet long, with a property room 121 feet by 107 feet. This was accompanied by an 81-feet-by 40-feet engine room, four brick buildings, and a smokestack. The electric plant included expansive facilities for incandescent lights (*Courier-Journal* 24 Apr. 1904). Apart from the auditorium space, other amenities of the facility might be pressed into service as backdrops for performances. In 1899 the manager floated a copy of Dewey's flagship in the lake as scenery for *H.M.S. Pinafore.*

Within the auditorium, a square room running 120 feet from the stage line to the rear wall, seven private boxes flanked the stage on each side (*Illustrated* 85). Beyond a horseshoe shaped parquette divided by a central aisle, the dress circle swept around in a vast semicircle. Besides the middle aisle, four others split the dress circle into six segments. Matting covered the aisles to reduce noise. Of the 3072 seats, 450 were in the parquette, 2130 in the dress circle, 450 in the balcony, and 72 in the private boxes. This large hall could be converted for balls or similar assemblages by installation of a secondary floor resting on trestles over the parquette (*Courier-Journal* 2 Mar. 1897). The more famous Chicago Auditorium by Adler and Sullivan employed the same technique.

The huge stage, 90 feet wide and 60 feet deep, incorporated a proscenium 50 by 27 feet. Above the stage rose a 52-feet high rigging loft and a 27-feet high fly gallery. A 10-feet deep cellar gave adequate space for traps (*Illustrated* 85). A portrait adorned the top of the proscenium arch, surmounting the inscription "Words, Words, Words-Shakespeare" (Gatton xii).

Taking advantage of the latest technology, Norton installed incandescent, arc, and gas lights. Running the complex required a vast and expensive physical plant. The Auditorium never suffered a fire, but the management installed seven 12-foot pocket doors as a precaution.

Details of the scenery and decoration can be abstracted from reports of the 1904 sale. The original scenery, still in use in 1904, had been painted by Albert, Grover and Burridge, a firm which specialized in such projects (*Courier-Journal* 15 May 1904). Theatrical notices sometimes specified the creators of Norton's scenery and props, as in the case of the one designed for the Fireworks Amphitheatre in 1894 (*Courier-Journal* 6 May 1894). He seems to have used mention of firms from outside Louisville as an audience draw. Local painter and stage carpenter Frank Bolton (McDonald) painted a considerable volume of scenery for the theatre (*Courier-Journal* 2 May 1909).

At the time of the sale, the theatre owned 285 "pieces set" and 138 drops. His props ranged from costumes to hassocks, lace curtains, and mirrors (*Courier-Journal* 24 Apr. 1904). Among the props were a set of dueling pistols used by Joseph Jefferson in *The Rivals*. Muskets, swords, helmets, and old supers' costumes aroused little interest from anyone other than junk dealers (*Courier-Journal* 6 May 1904).

Norton had owned a bronze bust of Edwin Booth, given to him by Lawrence Barrett. As Barrett requested, the bust went to the Player's Club in New York, but the granite block on which it rested at the Auditorium sold for $60 (*Courier-Journal* 7 May 1904). John T. Macauley bought a gilded throne chair and some scenery. This throne had been made for an appearance by Madam Adeline Patti by the London firm of Robson Baiths, producers of theatre props (*Courier-Journal* 15 May 1904).

Two hundred and four of the auditorium chairs went to a Baptist church. Frank Parfitt, who had operated the electrical facilities, bought a portrait of Mrs. Fiske and a framed poster of *The Rivals* cast, both of which had hung in the building (*Courier-Journal* 7 May 1904).

The sale raised about $2,000 from the stage properties and auditorium contents. Although the value of the scenery was estimated at $40,000, it sold for $400 (*Courier-Journal* 6 May 1904).

More publicity attended the 1904 demolition than had heralded the construction or any of the performances. Large advertisements specified dimensions, types of structures, and the electrical plant machinery to be sold. Among other proposed uses, there had been some discussion of converting the property for use by the Horse Show Association, but the plans fell through (*Courier-Journal* 21 Apr. 1904; 5, 7 May 1904).

Following the auction, the purchaser recycled the building materials into new structures and developed the site for housing. A real estate agent paid $900 for the Auditorium building and, as required by the purchase contract, demolished it within 60 days.

Outdoor theatres surged into popularity in the early 20th century on a wave of enthusiasm for natural settings. Proponents of open-air theatres stressed the importance of rustic design with earth stages, rustic seats, and limited scenery (Waugh 61). Shakespeare and the Greek plays were considered best suited to outdoor performances (17).

The zeal with which advocates championed outdoor settings partially stemmed from a belief that Shakespeare had originally been staged outdoors (Waugh 17). To enthusiasts, the new theatre form represented a return to the roots of drama paired with escape from the industrialized world. The Arts and Crafts movement, with its stress on naturalism also encouraged the new simplified theatres. Gustave Stickley's influential magazine, *The Craftsman*, ran articles on such settings.

The interest in natural settings for plays coincided with the time when Isadora Duncan shocked audiences with her interpretive "free" dance forms. One author wrote of outdoor theatres as corrective measures for over-sophistication and artificiality and of their democratic seating and the "spiritual effect" produced by the environment (Cheney vi).

Jefferson County possesses a classic example of the outdoor theatre in Bingham Amphitheatre at Glenview. Constructed in the 1920s for Judge Robert Worth Bingham, it was designed by New York architect Thomas Hastings. Hastings' friendship with Judge Bingham probably accounts for his role in the design of this theatre. Built of brick and stone, it featured Doric columns. It is said that the Bingham Amphitheatre was modeled on one in Italy ("Bingham...").

In the mid-20th century, Kentucky began to build theatres for outdoor dramas. Eventually there would be several such facilities offering summer seasons of predominantly historical drama. These have a different orientation from the early 20th-century idealistic outdoor theatres. The usual fare is populist and aimed at tourists, a different audience from that which attends plays in conventional theatres.

The idea originated with *The Lost Colony*, Paul Green's play presented at Roanoke, North Carolina. Outdoor dramas rapidly increased in popularity. Most center on a theme of local history (Davis 24). Kentucky, like other states, found them a lucrative tourist draw worth the investment of state dollars to construct the amphitheatres (24). Kentucky quickly offered three dramas, *The Book of Job* at Pine Mountain State Park in Pineville, *The Stephen Foster Story* at the Old Kentucky Home State Park in Bardstown, and *Stars in My Crown*, at Kentucky Lake State Park near Murray.

The state attracted some well-known writers of these historical dramas. Paul Green, a Pulitzer Prize winner, authored *The Stephen*

Foster Story. Kermit Hunter, writer of *Stars in My Crown*, also wrote several other plays, including North Carolina's *Horn in the West*. The state has continued to build these facilities and to successfully attract audiences.

Chautauqua

Early 20th-century Kentucky residents had access to theatre through a medium reminiscent of the first traveling troupes and the showboats. Tent Chautauqua brought drama into rural areas and into the lives of many people who otherwise would never have laid eyes on a stage. Chautauqua organizers and performers claimed as a prime contribution that individuals who viewed theatre as an entity wrapped in sin went away with more tolerance. Ultimately, permanent theatres must have gained more support and larger audiences as a result.

The relevance of Chautauqua and its tent theatre to an article such as this lies in its relationship to permanent theatres and to the general development of theatre. Similarities are strongest between small town opera houses and tents. Many Chautauqua performers came from a background of stock repertory, playing the opera houses in winter and Chautauqua in summer.

Most people associate the Chautauqua name with performers who arrived for an average of seven days in the summer, erected a large brown tent, and provided a wide ranging program of lectures, readings, music, and drama. The organizers of these events borrowed the name from a permanent Chautauqua in New York State (Morrison vii). Bishop John Vincent was largely responsible for the founding and development of the original Chautauqua. It started as training for Sunday School teachers and grew into an institution noted for summer programs of education, music, art, theatre, dance, and painting. In other words: culture. Despite the religious origins, Vincent avoided evangelistic gatherings of the tent-meeting type (Morrison 33).

His interest lay in providing education to people who lacked access to formal education (Vincent 176). Under Chautauqua's auspices, many communities organized Literary and Scientific Circles, providing people of like interests an opportunity to read and debate (Morrison 53). Struck with the success of the original Chautauqua, other gatherings appropriated the name.

In time, it occurred to some individuals that communities which would not support a permanent Chautauqua institution might patronize a short interval of such programs. The Chautauqua circuits were born of that idea. Precedent for centralized booking of lecturers had already been established by the lyceum movement. One of the better known lecture bureaus was that of James Redpath, one of whose Redpath Circuits brought Chautauqua to Kentucky (Case and Case 196).

In order to have Chautauqua, a community had to agree to raise the funds. This meant requiring a local committee to sign a contract assuming responsibility for the money (Morrison 178). At the scheduled time, Chautauqua would arrive, erect a tent, build a stage, present its performances over five to seven days and then depart. Chautauqua became a gala event in many areas, eagerly anticipated and well attended (Horner 77).

Drama was far from the only type of performance given at Chautauqua, but opera houses and theatres also tended to book assorted entertainment. Lexington in 1887 watched stereoptican views, heard musical performances, and listened to speeches (*Lexington Transcript* 2, 6, 17 July 1887). Inspirational talks exhorting the audience to aspire toward better lives gained great popularity in the nineteenth century and remained popular into the 20th century. Chautauqua leaned heavily to lectures of a type referred to as "Mother, Home, and Heaven" (Morrison 184; Slout 78). The circuits booked some well known speakers, such as Jacob Riis, author of *How the Other Half Lives*, and William Jennings Bryan, who developed a close association with Chautauqua through his numerous speeches (Morrison 186). Jane Addams was among the speakers at a 1907 Louisville Chautauqua (*Courier-Journal* 3 Aug. 1907).

Theatre came into the tents very gradually and with much initial dubiousness on the part of the organizers (Slout 54; Morrison 182). Chautauqua's rural audiences held a long tradition of distrust for actors. Plays first appeared as readings by a single person, who could be billed as a reader, entertainer, elocutionist, or impersonator, rather than an actor (Horner 37; Case and Case 52; Morrison 182).

In 1907 a Louisville Chautauqua featured a performer reading from *In a Balcony* (*Courier-Journal* 3 Aug. 1907). An elocutionist giving poems and dramatic recitations formed part of the program for Lexington's 1887 Chautauqua, although there was also a patriotic note in the eulogy for Garfield which constituted part of the program (*Lexington Transcript* 7 July 1887). An editorial at that time pointing out that a dramatic stage at Woodland would be desirable, praised the use of drama in Chautauqua (as long as it was moral) as an influence for good (*Lexington Transcript* 13 July 1887).

After Ben Greet and his performers began to work with Chautauqua in 1913, plays became more an established part of the offerings (Slout 55). In time, they ranked among the favorite parts of Chautauqua. By 1922 Chautauqua was offering a prize for clean "dramatic comedy suited to the tastes of the plain folk of the nation." (*Courier-Journal* 20 Aug. 1922). Chautauqua's reputation for respectable cultural events permitted even actors to become respectable under its name (Gould 79).

Drama presented in the Chautauqua tents was not avant garde. Audiences would have had little comprehension or interest in the psychological insights of O'Neill or the social criticism of Ibsen. "Toby" plays, which stressed the virtues of rural life while condemning the sins of the city, remained favorites with rural audiences (Case and Case 51). The success of Ben Greet's Shakespearean plays might seem surprising under the circumstances, but Shakespeare had also been a favorite with Victorians. The secret lies in the fact that Shakespeare can be enjoyed just as stories without looking for deeper meaning, especially if the play was bowdlerized. Removal of lines to which the audience might take offense sanitized the plays (Homer 181). Remoteness of time and place meant that audiences were not forced to see themselves in the plays, as they would in O'Neill's characters.

Given the physical conditions of performance, the type of plays, and lack of trained performers, quality was naturally highly variable (Case and Case 52). In defense of the sometimes questionable quality of the drama, an organizer of the Redpath Circuit, which operated in Kentucky, gave a still current defense familiar to critics of insipid television offerings. He figured they could not limit themselves to producing programs aimed only at the well-informed because no one would come (Harrison 98).

In Kentucky, Chautauqua appeared all over the state. The Redpath Circuit run by Harry P. Harrison set up in 11 communities, including Hopkinsville, Bowling Green, Danville, Cynthiana, Henderson, Harlan, Ashland, Paducah, and Morgantown. Harrison estimated that attendance at single shows averaged well over the 1,000 which he considered the break-even point (Harrison 94). Other circuits also scheduled performances in Kentucky. Because no national booking organization existed, any circuit which thought it profitable could schedule performances (Case and Case 201).

Organizers preferred erecting the tents in a park or similar place to approximate the original New York Chautauqua's lake-side setting (Case and Case 179). Lexington held its Chautauqua at Woodland

Park. One viewer wrote that "The great spread of tents presents a military appearance; put one in a mind of 'war lines'" (*Lexington Transcript* 1, 17 July 1887). Chautauqua was known for its large brown tents (as opposed to the white circus tent). During performances the sides were rolled up to reduce heat, a constant problem in the south (Scott 42; Harrison 94).

Wind and rain created another weather-related concern. Harrison wrote of a case in Bowling Green in which a storm bent the center pole, forcing the performers into using Bowling Green State Teacher's College's auditorium. Upon reflection, he decided the acoustics were better, anyway (Harrison 95). Wind from a storm in Lexington pulled the shorter tent poles from the ground and flung them about, to the considerable alarm of the audience, which promptly fled. "Many of the ladies gathered up their skirts, and lit out without regard to proprieties" (*Lexington Transcript* 8 July 1887).

During a performance in Owensboro, an attempt to shift rainwater from a sagging pocket above the stage resulted in a pole punched through the canvas and an irate wet performer. Other problems could occur. Mischievous boys in Henderson gathered a group of dogs near the tent where the animals howled in accompaniment to a cornet solo (Harrison 100).

Accounts by participants suggest that little scenery was available (Scott 28; Horner 46). Props might be supplied by local citizens. Some performers, such as the Ben Greet players, used no scenery (Harrison 199). Stages, significantly referred to as platforms, had to be simple to facilitate quick construction and rapid removal (Horner 46). Chautauqua tents lacked the luxurious drapery and decoration of the larger opera houses, which would likely have been deeply suspect to audience members alert for any sign of decadence.

Chautauqua began to die out in the 1920s and by the early 1930s had vanished. Technology had brought more sophisticated entertainment to rural audiences. Furthermore, regional theatre of all types was feeling the effect of the movies and of the centralization of theatre in New York. The need and demand for traveling troupes disappeared. To assert, as one organizer did, that Chautauqua was largely responsible for ending small town opposition to drama is an overstatement. Nevertheless, it played a role in luring more people into theatres.

Tent Shows
Chautauqua was not the only drama housed in a tent. From World War I until the Depression years, repertoire shows (also called

tent shows, tent rep, or Toby shows) traveled around the country. Traveling troupes of this kind originated with 19th-century companies who played the opera houses. At its height, there were around 400 companies (Klassen 1). These summer shows capitalized on the fact that in a pre-air conditioning era most theatres went dark during the weeks of heat. Legitimate theatre, vilifying them as little more than circus or medicine shows, never regarded tent rep with much favor, but the audiences felt differently about the Toby shows, especially in the central area of the United States (Meckel 3). A mid-west community might have five one-week shows during a summer (Slout 102). It has been suggested that these shows provided a valuable source of training for actors, as well as giving impetus to community theatre through the efforts of former actors (ix).

No aura of culture surrounded the plays, but no one could complain of salacious content. Most were either melodrama or comedy, in part because Broadway plays tended to have too many suggestive lines (Klassen 81). Managers presented plays under a variety of titles, sometimes to avoid payment of royalties and also to imply a wide range of offerings (79). Following the 19th-century habit of interspersing other entertainment with drama, tent shows included jugglers, knife throwers, chalk-talk artists, and singers. Toby plays attained particular association with tent rep.

Actors, an average of ten in a company, worked hard. Generally, three to seven plays had to be rehearsed in the two weeks before a company began constant travel. Most actors never signed Equity contracts (Klassen 114).

Tent size varied considerably, from 20 by 30 feet to 130 by 100 feet, seating 500 to 1,000 in the audience (Klassen 123). The usual two section division provided for "blues" or general admission in the back and a larger reserved section in the front. Seating often consisted of ten to twelve inch boards supported by stringers, wooden jacks, and rope lacing. Alternatively, folding chairs might be used (Slout 40). Lexington's Pavilion Theatre, capable of seating 1,800 people, in 1887 began with benches, but acquired 400 chairs when the Chautauqua finished its season. Regular admission cost 10 cents. All the reserved 20-cent seats converted to chairs (*Lexington Transcript* 1, 6, 7, 8, 10 July 1887).

More elaborate set-ups had raked wooden floors and occasionally, boxes. The average stage opening was 20 to 30 feet with a depth of 14 to 25 feet (Klassen 124). Usually, placement of boards on jacks produced the stages. Sometimes truck beds were pressed into service (Slout 46). According to one local newspaper, the open air during a hot July compensated for a small stage (*Lexington Transcript* 12, 19 July 1887).

One of the problems attendant upon performance in a tent was the pole, located by necessity directly in front of the stage (Slout 40; Meckel 54). The pole had to be there because the slope would otherwise be too low for stage rigging. As early as 1910, Driver's Improved Theatrical Tent was marketed, but dramatic end tents did not see much use until around 1920 (Slout 41; Klassen 312).

Generally, companies employed little scenery, although there were exceptions. Slip covers could alter the guise of seating. Diamond dye scenery, achieved by painting durable dyes on cloth, which could then be folded for easy packing, was one of the more popular forms (Klassen 124; Meckel 45). These cycloramas utilized top strings tied onto the framework above the stage and were tacked to the stage at the bottom. A curtain running the width of the tent hid the backstage area. At the curtain's center opening, a front curtain and specialty (olio) curtain parted to reveal the stage.

Lighting, provided by kerosene, calcium carbon, acetylene, gas, or electricity, was generally confined to overhead strips, footlights, and possibly small spotlights (Slout 46). None of the available techniques even approached the dazzling lighting effects of permanent theatres.

Tents may have been a pale reflection of city opera houses, but they did adopt the usual theatrical layout in a vastly simplified manner. Theatrical architecture influenced the relationship of stage to audience. The general scenery design drew from that used in the city theatres, although it lacked the splendor of major theatres.

Discussion of theatre architecture is incomplete without some consideration of the variations which coexisted with conventional buildings. The design of such settings reveal the influence of more permanent structures. Furthermore, alternative theatrical spaces are intriguing in their own right. Many people saw their first play and developed their concept of theatre from alternative theatres.

Works Cited

"Bingham Ampitheatre." Kentucky Historic Resources Inventory, 1979.

Bowmar Collection, Special Collections, U of Kentucky.

Case, Victoria and Robert Ormond Case. *We Called It Culture*. 1948. Freesport, NY: Books for Libraries P, 1970.

Cheny, Sheldon. *The Open-Air Theatre*. New York: Mitchell Kennerley, 1918.

The City of Louisville and a Glimpse of Kentucky. Louisville: Committee on Industrial and Commercial Improvement of the Louisville Board of Trade, 1887.

Courier-Journal
    19 July 1879.
    23 Sept. 1889.
    16 July 1893.
    6 May 1894.
    5 Aug. 1894.
    6 Feb. 1897.
    2 Mar. 1897.
    1 Aug. 1897.
    10 June 1900.
    28 Aug. 1903.
    21, 24 Apr. 1904.
    5, 6, 7 May 1904.
    15, 20 May 1904.
    18 July 1906.
    3, 5, 18 Aug. 1907.
    2 May 1909.
    8 May 1921.
    15 May 1921.
    20 Aug. 1922.
    3 Aug. 1933.

Creason, Joe. "Phoenix Hill." *Courier-Journal Magazine* 13 Nov. 1949: 49-51.

Davis, Harry. "Theatre of the People." Souvenir Program for Home is the Hunter, 1974.

Dimmick, Ruth Crosby. *Our Theatres To-day and Yesterday*. New York: H.K. Fly Company, 1913.

Gatton, John Spalding. *"Only for Great Attractions." The Amphitheatre Auditorium, Louisville, Kentucky: A Brief History and a Checklist of Performances 1889-1904*. Louisville: Delan Pub. Co., 1977.

Gould, Joseph E. *The Chautauqua Movement*. New York: State U of New York, 1961.

Hammon, Stratton O. "Phoenix Hill Park-Louisville, Kentucky." *Filson Club History Quarterly* 44 (Apr. 1970): 156-63.

Harrison, Harry P. *Culture Under Canvas*. New York: Hastings House, 1958.

Horner, Charles F. *Strike the Tents*. Philadelphia: Dorrance and Company, 1954.

Illustrated Louisville: Kentucky's Metropolis. Chicago: Acme Publishing and Engraving, 1891.

Johnson, J. Stoddard. *Memorial History of Louisville.* New York: American Biographical Pub. Co., 1896.

Johnson, Stephen Burge. *The Roof Gardens of Broadway Theatres, 1883-1942.* Ann Arbor: UMI Research P, 1985.

Klassen, Robert. "The Tent-Repertoire Theatre: A Rural American Institution." Dissertation: Michigan State U 1969.

Lexington Herald 1 Oct. 1905.

Lexington Transcript 1, 2, 6, 7, 8, 10, 12, 13, 17, 19 July 1887.

Meckel, Jere C. *Footlights on the Prairie.* St. Cloud, MN: North Star P, 1974.

Morrison, Theodore. *Chautaugua.* Chicago: U of Chicago P, 1974.

Ranck, G.W. *Ranck's Guide to Lexington Kentucky.* Lexington: Transylvania Printing Co., 1884.

Scott, Marian. *Chautauqua Caravan.* New York: D. Appleton-Century Co., 1939.

Siout, William Lawrence. *Theatre in a Tent: The Development of a Provincial Entertainment.* Bowling Green, OH: Bowling Green State University Popular Press, 1972.

Van Hoogstraten, Nicholas. *Lost Broadway Theatres.* New York: Princeton Architectural P, 1991.

Vincent, John H. *The Chautauqua Movement.* 1885. Freesport, New York: Books for Libraries P, 1971.

Waller, Gregory A. "Situating Motion Pictures in the Prenickelodeon Period. Lexington, Kentucky, 1897-1907." *The Velvet Light Trap* 25 (Spring 1990).

Waugh, Frank A. *Outdoor Theatres.* Boston: Richard G. Badger, 1919.

INSTRUCTION AND DELIGHT:
THEME PARKS AND EDUCATION

Margaret J. King

The lecturer who puts his students to sleep looks with a jaundiced eye on the man who keeps them bolt upright, who tries to entertain them as he teaches so as to make what is taught memorable and colorful.
—William Sloan, *The Craft of Writing*, 1979

Knowledge is important, but imagination is more important than knowledge.
—Albert Einstein

Experts, educators, and educatees alike agree that American education is in trouble. SAT and ACT scores have been on the decline for some years and there is widespread concern about how low they will go as well as when and why. There is also agreement that education is not going to get any better without some dramatic changes. The current popularity of such critiques as Allan Bloom's *Closing of the American Mind* and John Allen Paulos's *Innumeracy* testifies to this anxious state of affairs in the teaching arts.

The challenges to education in the information age are stern. No longer is it enough merely to inform. Education is now called upon to teach forms of judgment, discrimination, values, analytical skills, and problem solving never before imagined and well as something even more rare: to show people of all ages how to learn. The traditional trio of classroom. textbook, and teacher is simply no longer equal to the task. Nonetheless, education continues to operate as an enclave of elite culture battling for interest and respect in a universe of mass media, high technology, and the popular arts—the ecology of everyday life. What is called for is some way of bringing into better confluence these "two cultures" that have increasingly diverged over the past century. Creatively applying the tremendous success of theme parks and related forms offers perhaps the brightest prospect for this critical integration.

In "The Death of Good Taste," a lecture sponsored by the Clemson University Architectural Foundation, Dr. Roger Rollin

219

suggested teaching some connections between *War and Peace* and *Star Wars*. "Moreover," Rollin noted, "it would seem to make sense to provide students with some of the intellectual tools they badly need to understand their popular culture.... And we in humanistic education bear a major responsibility for helping people maximize their cultural options....."[1]

Imports from popular culture into schools is one leading-edge development. Television and computers are just two examples, but even more pervasive are the total environments of Disneyland and Walt Disney World—the theme parks. The rich fusion of entertainment and education at the Disney parks—and related "megaparks"—has been the basis of intense debate. The spatial free association of ideas that was for so long possible only in images and words has now developed, with high technology, into a three-dimensional artform. And though a stroll through Disneyland or World happens within a planned environment, the guest can endlessly vary the journey according to mood and interest. The quality and meaning of this experience has recently become the focal point for the museum and educational "events" world, where theme parks are being considered as a design model for attracting and engaging the visitor.

For a cultural audience raised on television, with a technological rather than a traditional humanities view of the world, theme parks offer the ideal setting and inspiration for education. Many of the innovations taken for granted as part of classroom and museum education enhancements, such as multimedia events, were born at the theme parks.

Education is hailed by theme parks as a central mission. "Disneyland," says the official brochure, "combines fantasy, history, adventure, and learning." Roy Disney's summation of Walt Disney World's outlook makes a similar claim: "May Walt Disney World bring joy and inspiration and new knowledge to all who come to this happy place [where all] can laugh and play and learn together" (qtd. in Pettit).

The Disney penchant for educating widely and well has always stayed several moves ahead of the priorities shift in U.S. education. Since the 1960s, the emphasis has been away from knowledge-building and analytical thinking as taught through the motifs of history and literature: the linear landscape of cause and effect, motive and action, personality and destiny prescribed in the study of warfare, economics, romance, and the search for the fulfillment of empire and self. New models of intelligence based on research in

Fig. 1. Symbolic and fantastic architecture, including geometric topiary and a waterfall that falls up, encode the collaboration of art and technology in EPCOT's Journey into Imagination. Photo credit: Jamie O'Boyle.

problem-solving and creativity have induced a fresh new agenda of curiosity, imagination, discovery, invention, and innovation. Suddenly students are being summoned to think in new paradigms (imagining scenarios like a nuclear holocaust or the eradication of all disease), to invent new solutions ("design the tallest building possible out of paper"), and to operate interactively (solving medical problems in trouble-shooting student teams rather than simulating solo practitioners).

E. Paul Torrance and Kathy Goff, researchers in creativity education, have declared, "Many educators have not fully recognized that changes in the direction of more creative education have occurred.... Practically every curriculum reform during the last 30 years has moved education in the U.S. to be more creative in nature (Torrance and Goff 139-40).

Entertainment as Education

Walt Disney has been called "the greatest educator of the twentieth century." In this oft-quoted accolade, Max Rafferty, Superintendent of Education for the State of California, was recognizing the power of the Disney enterprise to do far more than entertain. He saw in Disney's films, television, and print, and then in the theme park, the hand and mind of a creative innovator whose power drew on the American family audience's interest in learning, an impetus that closely parallels the desire to travel and explore other worlds, eras, and minds.

This perception about the nature of education has paid off many times over. Disney's genius for educating by starting with what is already known follows a well-known precept of teaching and of popular culture alike—consumer or student-oriented teaching. As Richard Beard put it in his book on EPCOT, "The organization that Walt fostered is a wizard at giving people facts they enjoy and remember" (Beard 35). It would certainly be safe to say that Disney has enjoyed more influence than anyone has suspected in educating every generation of Americans since the 1930s. Certainly as the artistic director of a major multi-talented enterprise—as filmmaker, artist, businessman, and creator of the City of the Future—Disney can readily be construed as America's Dean of Applied Creativity.

In the mass media age what we learn and what our children learn is most often absorbed outside the classroom: through magazines, sports, films, computer games, rock concerts, theme parks, malls, and shopping (now the major leisure activity in the U.S.) and through the sociable interchange that goes with all these. Time allotted to reading and formal instruction, of course, lags far behind these pursuits. Without a total re-thinking and overhaul, the classroom can no longer compete with the wide wonderful world of popular culture. The "Never-Never Land" of the theme park, the stagey themed atmospheres of restaurants and malls (which have now become major socialization centers), and the drama of both large and small screen are simply far more attractive, stimulating, and engaging.

Education begins with delight, with engagement, with the ring of the familiar. Teaching aids can be traced from designs first conceived for entertainment. After their integration into home life, the stereopticon and magic lantern of the late 19th century, followed by the Kodachrome slide, videodisc, and video game, have all made the migration from parlor and den into the halls of academe for a "second career" in education.[2] The first breath was drawn in enjoyment, not pedagogy.

Following the same fashion, formal education is already turning to alternatives in a quest to make the classroom a "learning center" rather than a traditional library/lecture hall/museum: video-assisted instruction, part-time programs, flexible schedules, field study, home learning through television and computers. From their inception, theme parks posed the groundwork for alternative (or at least supplementary) educations. Thirty years later and now more fully developed as a communications media in themselves, these alternative "academies" offer both challenges and promises to ideas about how people can be induced to explore, to learn, and to remember.

As time-honored extensions of the schoolroom, museums are naturally drawn to these advancing formats, and are emerging as a leading component in public education—sometimes complementing, sometimes being handed roles to take over from the overworked school curriculum (especially in the sciences). In Philadelphia, for example, the Franklin Institute's Futures Center, with its interactive science garden, hands-on-exhibits, and heavy computer use, is one prototype of this evolution of the "museum of the future" movement.

Since the mid-1950s, the Disney Corporation has pioneered and perfected the novel art form of themeing, a total sociology and aesthetic, which has been raised to a new height with the opening of EPCOT's Future World and World Showcase in the early 1980s.[3] Although often considered simply a form of highly successful mass entertainment, the theme park (or "atmospheric park," which it has also been called) (Schickel 13) has generated an ever-widening circle of influences, ranging from town planning and historic preservation to building architecture, mall design, and merchandising to home and office decor, exhibit design, crowd management, and video- and computer-assisted education. Inspired and propelled by thematic applications of technology and the use of themed motifs in decor, the extension of set design, and flights of fancy (along archetypal routes) in symbolic and fantastic architecture, the "Disney effect" is making itself seen and felt across the cultural board. As unlikely as it may seem at first blush, the models of many contemporary notions about the way public spaces should look and feel trace back to the gateways of the Disney parks. This includes the dimensions, kinetics, textures, sounds, and other character traits of the (other) places we go to encounter the world in stylized form: the Madonna Inns, Food Courts, Donut Worlds, and Magic Time Machine Restaurants, as well as the thousands of McDonald's outlets keyed to local themes.

Themeing
Throughout nearly three and a half decades of conception, development, and evolution, theme parks have exerted a surprisingly

disproportionate effect on American culture—both in mainstream and avant-garde endeavors. It is even possible that, as a result of that influence, there has been no more immediately successful or more all-encompassing art form in human history. Disney's is a multi-experiential approach, melding education, entertainment, food, souvenirs, travel, and other modes to achieve its effects (Schoener 38). Consider the attendance figures of 50 million a year to Disneyland, Walt Disney World, and Tokyo Disneyland—with another 11 million expected to visit EuroDisneyland in Paris after 1992.

The ancestors of the theme park are venerable, including pilgrimage place, fair, harvest rite, royal pleasure ground, theater, science exposition, history park, world's fair, and museum. The first generation was established and matured over a 30-year period. The spin-off progeny, the second generation, now includes such prominent features of the entertainment landscape as Knotts Berry Farm, Busch Gardens, King's Island, the "Six Flags" parks, Sea World, and Opryland. The third generation theme park offspring are showing up in themed entertainments and exhibitions, restaurant decor, historic redesign and rehabilitation, retirement and resort communities, retail and mall design, main street restoration, and in inventive extensions of and within traditional museums such as the Futures Center.

Theme parks serve as modern museums and history parks, often following even better than museums themselves the museum mandate to "endow knowledge, incite pleasure, and stimulate curiosity" (Commission on Museums for a New Century, 1984). Through the device of themeing and its shorthand stylizations of person, place, and thing, an archive of collective memory and belief, symbol, and archetype has been created.

"Imagineering" (a Disney trademark) is the brainpower of themeing: the dynamic synthesis of right- and left-brain talents, merging creativity with technical know-how. "It is precisely in this unique combination that [we have] excelled, and in creating Epcot Center we believe [we] will achieve new dimensions and dynamics in family entertainment and learning experiences," says Marty Sklar, Vice President of Creativity Development for WED Enterprises (qtd. in Beard 25).

This "bank" of popular culture has earned high interest, both inside and beyond the business of entertainment. It is an account open and available for educators of every style and subject to draw upon.

Fig. 2. The stuff dreams are made of: Hollywood Boulevard of the 1930s and 1940s, reduced and reconstructed to fit a collective cultural "memory" of a place we have never seen except as a pastiche of video images. Disney/MGM Studios, Walt Disney World. Photo credit: Jamie O'Boyle.

The following questions suggest themselves for a study of the interface between theme parks and education: What is being learned and taught through themed environments, and how? What is the relationship between education, entertainment, and acculturation? How can themed environments offer inspiration to schools, museums, libraries, and other formal and informal educational/ enrichment programs—in their operation and mission alike? What are the issues of education and accuracy versus "promotion," with its stylistic impulses and imperatives, within these environments? And must these forces necessarily be cast as conflicting ones? What are the interactions between popular culture and elite/educational/historic forms in the education process? And finally, how do theme parks educate, and to what extent has their ability to teach brought them such unprecedented successes?

An appreciation of how various publics are attracted, involved, and educated by theme parks, based on the approach of "themeing" to knowledge complexes, is generic to the innovative connections currently being sought between entertainment and education, in particular the problematic "cross-cultural encounters" between formal and informal education. (For example, in the work of George MacDonald and Stephen Alsford at the Canadian Museum of Civilization, a starring example of a new age museum.)[4] These emerging integrations offer exciting new opportunities and directions for educational institutions of all stripes for the coming century. The gathering wave of world trade, tourism, and migration lends an urgency to these opportunities they have never had before (King "Theme...").[5] At the same time, they construct an intellectual theme of growing importance in the world at large: the creative synthesis (or reunification) of popular culture with elite in myriad motifs, trends, subjects, and styles. As a case study, theme parks, rooted in the California and Florida prototypes, are also posing some solutions (or problem-solving frameworks) to some of the central concerns of modern civilization, both Western and international. "The parks transform formidable technology into something we can understand and look forward to enjoying," says Beard (35).

Disney's efforts have often hastened the process by which less advantaged and bookless children in the U.S. have acquired knowledge of history, lore, and myth that were previously held as a cultural monopoly by the better-off. The Disney classroom can be considered as a major acculturation on the American social scene, one that has "levelled up" millions of young by saving them from Dick and Jane banality. There is a price, of course—Disney versions of Snow White and Winnie the Pooh and Bambi may lack that poetic refinement of European verbal and graphic originals. But this issue of quality obtains in all the diffusions of education and literacy and never applied to Disney alone.

Indeed, it can be argued that the two great popularizers of the ecological movement were Rachel Carson (*Silent Spring*, 1962) and Walt Disney. Who would deny that all attitudes toward animals, wild and tame, natural and fantastic, have been mediated by Disney for at least 60 years?

Even so, it continues to be a point of pride with many American intellectuals that they have never (and refuse to) even set foot in any of these places. Analyzing the intellectual underpinnings of theme park content offers tremendous promise for mediating the battle of taste cultures, while showing potential to carry forward the whole enterprise of integrating elite and popular culture modalities.[6]

Concern with the political and social control of Disney's versions of the world—in particular, history, has prompted a generation of criticism based on the selective perception generated by Disney's brand of Midwestern conservatism—although this style, according to his biographers, is best viewed as a conservatism without commitment. These critiques take special aim at the Disney enterprise because of its special powers over the American mind. This power is attested to by the studios' great success in attracting generation after generation to the Disney oeuvre of film, parks, and merchandising.

Critical anguish is at heart, as Michael Wallace's recent review of Walt Disney as popular historian shows, an aghast perplexity about the state of education under the incursions of popular culture. "Nowadays it often seems as if the past gets presented to popular audiences more by commercial operators pursuing profit than by museums bent on education," says Wallace, "....blurring the line between entertainment center and actual museum" (Wallace 158-80). The construction of images and ideas in the Carousel of Progress, American Adventure, and the Hall of Presidents are the sourcebooks for the study of history transformed into popular culture.

Themeing is evocative as opposed to literal. Themeing is an involving form. It makes participants out of viewers. It collapses the traditional distance between the audience and the artifact. Contrast this participatory theory of art with the Western doctrine of art as disengaged, removed, and objectified, as in the conventional art museum, where velvet ropes carefully separate viewers from the thing viewed. Kant even offers the definition of "taste" as "disinterested judgment."

The parks are born of the dramatic, playful, holistic hyperbole of the video arts as contrasted to the cool, detached, analytical mentality of print media and traditional glass-case exhibit. As McLuhan noted in the *Medium is the Massage* (1967), environments out of the past become the content of new art forms. Thus the turn-of-the-century Main Street, USA, complete with gazebo and gaslights, becomes the retrograde symbol for the high-tech parks, with the even more ancient medieval castle centered as the crown jewel and polar star. In a similar vein, Disney nature films of the 1950s came to prominence just as the country was moving out of the countryside to regroup in city and suburb.[7] Both genres have been prime movers in the public's fascination with American history and with ecological issues.

Innovating on a popular culture stage rather than in an avant-garde studio, the Disney "Imagineers" have been leading-edge instigators in researching and developing concepts in the enchanted terrain between art and science. Examples are the arts of audio-

Fig. 3. The medieval architecture, music cues, folk art, and flag all imply Denmark, but the hills are Southern California. Both commercial and residential neighborhoods are themed to preserve the Danish heritage of Solvang, California. Photo credit: Jamie O'Boyle.

animatronics (called "animation in the round"), applications of computers to problems in communication and exhibition, new uses of video disk, electronics, and fiber optics, the remaking of historic artifacts by advanced engineering, the melding of space-age with neotraditional forms and functions, and the future-planning orientation of all park features. This innovation has a very human dimension as well. Walt Disney Seminars is a prominent player in management, marketing, and communications education and consulting, an "excellence" company at the forefront of training school, hotel, hospital, and museum executives as well as front-line workers in a variety of service industries.

In this vein is EPCOT, the Experimental Prototype Community of Tomorrow, at Walt Disney World. Originally planned as a residential community of 20,000, EPCOT combined some of the most advanced thinking in consumer science and ergonomics. Architect Peter Blake remarked in *Architectural Forum*, "Not even Corbusier at his brashest ever proposed anything so daring" (Blake 28).

History and Historiography

Just as the arts have been transformed by science, so have our shared concepts of history been put to the critical test by the "death of history." Vattimo's *The End of Modernity* asks what, at the end of the doctrine of Progress, awaits us? New doctrines are developing— not out of test-tube labs, but at "living history labs" like EPCOT's Future World, and shared symbols of designed environments like Main Street, USA, the gateways to the Disney parks East and West. Richard Francaviglia describes the importance of these recreations as symbol-places to be valued and appreciated as archetypal American experiences—especially in an age in which shared national identity has been weakened at the center and is under many pressures and, many feel, is reaching a breakdown (or meltdown) point (Francaviglia 141-56). The shared "anamnestic (memory assisting) response" elicited by the parks forms an important bond.

Part of this new tension between past and present is the sheer volume of data with which we are now faced and forced to deal; turning the massive overload of data into intelligence is a prime project for modern man, with pressure points aimed directly on the opinion leaders: our academic institutions, political advisors, and directors of informal education, including museum manager, publisher, religious spokesman, and network executive.

Everywhere there is a great need for more effective ways to organize and process information. The "knowledge clusters" of exhibits such as science (Living Seas, World of Motion, Wonders of Life), and communications (Communicore), provide a tactile, visual, and kinetic message about recent science information—as does, in a very immediate manner, the monorail, Mission to Mars, and Space

Mountain. Other examples are actual scientific experimentation such as plant cloning in "The Land," which U.S. Secretary of Agriculture Richard Lyng called "the cutting edge of biotechnology" at its dedication in 1988.

The Future

Philadelphia's Franklin Institute Futures Center, opened in 1990, is a design parallel to EPCOT's Future World pavilions following the Disney Method. This $58 million project spearheads the Institute's new momentum (actually a return to its original nineteenth-century mission) toward "an active education." Momentum has been fueled by *A Nation at Risk*, the Presidential Commission's 1983 report calling for a stepped-up science education (McKenna 1).

Historian Kenneth Keniston's incisive essay, "Stranded in the Present" (Keniston 40-43), describes the alienation of youth in the transformational 1960s as a function of alienation from history—both past and future. He diagnoses this modern malady as "asynchrony," time sickness, or the psychological loss of connection between generations in an age when the present is so radically different from the past that links to the future are either eroded or invisible. What is needed, Keniston suggests, are techniques beyond simply adapting to change. We need more: to find a way to assimilate change. This much taller order calls upon more universal and eloquent responses than our artists, scientists, or historians have been asked to give us in the past. In answer to these problems in historiography and in personal and social neurosis, this technique must be capable of mediating the "anxiety of historical dislocation" that has accompanied unguided technological and social change. We are planning now for a future that will be obsolete by the time we get there. This technique resides in what Keniston calls "aesthetic outlook," the translation of history into art—one of Disney's outstanding characteristics. (Think also of the many Disney history films, costume dramas that have brought the past to life in the popular imagination.)

Theme parks offer an intelligible stability in a world where change has become the rule, not the exception—and the pace of change has accelerated at mindbending rates. In addition, as a leading intergenerational learning laboratory, they answer many of the concerns of the generation gap. Two-, three- and four-generation tour groups come away from the Magic Kingdom and EPCOT with a new bond.

Change Management

In the theme park, historical and cultural archetypes set up a framework of reassurance, creating a safety zone amid the barrage of change. Vital to our mental health is coping with the great *terra incognita* of the future (including the near future), surely an educational issue of critical importance. Disney's response is a form of effective change management operating in part on the subconscious level of audience awareness. The wide acceptance and support commanded by the realms of Disney is an indication that they are connecting on too many levels and at too many points to be a mere diversion.

What are the key topics with survival value for modern living? An audit of leading themes at Disney's worlds tells the story:

Spatial:	The technology of Future World, Tomorrowland
Temporal:	History, collective and personal (Adventureland, Frontierland, American Adventure, Main Street, USA, World Showcase)
Psychological:	Change and mobility (Future World) in time and space (World Showcase)
Informational:	Social, psychic, cross-cultural (Future World, Fantasyland, Tomorrowland, Disney/MGM Studios)

In our world where the possibility of "staying ahead" has long ago disappeared beyond reach, just to know what is going on at any given time and place is an achievement of some magnitude. We can easily identify with Holden Caulfield in Salinger's *Catcher in the Rye* on his return to the New York Natural History Museum to assure himself that the hunter and deer in the prehistoric diorama are still in position as seen on his childhood visits. We are all feeling to some extent like aliens in our own age and country. The trend in "fish-out-of-water" films like *Back to the Future* testifies to a collective identity crisis.

Theme parks both supplement and compete with museums as stabilizers in this flux of modern change. This makes them especially interesting places to re-visit after having grown up in them. The entire baby boom generation is now in the process of discovering the drama in the "before" and "after" experience and impressions. As the theme park anticipates the future and plunges us into "then," carrying us all with it, it is interesting to note that certain features must in fact be updated. Thus the once-futuristic "Flight to the Moon" (Disneyland) was forced further out into the cosmos as "Mission to

Mars" after the moon landing had become history. For the same reason, the "House of the Future" in Tomorrowland quickly become outmoded as one of yesterday's tomorrows. An Innovations Plaza, including a Home of the Future, is planned for EPCOT in mid-1994.

Post-EPCOT "enclaves of the future," as Alvin Toffler calls them, will have the opportunity to take a lead in futurology by "reverting" to EPCOT's original conception as residential community—a fully functioning experimental "try-out" behavioral laboratory for new hard- and software, with everything from video telephones to home computer networks to moving sidewalks, solar power, and electronic elections.

Popular Culture and Tradition

While the parks are giving us the future, they also have been exemplary in restoring to public life many of the features—and with them, values—now banished from our megacities and suburbs (King, "Disneyland...").[8] Very few American cities can boast horse-drawn streetcars, outdoor cafes, boats and waterways, topiary landscaping, and a leisurely and safe pedestrian way of life. Along its now-famous River Walk, the city of San Antonio, Texas, has re-introduced walking, boating, and sidewalk dining to the heart of a major American metropolis. To this exercise in applied civic themeing, public acclamation has been resounding.

The Disney Experience continues to influence much else in America and now (with Tokyo and Paris models) international life, including the look and feel of our cities, public places, and learning environments. The universality of this tour (along with the integration of television into every aspect of daily life) is the backdrop against which all other attractions must be plotted. The contemporary "grand tour" around the global village could well be a procession from theme park to theme park as self-image crystal balls of far-flung world cultures. Given this premise, there is little practical sense in talking about museum-going, formal education, government programs, or any other communication-rich institution as independent of popular culture and its demands and effects.

Within the wraparound Circlevision or audioanimatronic theaters in Disney's Magic Kingdoms, transporting us to China, the Living Seas, prehistoric forests, or deep inside the mysteries of the human body, there is no distancing oneself from the images, movement, color, and music. These are totally enveloping experiences, sensory and mental, as close to "being there" as can be achieved without teleportation.

Fig. 4. Spaceship Earth, the centerpiece of EPCOT housing the AT&T Communications pavilion, melds space-age with neotraditional forms and functions. Photo credit: Jamie O'Boyle.

Popular culture works as the intermediary between history and its audience, the symbiosis of media event and artifact/architecture in which each feeds on and into the other in creative interplay. These parks are a living demonstration of how popular culture and history can be mutually reinforcing, supporting, and educational. It is never an "either/or" situation, even in the most seemingly "diametric" situations. As a case in point, in a recent issue of *American Heritage*, managing editor Richard Snow's acutely evocative essay on Disneyland, attributes to his visit there at age ten a lifelong interest and career in history, calling Disney's Main Street, USA "A triumph of historical imagination" (Snow 22-24). Moving toward the same aesthetic of engagement are the surrogate artifacts, hands-on, and interactive exhibits now part of museum and classroom learning. Disney's sense of intuition, risk-taking, and planning had much to do with setting these wheels in motion.

Archetypes

Comparisons with "literal restoration" history sites such as Williamsburg, Greenfield Village, and Slater's Mill are unavoidable. But in fact it is Disney's imaginative reconstructions, his archetypes based on stereotypes, that have served as inspiration for the Main Street architectural revivals of the 1970s. This renaissance was institutionalized as the 1977 Main Street program pioneered by the National Trust for Historic Preservation.[9] The use of archetypes is an intriguing aspect of themeing, because while they engage the visitor by drawing on and linking up with a built-in and built-up set of images about the world, including arts, cultures, peoples, and history, they must also somehow transcend that "flashpoint" to move on into deeper instruction.

The parks are an object lesson in the popular need for a shared vision and symbols of the past as well as of other places; the need to update these visions to express the cosmology of the present; and their attractiveness as a tangible index to ideas. It is no accident that the future should play its starring role at EPCOT in the late 20th century.

There is an especially active debate around culture parks like the World Showcase at EPCOT, the Polynesian Culture Center, and "real-life" re-creations such as Sturbridge Village. It is within such "hyper-real" environments that the education staff—curator, education director, and exhibit designer—must deliberate on how to carry this focus forward and to fruition once the audience has been effectively captured.

Romanticized and fictional evocations have long enjoyed a lofty status in the novel, play, poem, painting, architecture, and film. In their new manifestation "in the round," they now deserve reevaluation as important historo-cultural mediators.

The archetypes within themed environments can advise as well as caution in this endeavor (the forced foreshortening of time and space in Adventureland and Frontierland are obvious instances). At a museum directors' planning meeting held at Walt Disney World, Francois Barre, Grand Halle Director at Parc La Villette science museum in Paris, described the Disney World experience as one in which visitors can "rediscover their own memories, even fantasies. They are immersed in a universe where everything was at once true and false; false because it consisted only of background and illusion, but true because it existed in everyone's heart and dreams. It was not just an amusement park, but an environment stimulating new ideas" (Schoener 39).

The problem with the past is that it must be assimilated with the psychic equipment of the present. History is unruly, rampaging, inscrutable, and inaccessible. Public education faces this problem on a vast scale on a daily routine. The task seems to be, at its source, one of communication: taking the raw materials of information and artifacts to weave them into patterns that are orderly, beautiful, engaging, true.

In any event, at whatever level, the picture windows into the past must be set on the terms of the visitor, not the educator. Walt Disney's greatest asset in this regard was his close and unwavering identification with his audience. He was always one of them and never withdrew to a position above the crowd, except perhaps in his charmingly civic conceit of reserving a private apartment for himself above the firehouse on Disneyland's Main Square.

William Thompson, in *At the Edge of History*, pinpointed the cosmic place of the theme park: "Disneyland is the technological cathedral of the 20th century, as the Gothic cathedral summed up the world in the medieval town" (21). An ironic measure of Disney's place in the American mind is the answer to the question of what man-made structure can be seen from the moon. The response is just as often "Spaceship Earth at Walt Disney World" (Buckminster Fuller's geodesic globe at the entrance of Future World) as the correct answer, which is the Great Wall of China. Of course it is understood that the universe is now far more expanded, less knowable, and more uncertain than ever, mainly because of man's efforts to control and re-create it. Theme parks are a superb response to this principle, a glowing showcase of the inside of our own minds. They are full of clues for the pursuit of what historian David Lowenthal has termed the "search for sensibility." The prime job of the modern historian (*The Past is a Foreign Country*), is the exploration of ways of seeing, thinking, and feeling that have shaped the past and are molding the present.

Engagement

Philosopher Arnold Berleant, in a book titled *The Art of Engagement*[10] studies problems of presentation and experience in public environments. In an interview discussing his book, Berleant expresses the frustration of "museum fatigue" in this way: "No matter how interesting, I can't spend over an hour and a half in a museum. I always go home exhausted. There must be a better way to interact with collections" (Berleant interview). There have to be better, less taxing ways to an exhibit-assisted education—and the key will lie in the entertainment modalities that theme parks have been affording their "guests," Disney's term for visitors, which he used advisedly. While even one hour may be considered a long time to spend in a museum (the North American average is actually closer to just 50

Fig. 5. Shopping is now the major U.S. leisure activity and an ideal medium for themeing at The Forum Shops at Caesar's Palace, Las Vegas. A total indoor environment featuring a Roman village of winding cobblestone streets, plazas, shops, fountains, and an arched painted sky with a computer-controlled sunrise every hour. Photo credit: Jamie O'Boyle.

minutes), visitors routinely spend eight hours or longer strolling, sitting, eating, riding, and otherwise enjoying theme park environments. It is not unusual to find family or friends spending an unbroken *week* hard at play at Walt Disney World and EPCOT—and then returning home to remark how sorry they are that there wasn't time to see it all! Returning visitors are a major factor in the unbeatable attendance records (25 million a year at Walt Disney World) at these places.

Theme parks must process incredible numbers of visitors per day—and at increasing rates. Recently, Walt Disney World's gates have had to close in midmorning because of capacity conditions. But by ingenious planning and management of space, light, and noise control, they manage to avoid many of the problems museums and other exhibitors are experiencing by oversubscription, especially in the intimate intensity of science "discovery centers." Of particular concern to science parks is the difficulty of controlling hands-on exhibits that require concentrated one-on-one activity—especially difficult with those who stand most to benefit from them: school groups. "These exhibits are built for one-on-one, not 3,000 on one," says Wendy Pollack at the Association of Science-Technology Centers (ASTC).

One of the problems of designing good exhibits is just this situation: the more absorbing and personal, the more difficult to access. One solution to this problem posed at the theme parks is in the "dark rides," transporting the rider on an intimate and close-up "trip" through the exhibit in two-seat trams wired for sound. These modules give a feeling of privacy and "up-close" vision while they cut to almost nothing the feeling of crowding and competition for personal space and visibility that can compromise the best-laid exhibit design. For example, in the new exhibit "Body Wars" in the Wonders of Life pavilion sponsored by MetLife at EPCOT, the audience is "shrunk" to take a "Fantastic Voyage" through the human body via film and flight simulation technology. A neighboring attraction, "Cranium Command," takes viewers on a strange tour through the workings of the brain of a 12-year-old boy.

On the broad scale, within the sprawling megapark of indoor-outdoor "museumettes" at the Disney parks and EPCOT, visitor movement is very skillfully engineered: more so for being inobvious and invisible. The radius of walkways, paved with a rubber compound to lessen foot stress, is one strategy to sidestepping the chaos that could so easily be loosed upon these places with the wrong systems in place. The genius of the plan is that within any single theme area no "foreign" theme is allowed to intrude, reducing the "overchoice" or information overload that can plague the visitor who feels he is being offered too much at a time on too many plates—attractive as each one may be (a common complaint at World's Fairs, for example). The central medieval castle stands alone above other monuments as a navigator's point. This is more than security and crowd control. It is an aesthetic of comfort and freedom as an answer the challenges of urban congestion. The result is a national "field of care," places charged with feeling, fondness, and connection for us all.

Evaluation

Assessment of the learning process is another vogue in which Disney, on a somewhat different front, has led the way. The lessons of the theme parks have already proven to be of unexpected but welcome assistance in addressing these problems.

In 1979 the National Science Foundation held a special symposium for science museums, at which a marketing researcher for Walt Disney World was invited to speak. The museum participants were somewhat astonished to learn Disney's annual budget for this activity—$1.5 million for visitor studies, including regular schedules for indexes from zip-code data to in-depth profiles. "At that point, museums were paying very little attention to their visitors, and a lot to their donors," says Minda Borun, Assistant Director of Programs at the Franklin Institute. "Over the past ten years, that has turned around." Now that museums increasingly depend on admissions income, the emphasis has begun to swivel considerably. Following the lead of theme parks, a consumer orientation is setting the tone for the way museums are reorienting along customer-service lines. They are asking how well their exhibits and programs are teaching and what they can do to reach more people more effectively. These are marketing questions. Museums, along with churches, university presses, orchestras, and arts councils, are learning to think like businesses—in patterns already etched by the great entertainment centers Disney founded.

The stakes for theme parks, major cultural institutions, and education alike are somewhat similar in that all are "big-ticket items" within their categories. Marketing studies show that high quality (with a learning component) can motivate people to drive farther, pay higher entry fees, plan longer, and defer other purchases. With recent price hikes at both theme parks and colleges, there seems to be no limit to what the consumer is willing to pay for such "quality" experiences.

The Greying of America

The nontraditional student is the newest target audience for higher education, and is here to stay. A glance at the demographics for the coming century should be instructive in correcting the notion that theme parks are attractive mainly to families with young children and to school groups. With the upward trend of life expectancy, already the ratio of adults to children in museums (science, leisure time) is over 3 to 2 (Source: ASTC). Contrary to their stereotype as a child's fantasy world, the Disney parks have always hosted far more adults than children—by a ratio of over 4 to 1. An interesting sidenote is that EPCOT reports a median age a full seven years higher than Disney World in general (Dychtwald 133). Disney World's mammoth scale, its vast acreage, and multitude of options, including new mini-parks such as Pleasure Island and Typhoon Lagoon, has led many visitors to view it as an adults-only experience and to leave the children at home. Increasingly, institutions of all types will be serving an older client base. By the year 2025, the Population Reference Bureau predicts, Americans over 65 will outnumber teenagers two to one (21).

The upcoming generation of older culture consumers, the baby boomers, will be the largest in history, and this is a cohort born and bred not only to continuing education in all its forms but to the theme park (where continuing education for credit is, in fact, now being offered).

Disney also offers its own brand of education. For adults (over 16), there are special lecture tours: "Hidden Treasures of the World Showcase," and "Gardens of the World." There are continuing education programs for credit in conjunction with Florida State University in Marketing and Communication. The Earth Shuttle Program offers class trips through EPCOT with special lesson plans. For 10-15-year-olds, there are the Wonders of WDW Program specializing in arts, nature, and entertainment.

In addition, EPCOT outreach and the EPCOT Teachers' Center provide a host of resources—print and electronic—to educators and students to extend the learning curve sparked by the parks. A computer-driven exchange network for educators is up and running but looking for wider and better applications than just "teacher network." These efforts are all part of the Disney "continuing commitment to excellence in education," in the brochure phrasing.

Presentation philosophy as taught by Disney, together with the whole cadre of themeing means and motifs, can flex to fill in the many gaps that continue to pop open between what is taught and what needs to be learned. With the era of chalk and primer already far behind, the whole panoply of popular culture—private, nonprofit, business, and public—offers itself as a rich and accessible research collection.

Properly plumbed and connected, the resources of the theme park offer exciting channels for the transformation of education into the well-rounded, interactive, and integrated adventure it must become in modern life.

Acknowledgment

The author wishes to thank Professor Reuel Denney for his generous assistance in reading and commenting on this chapter.

Notes

[1]Roger Rollin. "The Death of Good Taste." Revised version of a public lecture sponsored by the Clemson University Architectural Foundation. Clemson, SC, 1987.

[2]Rod Murray, Director of the Office of Academic Computing, made this observation in his Nov. 1989 progress report to the Thomas Jefferson University Medical College (Philadelphia) based on the university archival collection.

[3]Disney has been particularly instrumental as a "translator" of European children's literature into American plots and images (as can be seen in Fantasyland) to the extent that many Americans believe these tales to be original Disney creations. Disney's creation and re-cycling of American heroes is another key study: see Margaret J. King, doctoral dissertation, "The Davy Crockett Craze: A Case Study in Popular Culture." Dept. of American Studies, University of Hawaii, 1976.

[4]See for example "The Museum as Hypermedium," "Museums as Bridges to the Global Village," "Museums in the Marketplace," "EPCOT Centre in Museological Perspective," and "The Canadian Museum of Civilization: A Museum for the Global Village" (1987-89).

[5]See also M. King, "The Theme Park Experience." World Futures Society special issue, *Tomorrow's Museums*. (Washington, D.C.) Nov./Dec. 1991: 24-31.

[6]The director of a cultural museum reported to me that he visited the Bishop Museum of ethnology in Honolulu while he shunned the Polynesian Culture Center, the largest single attraction in the islands, and the main source of popular impressions and beliefs about Polynesia. He came home without ever experiencing the most important source of ideas on his museum's subject area!

[7]See Reuel Denney's new Introduction to the reissue of The *Astonished Muse*, New Brunswick, NJ: Transaction Publishers, 1989, for his discussion of animals in American civilization. "In the cinematic media, no one has paid greater attention to animals—first in cartoons and later in natural form—than Walt Disney" lvii.

[8]See also William F. Whyte on destruction of inner city pedestrian values.

[9]Richard Francaviglia discusses this topic in "After Walt Disney: The Role of Historic Image-Building in the Preservation and Revitalization of Main Street U.S.A.," paper presented at the annual meeting of the Organization of American Historians, St. Louis, MO, Apr. 1989.

[10]A condensed version appears as a chapter, "Experience and Theory in Aesthetics." *Possibility of the Aesthetic Experience.* Ed. M.H. Mitias. Dordrecht, Netherlands: Martinus Nijheff, 1986.

Works Cited

Beard, Richard. *Epcot Center: Creating the New World of Tomorrow.* New York: Harry Abrams, 1982. 35.

Berleant, Arnold. Personal interview. Apr. 1989, Philadelphia, PA.

———. *The Art of Engagement.* Philadelphia: Temple UP, 1991.

Blake, Peter. "The Lessons of the Parks." *Architectural Forum* June 1972: 28.

Carson, Rachel. *Silent Spring.* New York: Houghton-Mifflin, 1962.

Dychtwald, Ken. *Age Wave: The Challenges and Opportunities of an Aging America.* Los Angeles: Tarcher, 1988. 21, 133.

Francaviglia, Richard. "Main Street, U.S.A.: A Comparison/Contrast of Streetscapes in Disneyland and Walt Disney World." *Journal of Popular Culture* Summer 1981: 141-56.

Keniston, Kenneth. "Social Change and Youth in America." *Confrontation.* Ed. Michael Wertheimer. Glenview, IL: Scott Foresman, 1970. 40-43.

King, Margaret J. "Disneyfication: Some Pros and Cons of Theme Parks." *Museum.* Paris: ICOM/UNESCO, Winter 1991: 6-8.

———. "Disneyland and Walt Disney World: Traditional Values in Futuristic Form." *Journal of Popular Culture* Summer 1981: 116-40.

———. "Theme Park Thesis." *Museum News.* Sept.-Oct. 1990: 60-62.

McKenna, Brian. "The Franklin Institute: Selling the Future." *Philadelphia City Paper* 13-20 Jan. 1989, no. 231: 1.

Pettit, Robert B. "Disney Theme Parks as Shrines of the American Civil Religion." Popular Culture Association annual meeting, Atlanta, GA, 1986.

Schickel, Richard. *The Disney Version*. New York: Simon & Schuster, 1968. 13.

Schoener, Allon. "Can Museums Learn from Mickey and Friends?" *New York Times* 30 Oct. 1988: 38-39.

Snow, Richard. "Disney Coast to Coast." *American Heritage* Feb./Mar. 1987: 22-24.

Thompson,William. *At the Edge of History*. New York: Harper & Row, 1971. 21.

Torrance, E. Paul and Kathy Goff. "A Quiet Revolution." *Journal of Creative Behavior* 23.2 (1989): 139-40.

Wallace, Michael. "Mickey Mouse History: Portraying the Past at Disney World." *History Museums in the United States*. Eds. Warren Leon and Roy Rosenzweig. Urbana: U of Illinois P, 1989. 158-80.

CONTRIBUTORS

Ray B. Browne, Chair of the Popular Culture Department, Bowling Green State University, *emeritus*, is author of more than 50 books, Secretary-Treasurer of the Popular Culture Association and the American Culture Association, and editor of the *Journal of Popular Culture* and the *Journal of American Culture*.

Marilyn Casto is an Associate Professor, Department of Consumer and Family Sciences, Western Kentucky University, Bowling Green, Kentucky.

Susan F. Clark is an Assistant Professor of Theatre History and Criticism at Smith College in Northampton, Massachusetts, specializing in American theatre. She is currently preparing an anthology text for classroom use. Dr. Clark also serves as the Executive Director for Kristin Linklater's Company of Women, Inc., a non-profit multi-cultural theatre company.

Adam Colin is completing a Masters in the Anthropology of Tourism and is Research Assistant with David Crouch at Anglia University, England.

David Crouch teaches culture and leisure at Anglia University, Cambridge and Chelesford, United Kingdom. His book, *The Allotment: Its Landscape and Culture,* will be available in paperback in 1994. He researches and publishes widely on place and cultural identity.

Bruce C. Daniels, Professor of History at the University of Winnipeg, Manitoba, Canada, is a former editor of the *Canadian Review of American Studies* and the past president of the Canadian Association for American Studies.

Anne K. Kaler, Professor of English at Gwynedd Mercy College near Philadelphia, conducts panels at the national and Mid-Atlantic Popular Culture Association/American Culture Association conferences on Popular Romance Writers. Her book, *The Picara,* was published by Popular Press. She has also published numerous book chapters and articles. Her interests lie in scholars on romance, myth, women's studies, Friar Tuck and Shakespeare.

243

Judith L. Kapferer teaches sociology and cultural studies in the School of Education at Flinders University in South Australia. She has published widely in these fields, and in the cultural and social analysis and critique of nationalism, tourism and government policy.

Margaret J. King was the first to earn a graduate degree in Popular Culture at the Center for the Study of Popular Culture. Her doctoral work is in American Studies and cross-cultural topics at the East-West Center. As a cultural specialist, she writes and consults on theme parks, themeing, museums, the popular arts, education, creativity, and lifestyles. She is on the faculty of General Studies at Thomas Jefferson University in Philadelphia.

Michael T. Marsden is Dean of the College of Arts and Sciences and Professor of English at Northern Michigan University in Marquette, Michigan. He is also Co-Editor of the *Journal of Popular Film and Television*.

Doug A. Mishler is a student in the Department of History, University of Nevada. He is currently completing his dissertation, "The Greatest Show on Earth: The Circus and the Development of Modern American Culture."

Terry Donovan Smith has served as a lecturer in dramatic literature at California State University, Northridge and is currently in the doctoral program at The University of Washington's School of Drama. He is also a professional stage director and actor.

Mehran Tamadonfar is an Associate Professor of Political Science at the University of Nevada-Las Vegas. He is the author of *The Islamic Polity and Political Leadership: Fundamentalism, Sectarianism, and Pragmatism* and numerous articles and book chapters on the politics of the Third World.

Les Wade is an Assistant Professor in the Department of Theatre, Louisiana State University, Baton Rouge, Louisiana.

George E. Weddle is a graduate student in the American Studies program at Purdue University. His areas of concentration are American cultural and intellectual history and the sociology of religion. He is currently working on his dissertation entitled "Religion, Competition, and the Frontier: Indiana, 1800-1860."